UNDERSTANDING
the New Testament

UNDERSTANDING
the New Testament

1ST AND 2ND TIMOTHY,
TITUS, AND PHILEMON

WILLIAM VICTOR BLACOE

CFI
SPRINGVILLE, UTAH

ISBN 13: 987-1-59955-900-1

Published by CFI, an imprint of Cedar Fort, Inc., 2373 W. 700 S., Springville, UT 84663
Distributed by Cedar Fort, Inc., www.cedarfort.com

LIBRARY OF CONGRESS CATALOGING-IN-PUBLICATION DATA

Blacoe, William Victor, 1954- author.
  Understanding the New Testament : 1 & 2 Timothy, Titus, & Philemon /
William Victor Blacoe.
      pages cm
  Includes bibliographical references and index.
  ISBN 978-1-59955-900-1
  1. Bible. N.T. Pastoral Epistles--Commentaries. 2. Bible. N.T.
Philemon--Commentaries. 3. Church of Jesus Christ of Latter-day
Saints--Doctrines. I. Title.
  BS2735.53.B58 2011
  227'.83077--dc22

                        2011006540

Cover design by Angela Olsen
Cover design © 2011 by Lyle Mortimer
Edited and typeset by Megan E. Welton

Printed in the United States of America

10 9 8 7 6 5 4 3 2 1

Printed on acid-free paper

CONTENTS

ACKNOWLEDGMENTS

Gratitude and appreciation is due to my wife, Reingard, for her enduring sacrifice and support in the preparation of this project. Specific appreciation is also due to those who contributed to the diligent proofreading and grammatical suggestions—Gloria Paakanen (English), Giles François and Lars Enger (Greek), and Terry Niederhauser and incognito (Hebrew). Further gratitude is due to many translators and specialists in several countries who provided insightful understanding on a multiplicity of terms and interpretations in different languages. A posthumous applause to Biblical commentators in past centuries—in particular, the nineteenth century, from which this work liberally draws. This work is perhaps a dedication to so many whose efforts in a bygone era have dwindled into obscurity on the shelves of libraries across the Christian world.

INTRODUCTION

In the centuries of the Middle Ages in Europe, the populace was kept from learning to read and write. Through the process of ignorance, access to personal scripture study was hindered. Many longed for the truth but could not possess it; they could not find it. Possession of even a few hand-written sheets of Biblical text was a crime punishable by a torturous death. The Biblical translator William Tyndale was strangled and then burned at the stake in 1536 for the heresy of translating the Bible into English. In the passionate search for gospel truth, individuals, families, and even whole communities endured significant intimidation and loss of personal freedom. People forsook their homes and emigrated to foreign lands in search of liberty and freedom to possess and study the Holy Bible. The passionate zeal to become a better Christian motivated generations to read and learn from the written words of earlier prophets and apostles.

In the twenty-first century human quest for access to information, that which was once sacred is ignored as old-fashioned and irrelevant. We now live in an age where there is no practical shortage of access to information. Thousands of books are published, and millions of pages are added to the Internet each day. This is not an age of information shortage but of interpretation and application in a time of information plenty. We are overwhelmed with access to information but dwindling in understanding. We systematically feed our mind with the fleeting crumbs of take-away knowledge, and bypass the opportunity to feast upon the Divine Word. The opportunity exists to elevate the mind; instead we see the degradation of the human soul.

The study of the Holy Bible should not be an academic exercise but rather a dynamic rediscovery of the spark of divinity that we are all born with. Scripture study should be an enthusiastic exercise that motivates, excites, satisfies, and yet leaves one wanting to return for further light and knowledge.

In the words of C.S. Lewis, "We have to be continually reminded of what be believe. Neither this belief nor any other will automatically remain alive in the mind. It must be fed."[1] The distractions of worldliness are loud and profuse; we need to learn from the faith of our fathers and embrace Christianity, not only in our life but in our living. "It is not being gilded over with the external profession of Christianity that will avail us. Our religion must be a vital principle, inwardly to change and transform us."[2]

Permit me to share my excitement and discoveries as we learn together from those who have left to us their legacy of recorded scriptural understanding. Let us speak "of these things; in which are some things hard to be understood" (2 Peter 3:16), only obscured by almost two millennia of cultural misunderstanding.

No original Greek text of any New Testament content exists today as penned by its original author. A profusion of manuscripts—all with different varia-

tions in text—exist today. No definitive text has yet been achieved, though there are common consensus Greek texts. The primary example is *Novum Testamentum Graece*, the first edition of which was printed in 1514 and published in 1520. *Novum Testamentum Graece* (now referred to as the Nestle-Aland edition) is now in its 27th edition. This work is managed by the Institute for New Testament Textual Research, at the University of Münster, Westphalia, Germany. Variations between New Testament Greek texts are minutely monitored and catalogued for comparison. Based upon the best consensus of the current various Greek manuscripts, a decision is made and the choice of Greek wording is selected. The 27th edition consists of 7,947 verses, 4,999 of which are variation free. This equates to 62.9 percent of the New Testament verses being consistent, and 37.1 percent being inconsistent. More than one in every three verses of the New Testament in Greek manuscripts is different—in minor or major variation! The First Epistle of Paul to Timothy has the highest accuracy at 81.4 percent, and the Gospel according to Mark has the lowest accuracy at 45.1 percent. This leaves us with the understanding that more than half of this Gospel account is possibly *not* specifically according to Mark! Since we cannot reach a definitive consensus on the Greek text, we will never reach a consensus on any language translation.

This is the first volume in what may prove to be a series of translation revision and commentary on the New Testament of the Holy Bible. Centuries of scholarship working with extant Greek text has produced a wonderful legacy of biblical resource materials. How blessed we are with such a considerable store of Bible translations that enable us to enlarge our comprehension of complex passages, Jewish and Greco-Roman idioms, and cultural writing styles.

An enormous debt of gratitude is owed to so many clerics, scribes, archivists, and translators who have preserved and increased the legacy of Biblical understanding we now have. Even in our present day, several individuals from reputable Christian denominations continue to champion the cause of Christian education and New Testament study. This work draws liberally upon the scholarly works of centuries of biblical champions, translators, and commentators, in most European languages. Their insightful observations on several doctrinal and historical points have enhanced and enabled the production of this work.

William Victor Blacoe
Rodenbach, Hessen, Germany
19 January 2011

ENDNOTES

1. Lewis, *Mere Christianity*, 141.

2. Archbishop Tilliston quoted in Adam, *The Religious World Displayed*, 1:xxii.

GETTING THE MOST FROM

UNDERSTANDING THE NEW TESTAMENT

Each verse from 1 and 2 Timothy, Titus, and Philemon is included inline, calling special attention to variants in translation.

Key terms and phrases, along with a comparison of their language(s) of origin are included after each verse.

Additional commentary regarding contemporary culture, customs, and geography provides context for each verse.

Introductions to groupings of verses offer the gospel scholar increased contextual understanding of themes, culture, and language.

Unprofitable (Greek *achrestos* ἄχρηστος) means unprofitable in the sense of being useless. If Onesimus had been unprofitable in the sense of being hurtful or aggressive, then he would have used the word *achreios* (ἀχρεῖος) used in reference to the parable of the unprofitable servant in Matthew 25:30.

. . . make use of.[41]

a comparative . . . ly Luke is with . . . oring him in . . . ofitable [*euchres* . . . or the ministry"

. . . in Greek that is . . . this verse. The . . . *emas* Ὀνήσιμος) . . ." or "useful." . . . again verses 10–11 we understand his pun: "I [Paul] entreat thee [Philemon] for my son, Onesimus [*Useful*], whom I have begotten in my bonds: which in time past was to thee *useless*, but now *useful*, to thee and to me." By implication, we could read the following: "Previously *Useful* was *useless* to you, but now *Useful* has become *useful* both to you, Philemon, and to me, Paul." Onesimus is a changed man in his rebirth as a faithful Christian (*Christianos* Χριστιανός). There is an obvious similarity in Greek between *Useless*, *Useful*, and *Christian*—compare above. This may have been intended by Paul as a subtle additive.

[1:12] Whom I have [returned to you][42] ~~sent again:~~ [that is mine own inward affection,] ~~thou therefore receive him, that is, mine own bowels:~~

Sent again (Greek *anapempo* ἀναπέμπω) is a legal term denoting "send up to a higher authority."[43] There is a specific intention in the use of this word by Paul. At the time of writing this letter, Paul was in Rome pending the judicial decision of the Imperial court. He had appeared before a lower provincial court in Caesarea and had exercised his right of citizenship by declaring, "I appeal unto Caesar" (Acts 25:11). As the charge against Paul was deferred to the higher judicial authority, so too is the charge against Onesimus deferred to the higher judgment of Philemon.

Mine own (Greek *emos* ἐμός) is a term generally equated with children in relation to their parents.[44] Paul is pleading with Philemon to receive Onesimus hospitably. He expresses his own anxiety concerning the reception Philemon will extend to Onesimus. "The message of Christianity is primarily to individuals, and only secondarily to society. It leaves the unit, which it has influenced to influence the mass. . . . It acts on spiritual and moral sentiment, and only afterwards and consequently on deeds or institutions."[45]

[1:13] Whom I [was desirous to retain] ~~would have retained~~ with me, [so] that in thy stead he might have [minister to] ~~ministered unto~~ me [during

my imprisonment for] ~~in the bonds~~ of the gospel:

Paul indicates that Onesimus was useful to him and that he was "desirous to retain Onesimus"—he had need of him.

Bonds of the gospel (Greek *desmois tou euaggeliou*, δεσμοῖς τοῦ εὐαγγελίου) is complicated to translate. It might well be translated "the bonds for the gospel."[46] Once again, the gospel is a gospel of freedom, not of bondage. Idiomatic forms of expression are cumbersome when translated to some languages. The first rule of translation is to preserve the concept and message and not the literal meaning of words.

[1:14] But without thy [consent, I would not take the liberty] ~~mind would I do nothing; that thy~~ [good deed might not be imposed] ~~benefit should not be as it were of necessity, but~~ [voluntarily] ~~willingly.~~

It is as though Paul were indicating to Philemon that he has his best interests at heart respecting the request to change the status of Onesimus. Though the translation above provides better clarity, the concept is still vague to the modern English reader. The message of this verse is, "I wanted to give you the opportunity to do me a favor."

A NEW TRIPARTITE RELATIONSHIP (PHILEMON 1:15–21)

It is obvious from the contents of this letter that Paul and Philemon had an established relationship reaching back many years. The contents also echo the

relationship that has recently developed between Paul and Onesimus. However, the letter now invites Philemon to discover a new relationship with Onesimus—no longer as a slave, but now as a friend in a three-way relationship which includes Paul.

[1:15] For Perhaps [for this purpose he was separated] ~~he therefore departed for~~ a season, that [everlastingly] thou [may] ~~shouldest receive him for ever:~~

Thou shouldest receiv (ἀπέχω) means to rec . . . implication, though . . . Onesimus was as a ru . . . return and everlasting . . . than compensate in the . . . tive. Paul plays down t . . . runaway and charges . . . departing or separating . . . temporarily, as thoug . . . assignment instead of b . . .

[1:16] Not now as a [slave] ~~servant~~, but above a [slave] ~~servant~~, a brother beloved, [especially] ~~specially~~ to me, but how much more [now] unto thee, [as a man] ~~both in the flesh~~, and [as a brother] in the Lord?

Servant (Greek *doulos* δοῦλος) is a slave in the regular sense of the designation. See appendix C.

Verses 15–16 must be read together to preserve the message: "[15] Perhaps the reason he was separated from you for a

Part One

1 TIMOTHY

1 Timothy

———— ❧ ————

PROLOGUE

The year is AD 51, and the forty-six year-old Apostle Paul (Paulus) is on his second missionary tour in company with Silas (Silvanus). They arrive in the hinterland towns of Lystra and Derbe on the Galatian plateau (Acts 16:1). The expanded Christian congregation now includes a local family consisting of a grandmother, mother, and her son. The name of the grandmother is Lois (2 Timothy 1:5). The "believing" mother, Eunice (2 Timothy 1:5), "was a Jewess" (Acts 16:1), and the unconverted "father was a Greek" (Acts 16:1). Luke curtly records that their son, "named Timotheus" (*Timotheos* Τιμόθεος) (Acts 16:1), or Timothy—though yet a young man—"was well reported of by the brethren that were at Lystra and Iconium" (Acts 16:2). We may wonder how it was possible for a daughter of the House of Israel to marry a Gentile. In Palestine, Jewish Eunice would probably not have ventured to marry outside the covenant. Yet here, in a remote corner of heathendom, there was no righteous son of Israel to be found. As with many in a similar predicament, the ancestral religious heritage diluted.

Considering these communities are so small, we may conclude that Paul met young Timotheus on his first missionary endeavor with Barnabas years earlier. Circumstances

1

indicate that Paul purposed to take young Timotheus with him as a traveling companion on the rest of their journey. A major aspect of the Paul's preaching method was to focus on the local synagogue in each town they visited, so there remained an open issue with Timotheus to be resolved. To avoid vindictive reproach from the local "Jews which were in those quarters," Paul had Timotheus "circumcised . . . for they [all] knew all that his father was a Greek" (Acts 16:3). We are aware that Paul suffered the unnecessary punishment of the thirty-nine stripes on three occasions (See 2 Corinthians 6:5; 11:23–24) to maintain his access to the synagogue; therefore, we may assume that Paul expected Timothy would have greater freedom of access as a circumcised Jew rather than being percieved as an uncircumcised heathen. From this time, the life of Timothy is part of the unfolding history of Paul.[1]

THE MACEDONIAN AFFAIR

Later that year (AD 51), while in the Macedonian town of Berea, Jewish antagonists "of Thessalonica" came "and stirred up the people" (Acts 17:13). The net result was a clandestine departure of Paul by sea to Athens, "but Silas and Timotheus abode there still" (Acts 17:13). From Athens, Paul sent instructions back to Berea "unto Silas and Timotheus for to come to him with all speed" (Acts 17:15). Eventually, "when Silas and Timotheus were come from Macedonia" (Acts 18:5) they shortly thereafter returned to Thessalonica with the First Thessalonians Epistle containing the introductory greeting from "Paul, and Silvanus,

and Timotheus" (1 Thessalonians 1:1). We know that Timothy was courier of the epistle, being identified in the actual letter, for Paul wrote that he "sent Timotheus, our brother, and minister of God, and our fellow-laborer in the gospel of Christ, to establish you, and to comfort you concerning your faith" (1 Thessalonians 3:2).

Paul probably indicated that he would proceed on to Corinth and that upon their return journey from Thessalonica, they would find Paul there. They caught up with him at Corinth in later AD 52 (Acts 18:1, 5), and the missionary contingent "continued there a year and six months, teaching the word of God among them" (Acts 18:11). During this extended sojourn in Corinth, the Second Thessalonian Epistle was composed and dispatched. The opening verse indicates that Timothy was present with Paul, and may even have been one of the scribes of the letter. The letter greeting states that it is from "Paul, and Silvanus, and Timotheus, unto the church of the Thessalonians" (2 Thessalonians 1:1). Paul attests the missionary service of Timothy in Corinth years later in reflecting back on those months together. "For the Son of God, Jesus Christ, who was preached among you by us, even by me and Silvanus and Timotheus" (2 Corinthians 1:19).

TIMOTHY AGAIN IN MACEDONIA AND ACHAIA

During Paul's third missionary tour, we hear of Timotheus in AD 56 in companionship with Erastus departing from

Ephesus for an assignment to Macedonia and Achaia (Acts 19:22). That would encompass Philippi through to Corinth—though they would not actually arrive in Corinth until early the following year.[2] We know that Paul planned for Timothy to proceed to Corinth from his own remarks to the Corinthians: "Now if Timotheus come, see that he may be with you without fear: for he worketh the work of the Lord" (1 Corinthians 16:10). Within this same epistle, Paul declares, "Timotheus . . . is my beloved son, and faithful in the Lord" (1 Corinthians 4:17).[3] Following the dispatch of the First Corinthian Epistle, Paul departed for Philippi. To his surprise, he found Timothy still at Philippi. While there, he composed and dispatched the Second Corinthian Epistle in the summer of AD 57. The opening verse of this epistle includes Timothy in the greeting: "Paul, an apostle of Jesus Christ by the will of God, and Timothy our brother" (2 Corinthians 1:1). There is no information to indicate if Timothy accompanied Paul en route to Corinth. Considering the original intent of Timothy to continue at Corinth, we may assume that he did so. Indications are that Paul wrote the Roman Epistle while residing at Corinth—possibly in February of AD 58. This epistle includes the following greeting: "Timotheus my workfellow, and Lucius, and Jason, and Sosipater, my kinsmen, salute you" (Romans 16:21). Following a short *intermezzo*, Paul returns to Ephesus. "There accompanied him into Asia [Minor] Sopater of Berea; and of the Thessalonians, Aristarchus and Secundus; and Gaius of Derbe, and Timotheus; and of Asia, Tychicus and Trophimus" (Acts 20:4).

FURTHER SPORADIC APPEARANCES OF TIMOTHY

At the writing of the Colossian and Philippian Epistles in AD 62, Timothy was present with Paul in Rome (Colossians 1:1; Philippians 1:1). The Philippian Epistle also indicates that Paul intended to send Timothy soon to Philippi (Philippians 2:19). During the first imprisonment at Rome, Timothy was also present during the composition of the private letter to Philemon concerning the runaway slave Onesimus (Philemon 1). The completion of the Hebrews Epistle possibly occurred in early AD 63. An aside comment from Paul indicated that sometime prior to this Timothy had been imprisoned. Paul simply states, "Know ye that our brother Timothy is set at liberty" (Hebrews 13:23). Further, the postscript attached to our rendition of this epistle indicated that Timothy scribed the epistle (Hebrews postscript).

THE TIMOTHY EPISTLES

The years are passing, and we eventually come to the composition of the First Timothy Epistle possibly in May AD 67. Traditional indications are that Timothy is enjoying a period of extended residence at Ephesus. This first epistle includes extensive guidance and counsel to Timothy on the organization of the Church congregations and specific counsel for members—male and female, free and slave, rich and poor, widow and orphan, self-reliant and dependent upon Church support. The two Timothy epistles together with the epistle to Titus form the three documents collectively referred to as the Pastoral Epistles of Paul. He wrote these pastoral or ecclesiastical letters to individuals and not to congregations. In addition to the three Pastoral Epistles, we group the short Philemon letter of twenty-five verses. This is not an ecclesiastical epistle, but a private letter. Biblically, the Philemon letter appears together with the three Pastoral Epistles.

1 Timothy

COMMENTARY

The New Testament contains a collection of letters designated as *epistles*. In the first century, a letter in Latin was an *epistula* or *epistola*, and an *epistole* (ἐπιστολή) in Greek.[4] This is the first of a pair of surviving epistles written by Paul to Timotheus.

INTRODUCTION (1 TIMOTHY 1:1–2)

These two verses present the non-Trinitarian nature of "God our Father and Jesus Christ our Lord" (1:2). Paul refers to Jesus the Christ as Savior, a title adapted from the Greek divine title *Soter*. This title is normally applied to the Greek pagan god Zeus (Zeus Soter), and his daughter Artemis (Artemis Soter).

❧

[1:1] **Paul, an apostle of Jesus Christ [according to]⁵ ~~by~~ the [decree] ~~commandment~~ of God our Savior,⁶ and Lord⁷ Jesus Christ, [and]⁸ ~~which is~~ our hope;**

The name Jesus the Christ is a praenomen and a cognomen:

English	*Jesus the Anointed One*
Latin	*Iesu Christi* ⁹
Greek	Ὁ Ἰησοῦς ὁ Χριστός
	(*O Iesous Christos*)¹⁰

5

Hebrew   יֵשׁוּעַ הַמָּשִׁיחַ

(*Yeshua HaMashiach*)[11]

Though we refer to the Messiah as *Jesus* (Greek *Iesous*, Ἰησοῦς or *Iesoun* Ἰησοῦν), this is only the translation of his Hebrew name (*Yehoshua* יְהוֹשׁוּעַ or *Yehoshua* יְהוֹשֵׁעַ), meaning "Jehovah-saves." He has the same name as the Old Testament prophet known to us as *Joshua*, who succeeded Moses. As a point of interest, the prophet Joshua is also translated Jesus twice in the New Testament.[12] It would have been correct to call the Messiah; *Joshua* (Hebrew), instead of *Jesus* (Greek) in the New Testament, but tradition dictates that we retain the Greek name of Jesus.[13]

Christ is *Christos* (Χριστός) in Greek, and *Messiah* (*Mashiach* מָשִׁיחַ) in Hebrew—meaning "the Anointed One" or a "consecrated person," such as a king or priest.

The **commandment** (Greek *epitage* ἐπιταγή) is an injunction or decree. This word especially referred to "oracles or divine commands,"[14] and even a royal decree. Jerome correctly translated this word to *imperium*, meaning "decree."[15] *Command* or *commandment* is a correct translation; however, Paul is not using the word in the sense of the Ten Commandments. He is emphasizing the "imperial power of God" (Latin *Imperium Dei*) over the *imperium* of the emperor.

Savior (Greek *Soter* Σωτήρ) means "deliverer" and is consistently translated *Saviour* in the New Testament. "The term *soter* was a common description in the Hellenistic world for a God who rescues, helps, heals, or in some way intervenes on behalf of someone or some group. Indeed, the most powerful deity in the Greek pantheon was called Zeus *Soter* [Ζεύς Σωτὴρ[16]], and his daughter Artemis was called Artemis *Soteira* [Ἀρτεμᾶς Σώτειρα[17]]."[18] We may conclude that the purpose of Paul was to displace Zeus and the Greek pantheon of gods with the *Great God* (*Soter*). "Other persons were called 'Savior' in Ephesus, including the emperor, so there can be little doubt that Paul's acclamation has a counter-cultural element to it."[19] Usually the application of *savior* is applicable to "deliverance from physical peril; but here the fuller meaning is intended, as one who has set us free from the guilt and power of sin."[20]

This first verse is of a very peculiar composition. Paul makes mention of God three times in different titles in one sentence—(1) Jesus Christ; (2) God our Savior; and (3) Lord Jesus Christ. In the first instance, *Jesus the Christ* (*O Iesous Christos*, Ο Ἰησοῦς Χριστός) has reference to the divinity that empowered Paul with apostolic authority. The second is unusual in that Paul unconventionally refers to Heavenly Father as Savior (*Theos Soteros*, Θεος Σωτῆρος). "He calls God *the Savior*, a title which he is more frequently accustomed to assign to the Son; but it belongs to the Father also, because it is he who gave the Son to us."[21] Heavenly Father is the *Soter* (as explained above) that is able to offer salvation to his children through the merits of His Son. This interpretation may also apply to Jude 25, "To the only wise *God our Savior*, be glory and majesty, dominion and power, both now and ever."[22] The third title has reference to Jesus Christ in his role as *Lord* (Greek *Kurios* Κύριος) meaning "supreme in authority." He is the Lord Jesus Christ of our hope. This hope is "not merely the object of it, or the author of it, but its very substance and foundation."[23] Our faith is *in* Jesus the Christ, and our hope is *on* the offered redemption.

[1:2] **Unto Timothy, my [righteous]** ~~own~~ **son in the faith: Grace, mercy,**[24] **and peace, from God our Father and Jesus Christ our Lord.**

INCORRECT TEACHINGS CORRUPT THE FAITH (1 TIMOTHY 1:3–7)

Paul speaks to Timothy using Greek words applicable to a senior officer giving orders or instructions to a junior officer. The Church at Ephesus is under attack from the incorrect teaching and erroneous doctrines of pretentious individuals. Timothy is to repulse these individuals and teach the correct principles with a clear conscience and a pure heart.

———— ❧ ————

[1:3] **As I [was departing for Macedonia, I urged]**[25] ~~besought~~ **thee to [remain]**[26] ~~abide still~~ **at Ephesus,** ~~when I went into Macedonia,~~ **that thou mightest**

[give orders to][27] ~~charge~~ [those individuals] ~~some~~ that they teach no other doctrine[s],[28]

Thou mightest charge (Greek *paraggello* παραγγέλλω) means "to pass on an announcement"—order, charge, or command.[29] *Paraggelia* (παραγγελία) is the "command or order issued to soldiers"[30] (See appendix B, "The Imperial Roman Army").

That they teach (Greek *heterodidaskaleo* ἑτεροδιδασκαλέω) means those who teach different doctrine, or teach the same doctrine "differently, [and thereby] teach false doctrine."[31] The root word *heteros*[32] meaning *different* is "distinguished from *allos*"[33] meaning "another of the same kind."[34] This unique word appears twice in this epistle; here and in 6:3. This word has come into English as *heterodox* meaning "at variance with a commonly accepted doctrine in religion . . . [by implication] opposed to *orthodox*."[35]

[1:4] **Neither give heed to [myths]** ~~fables~~[36] **and [interminable]**[37] ~~endless~~ **genealogies, which [promote controversies]**[38] ~~minister questions,~~[39] **[instead of the]** ~~rather than godly edifying~~ **[stewardship of God]** ~~which is in faith: so do.~~[40]

Fables (Greek *muthos* μῦθος) "is that which is a simple account which attempts to explain reality; yet is unreal and fabricated, having only the appearance of truth, no truth actually contained therein."[41] Paul is perhaps making a play on words between *mythos* meaning *mythical*, as diametrically opposed to *logos* (λόγος) meaning "historic truth."[42]

Genealogies (Greek *genealogia* γενεαλογία) has reference to the claim to noble descent. Jesus encountered certain Jews asserting a purported hereditary superiority. He issued a stern rebuke at the time: "Think not to say within yourselves, we have Abraham to our father: for I say unto you, that God is able of these stones to raise up children unto Abraham" (Matthew 3:9; Luke 3:8). Even in Crete, certain Jews claimed Abrahamic, priestly, or rabbinical pedigree.[43] The Bible is replete with genealogical tables, not only of royal lineage of Abraham, Moses, and Solomon, but also of Jesus. Genealogical records are not the issue in this remark by Paul, but purported superiority through biological descent. Such claimants usurp the divine association of the patriarchs to themselves, as though the righteousness of Adam, Enoch, Seth, Abraham, or Moses was not only their heritage but also their own status. This is evidenced by his use of the word *endless* (Greek *aperantos* ἀπέραντος) meaning "interminable" to emphasize the futility of their claims. This verse singles out the Jewish converts with this reproach for their speculative theology[44] and sense of superiority. Paul draws attention to this genealogical issue again in Titus 3:9.

In evaluating this verse, the focus is

always on the "myths and interminable genealogies." However, the message of Paul is contained in the latter part of the verse when he indicated that the true heritage these Jewish converts should lay claim to is in the present and not the past. He said, "Instead" they should focus on, and lay claim to the virtues "of the edifying stewardship of God in faith."

[1:5] Now the [objective] ~~end~~ of [this instruction] ~~the commandment~~ is [love] ~~charity~~ out of a pure heart, and of a good conscience, and of [sincere][45] faith ~~unfeigned:~~

Paul is offering an explanation to Timothy why he included this statement when he already knew it. "Bad theology leads to bad ethics, or to put it the other way around, bad ethics are a sign of bad theological thinking about the faith."[46] In respect of "a good conscience" see appendix D, "Conscience, Ethics, and Morality."

[1:6] From which some [people] having [deviated from the truth and] ~~swerved have~~ turned [to] ~~aside unto~~ [senseless discourse] ~~vain jangling;~~

Having swerved (Greek *astocheo* ἀστοχέω) means to take aim as with a bow and arrow or a javelin at a target and then to miss the mark. In a spiritual sense, the message of Paul implies that their aim was to remain on the path of truth, but now they have deviated from that objective. Years earlier, in writing to the Philippians, Paul declared,

"I *press toward the mark* for the prize of the high calling of God in Christ Jesus" (Philippians 3:14; emphasis added). It was not his intention to miss the objective to declare redeeming grace of the gospel (compare 1 Timothy 6:21 and 2 Timothy 2:18).

[1:7] Desiring to be teachers of the Law; understanding neither what they say, nor [what] ~~whereof~~ they [confidently][47] affirm.

Teachers of the law (Greek *nomodidaskalos* νομοδιδάσκαλος) refers to one who is an expounder of the law, such as a Rabbi. During the mortal ministry of Jesus the Christ, the learned doctors of the law sought to instruct Jesus respecting the meaning and intent of the Mosaic law.[48] They never did comprehend that they were seeking to contradict the actual Divine Lawgiver himself. These doctors did not understand what they were confidently affirming; the deception of their apostasy was so complete that they never recognized their confidence was in an erroneous interpretation. Jesus declared unto those doctors, "Ye know not the scriptures, neither the power of God" (Mark 12:24). On one occasion, the chief among the doctors, "Caiaphas, being the high priest . . . said unto them, Ye know nothing at all" (John 11:49). Unfortunately, not even Caiaphas understood the inspiring truth of that declaration he uttered. "Ministers need to be reminded that the gospel is not good advice, but good news. It is not

a code of laws, nor is it merely a system of ethics, but the proclamation of the redeeming work of God, our Savior. It is a message of the infinite grace offered in Christ who is 'our hope.' "[49]

[1:8] But we know that the Law is good,[50] if a man [legitimately uses it][51] ~~use it lawfully~~;

Law in this verse refers to the Mosaic law. "The law is good" does not imply that the Judaizers are right in their attempts to impose Mosaic standards on the Christian church. The Mosaic "law is good, *if* a man legitimately uses it." Mosaic rites pointed adherents toward the coming Messiah. Unfortunately, the symbolism was lost, and the ritual itself became the objective. The Torah scroll became mystically holy, but the Messianic message evaporated.

[1:9] Knowing this, that the Law is not [laid down][52] ~~made~~ for a righteous man, but for the lawless and [undisciplined] ~~disobedient~~, for the ungodly[53] and for sinners,[54] for [profane] ~~unholy~~ and [excommunicated] ~~profane~~, for [patricide][55] ~~murderers of fathers~~ and [matricide][56] ~~murderers of mothers~~, for [homicide][57] ~~manslayers~~,

Ungodly (Greek *asebes* ἀσεβής) is a word usually associated with disloyalty to the emperor—in respect of his divine role. This concept was also adapted to the Christian concept of disloyalty to the gospel and Jesus as the Christ.[58] The general translation of this word is *ungodly* in English, which appropriately means "having no reverence for God"[59] or divinity.

Unholy (Greek *hnosios* ἀνόσιος) means "impious, profane, faithless, and even cruel."[60] This word is the inverse form of *holy* (*agios* ἅγιος) meaning "sacred (physically pure, morally blameless or religious, ceremoniously consecrated)."[61]

Profane (Greek *bebelos* βέβηλος) is an unusual word meaning "*accessible* (as by crossing the doorway)."[62] This designation came to describe a person who is "excluded, excommunicated," for being "profane, unhallowed, common, [and] vulgar."[63]

Murderers of fathers (Greek *patraloas* πατραλῴας) and murderers of mothers (Greek *metraloas* μητρόλῴας), are equivalent to the Latin words *parricidium* and *matricidium*, from which the English words *patricide* and *matricide* derive. Both of these Latin words convey the notion of "a crime against a sacred and inviolable person."[64] The last word in this verse is *manslayers* (Greek *androphonos* ἀνδροφόνος). This word means "premeditated murder" and is equivalent to the English word *homicide*. Jerome preserved this meaning in Latin with *homicidis*.[65] This is the only occurrence of this word in the Greek New Testament. The Spanish translation preserves these three words as "*para los parricidas y matricidas, para los homicidas.*"[66]

Patricide and matricide (*parricidium*) are

proscribed crimes in the *Lex Cornelia de sicariis et Veneficis* implemented by the dictator Sulla. The law decreed that "he who killed a father or mother, grandfather or grandmother, was punished (*more majorum*) by being whipped till he bled, sewn up in a sack with [animals] . . . and thrown into the sea."[67] The *Lex Pompeia de Parricidiis*, "extended the crime of parricide to the killing (*dollo malo*) of a brother, sister, uncle, aunt . . . and a mother who killed a [son or daughter]."[68]

To be expected, these crimes appear in the Mosaic code: "And he that smiteth his father, or his mother, shall be surely put to death" (Exodus 21:15). The word *smite* (Hebrew *nakah* נָכָה) means "to strike."

[1:10] For [male-prostitutes][69] ~~whoremongers~~, for [sodomites][70] ~~them that defile themselves with mankind~~, for [enslavers][71] ~~menstealers~~, for liars,[72] for [perjurers][73] ~~perjured persons~~, and ~~if there be~~ any other thing ~~that is~~ contrary to sound[74] doctrine;

For whoremongers (Greek *pornos* πόρνος) means "a male prostitute" or "paid fornicator." Usually translated to *fornicators* in English, the term is specific to male prostitution.

For them that defile themselves with mankind (Greek *arsenokoites* ἀρσενοκοίτης) simply translates as a *sodomite* or *homosexual*.[75]

For menstealers (Greek *andrapodistes* ἀνδραποδιστής) is a "slave dealer," or "kidnapper." This is the only incidence of this word in the New Testament. The word derives from *andrapodon* (ἀνδρά- ποδον) meaning to "enslave, especially of conquerors, sell the free men of a conquered place into slavery."[76] An animal was *four-footed* and the slave was *two- footed*—differing only from animals in that he walked on two legs instead of all four appendages. The noun form *andra- podistes* was therefore derogatory in its intention, applied to the slave-trader who enslaves free men for profit. See also appendix C, "Slaves (*Servus*)."

[1:11] According to the glorious Gospel of the blessed God, [with] which [I] was [entrusted] ~~committed to my trust~~.

In this verse, Paul asserts that the declarations of the previous verses were not of his own opinion. He indicates that the statements were "according to the glorious Gospel."

THE ILLUSTRATION OF DIVINE MERCY (1 TIMOTHY 1:12–17)

In these verses, Paul openly portrays his own evil state prior to conversion, and how he "obtained mercy" from God. If the grace of God can redeem Paul from his sinful condition, then he also "came into the world to save [other] sinners."

[1:12] And I [am thankful to] ~~thank~~ **Christ Jesus [the]** ~~our~~ **Lord, who hath [empowered]** ~~enabled~~ **me, for**

that he [accounted] ~~counted~~ **me faithful, [appointing]**[77] ~~putting~~ **me [unto]** ~~into~~ **the ministry;**

[1:13] [Even though I] ~~Who~~ **was [formerly] before a blasphemer, and a persecutor, and [a doer of outrage]**[78] ~~injurious~~**: [yet]** ~~but~~ **I obtained mercy, because I did [act]** ~~it~~ **ignorantly in unbelief.**

Blasphemer (Greek *blasphemos* βλάσφημος) means "abusive" or "speaking evil": the application is "calumny and slander towards man, or impious towards God."[79] Additionally, the word also related to profanity toward sacred things.[80] We know of the pious Pharisaic heritage of Paul of Tarsus in the Jewish portion of his life. The blasphemy of which he accuses himself is unrelated to elective opposition towards God. Paul did, however, oppose with indignation the early Jewish converts to Christianity, and, therefore, he indirectly blasphemed toward God.[81]

Unbelief (Greek *apistia* ἀπιστία) is the negative form of "belief." Paul was not formerly a Gentile ignorant of the *Law* of God, yet he vehemently opposed God from raising man from a lower *law* to a higher *Law*—the Gospel of Jesus Christ. In this condition, his opposition was literally ignorant apostasy, until he was divinely called to repentance in a Damascus suburb.

[1:14] [But] ~~And~~ **the grace of our Lord [abounded beyond normal]** ~~was~~

exceeding abundant with faith and love which is in Christ Jesus.

Exceedingly abundant (Greek *hyperpleonazo* ὑπερπλεονάζω) means to over *abound*.[82] The message of this verse appears in the following paraphrased rendition: "But the grace of the Lord *overflowed its wonted channels*, and a stream of faith and love in me, having Jesus Christ for its source and life, flowed side by side with this full flood of grace and mercy."[83]

[1:15] [And] This is a faithful [is the word][84] saying, and worthy of all [acceptance] acceptation, that Christ Jesus came into the world to save sinners;[85] of whom I am [the primary][86] chief.

Even though not a direct quote, the same concept is expressed in Luke 5:32, "I *came* not *to call* the righteous but *sinners to repentance*." Doctrinally, this verse validated that Jesus was foreordained to come into this world as the Messiah. Paul here declares that "Jesus *came* . . . to save sinners." Corroboration of this understanding is included in the words of Jesus, "I go unto him that *sent* me" (John 7:33; 16:5; emphasis added). Further, Peter as the senior apostle, declared that Jesus "was *foreordained before the foundation of the world*" (1 Peter 1:20; emphasis added). To these solemn witnesses we add, "Behold, *I am he who was prepared from the foundation of the world to redeem my people*" (Ether 3:14; emphasis added).

[1:16] [However] Howbeit for this [reason] cause I [received] obtained mercy, that in me [primarily] first Jesus Christ might shew forth all longsuffering, for a [prototype][87] pattern to them which should hereafter believe [in] on him [unto] to [Everlasting] Life everlasting.

Longsuffering (Greek *makrothymia* μακροθυμία) or *longanimity*, is to "possess a disposition to endure patiently; unlimited patience,"[88] or "forbearing patience." The English word *longanimity* comes from Latin *longanimitas* meaning "a disposition to endure patiently."[89]

[1:17] Now unto the King [Eternal] eternal, immortal,[90] invisible, the only wise God, be [honor] honour and glory forever and ever.[91] Amen.

Eternal (Greek *aion* αἰών) means an unbroken and uninterrupted duration of times. In this verse, Paul calls God *King of the ages* (Greek *basilei ton aionon*, βασιλεῖ τῶν αἰώνων). The Greek word, *aion* transliterated to English as *eon*, also meaning an incalculable, unending period of time. Therefore, the phrase used by Paul means "King of the æons." Paul "so names God with evident allusion to the Gnostics, who dream of orders of æons in which the being of the Godhead is unfolded. God is Lord over them all."[92]

This verse is merely quoting the divine title; Paul did not coin the term "King of the ages." It existed as early as the second century BC in the Book of Tobit: "Praise the Lord of Righteousness, and exalt the *King of the ages.* . . . Give thanks worthily to the Lord, and praise the *King of the ages.*"[93] Also in the Book of Enoch, "And they said to the Lord of the ages: Lord of lords, God of gods, King of kings (and God of the ages)."[94] Further, "And I Enoch was blessing the Lord of majesty and the King of the ages."[95] Respecting earthly monarchs, their rule "does not extend into successive ages,"[96] whereas, the rule of God does.

> **Immortal** (Greek *aphthartos* ἄφθαρτος) means undecaying in the sense of uninterrupted continuance and is usually translated *incorruptible.* "Of all who have dwelt upon this earth, the Son of God stands out alone as the only one who possessed life in himself and power over death inherently."[97]

CONTRASTING TIMOTHY WITH APOSTATES (1 TIMOTHY 1:18–20)

Paul casually refers to prophetic pronouncements previously uttered respecting Timothy and his missionary success. Then he contrasts the *faith* and *good conscience* of Timothy, against the apostasy of Hymenaeus and Alexander who with Gnostic philosophy shipwrecked their own tender faith, and sought to corrupt the tender faith of the emerging Church membership.

[1:18] This charge I [entrust] ~~commit~~ unto thee, ~~son~~ Timothy [my child], according to the prophecies [previously made concerning][98] ~~which went before on~~ thee, that thou by them [might fight the] ~~mightest war a~~ good [fight] ~~warfare;~~

We never discover what the prophetic pronouncements were upon Timothy. A prophecy concerning Timothy was probably made at the time he was set apart to his current missionary assignment. We assume that Paul uttered the blessing, or was at least present when it was pronounced.

[1:19] [Having] ~~Holding~~ faith, and a good conscience; which some having [repudiated] ~~put away~~ concerning faith [are shipwrecked] ~~have made shipwreck:~~

The first portion of this verse has reference to Timothy, whereas the latter portion has reference to the apostates. This verse transitions the comparison between the faithfulness of Timothy in verse eighteen and the faithlessness of Hymenaeus and Alexander in verse nineteen. The use of the word *shipwrecked* by Paul is significant.[99] By the time he wrote the Second Epistle to the Corinthians, Paul indicated, "Thrice I suffered shipwreck, a night and a day I have been in the deep" (2 Corinthians 11:25). In respect of "a good conscience" see appendix A, "Conscience, Ethics, and Morality."

[1:20] [Namely] ~~Of whom is~~ Hymenaeus and Alexander; whom I have delivered unto Satan, [in order] that they may learn not to blaspheme.

I have delivered unto Satan (Greek

paredoka to Satana, παρέδωκα τῷ Σατανᾷ) is a phrase that is variously interpreted. Some theological scholars interpret this as excommunication from the Church, while others dispute this understanding. The difficulty is that he does not actually use the words for *excommunicate* (*aphorizo* ἀφορίζω and *anathematizo* ἀναθεματίζω) or *excommunication* (*aphorismos* ἀφορισμός and *anathematismos* ἀναθεματισμός).[100] From the content of this verse, we consider Hymenaeus and Alexander to be among "the earliest of the Gnostics"[101] who apostatized from the Church. The only legitimate interpretation of being "delivered unto Satan" is excommunication.

SUPPLICATING PRAYER FOR CIVIL LEADERS (1 TIMOTHY 2:1–8)

In the next few verses, Paul invites all to pray *for kings, and all in authority* (v. 2). Specifically, Paul is asking that they pray "for" (v. 2) and not *unto* those kings. The Gentile adherents prayed *unto* the divine Augustus and the divine Claudius. Paul instructs the Christians to pray *for* current reigning rulers, indicating that it "is good and acceptable before God, our Savior" (v. 3). Though the Roman Senate voted divinity upon certain emperors, such a vote was invalid. These human emperors possessed no powers to intercede for mortal man. Whereupon Paul declares, "There is one God and one mediator between God and men, the Man Christ Jesus" (v. 5). The divine Christ

condescended to become a mortal *man,* so that he might intercede as a divine *Man.* Christ received his status of divinity from God prior to becoming a mortal man. The emperor received his divinity from the mortal members of the Senate. Roman senators could not bestow an emperor with mediatory powers; but God could make "the Man Jesus Christ," a "mediator between God and men" (v. 5).

[2:1] [Therefore first of all,] I exhort ~~therefore, that, first of all~~ [to be made], [petitioning] ~~supplications,~~ prayers [of supplication], ~~intercessions,~~ and [thanksgiving] ~~giving of thanks, be made~~ for all men;

[2:2] For kings, and ~~for~~ all ~~that are~~ in authority; that we may lead a [tranquil] ~~quiet~~ and [quiet] ~~peaceable~~ [existence] ~~life~~ in all godliness and [reverence] ~~honesty.~~

Honesty (Greek *semnotes* σεμνότης) characterizes a person of reverence and respect. Perhaps Paul is comparing the temporal authority of imperial and political leaders with the acceptability that God has for those who live by the celestial standard of godliness and reverence. This verse is the objective of the petitioning prayer of the previous verse. In simple language, Paul asks that the members of the Church pray that temporal authorities will leave the

Christians in peace to work out their salvation and thereby come closer to the divine standard.

[2:3] For this is good and acceptable [before] ~~in the sight of~~ God our Savior;

[2:4] Who [desires][102] ~~will have~~ **all men to be saved, and to come [to a full] ~~unto the~~ knowledge of the truth [which is in Christ Jesus, who is the only begotten Son of God,]**[103]

All may receive the initiation of Christian knowledge of the truth. The Gnostic perception was that "the vulgar throng are excluded" from such initiation.[104] Years earlier, in the Colossian Epistle, Paul made it plain that the objective of the Gospel of Jesus Christ was to teach every man the knowledge of the truth—not just a select few.

"To whom God would make known what is the riches of the glory of this mystery among the Gentiles; which is Christ in you, the hope of glory: whom we preach, warning every man, and *teaching every man in all wisdom*; that we may present every man perfect in Christ Jesus" (Colossians 1:27–28; emphasis added).

[2:5] [And ordained to be a][105] ~~For there is one God, and one~~ **mediator between God and [man; who is one God, and hath power over all]**[106] **men, the Man**[107] **Christ Jesus;**

In the context of this verse, **men**

(*anthropon* ἀνθρώπων) and **man** (*anthropos* ἄνθρωπος) are the same word. We are born of mortal parentage, whereas Jesus was born of a mortal mother and a divine Father. "In the language of Adam, Man of Holiness is his name, and the name of his Only Begotten is the Son of Man, even Jesus Christ" (Moses 6:57). When we read *man* in lower case it refers to us mortals; whereas, *Man* capitalized refers to God—specifically Jesus the Christ.

[2:6] Who gave himself a ransom for all, to be testified in due time.[108]

Ransom (Greek *antilytron* ἀντίλυτρον) is a combination of two words and means redemption price—"the preposition, *anti*, stresses a substitutionary 'ransom,' "[109] and conveys the meaning of an "*antidote* or *remedy*."[110] This is the only occurrence of this Greek word in the New Testament.

In due time (Greek *kairos* καιρός) has broad application, and in a very loose sense, *kairos* means "due measure"[111] or "a time suitable for a purpose."[112] Simply stated, God has scheduled the phases of the mortal probation, judgment process, and redemptive actions.

[2:7] Whereunto I [was] ~~am~~ ordained a preacher, and an apostle, (I speak the truth in Christ, and [do not] lie ~~not~~;) a teacher of [nations] ~~the Gentiles~~ in faith and [truth] ~~verity~~.

Am ordained (Greek *tithemi* τίθημι) is a word that is open to wide interpretation.

The word expresses "appointment to any form of service."[113] A particular use of *tithemi* (τίθημι) in context is "set a stool or chair for him."[114] We may conjecture that Paul is referring to the act of ordination, in which he sat down on a chair, and Peter laid hands upon his head and ordained him a minister and an apostle. If this conjecture is correct, then Paul is recollecting the occasion of his own ordination: "As they ministered to the Lord, and fasted, the Holy Ghost said, [set apart unto] ~~separate~~ me Barnabas and Saul for the work whereunto I have called them. And when they had fasted and prayed, and *laid their hands on* them, they sent them away" (Acts 13:1–2; emphasis added).

The Gentiles (Greek *ethnos* ἔθνος, Hebrew *goy* גּוֹי) means a *race*, a *tribe*—especially foreign. From this Greek word is derived the English word *ethnic*.

[2:8] I [desire][115] ~~will~~ therefore, that [the] men pray everywhere, lifting up [pure] ~~holy~~ hands,[116] [devoid of] ~~without~~ [indignation] ~~wrath~~ and [wrangling] ~~doubting~~.[117]

Holy (Greek *hosios* ὅσιος) with reference to "hands" means *hallowed*, *pious*, *sacred*, or *sure* hands—specifically undefiled by sin. Jerome retained the meaning in Latin with the translation *puras manus*[118] (*pure hands*).

Wrath (Greek *orge* ὀργή) means *violent passion*, *indignation*, or a negative form

of any *natural impulse*.[119] In the context of this verse, *without wrath* (*choris orges*, χωρὶς ὀργῆς) suggests to "remit one's anger"[120] and become more self-disciplined—the Polish translation *gniewu*[121] means *indignation*.[122]

Doubting (Greek *dialogismos* διαλογισμός) means "internal consideration (by implication, *purpose*) or (external) *debate*."[123] A Polish translation expresses this word as *poswarku*,[124] meaning *quarrel*, *altercation*, or *wrangle*.[125] The term "devoid of indignation and wrangling" in this verse is applicable to both the "sincere prayer" and the "pure hands."

COUNSEL TO WOMEN (1 TIMOTHY 2:9–15)

Paul directs the counsel in verses 9–10 at the rich women who can afford the ever-changing Roman opulent hairstyling and clothing. Their condescending nature is in contrast to the circumstances of the other female members of the Church in humble conditions.

The discourse of verses 11–15 is not of a general nature, but directed to a woman or women who were in the process of undermining the priesthood authority of those men ordained to preside in the Church. We never discover whom this woman or these women were, only this response to a local condition of which Paul was aware. Verse fifteen is actually aimed at not only women but also their husbands as indicated by the emphasis on *they* and not *she*.

[2:9] In like manner also, that women adorn themselves in [decent] ~~modest~~ apparel, with [modesty] ~~shamefacedness~~ and [discretion] ~~sobriety~~; not with [braided] ~~broided~~ hair, or gold, or pearls, or [expensive garments][126] ~~costly array;~~

Modest in apparel (Greek *kosmios* κόσμιος) means *orderly* or *decorous*. This is probably equivalent to "the Latin *habitus* [referring] not solely to dress but also to demeanor."[127] The word can mean "well conditioned in appearance and maintenance," or philosophically, in "an acquired perfect state or condition."[128]

Shamefacedness (Greek *aidos* αἰδώς) means "bashfulness toward men or modesty toward God."[129] In particular, this word expresses the "sense" of something as in sense of honor or sense of respect.[130] The word *aidos* appears only twice in the New Testament. The other incidence is in Hebrews 12:28, where it is translated *reverence*.

Broided hair (Greek *plegma* πλέγμα) means *braided* hair. Peter also makes reference to female excesses when he said, "Let it not be that outward adorning of plaiting the hair, and of wearing of gold, or of putting on of apparel" (1 Peter 3:3). The *plaiting* (Greek *emploke* ἐμπλοκή) used by Peter is a different word that also means "elaborate braiding of the hair."[131]

Women "originally dressed their hair with great simplicity, but in the Augustan period, a variety of different head-dresses came into fashion."[133] The new fashionable *coiffure* (hairstyles) was to braid the hair very high at the front of the head, and low at the back. Livia, the wife of August, enhanced the fashion of braiding her hair in tiers (steps) for attending the imperial court, in marble bust representation, and appearing on Roman coinage. The hair braid fashion moved to a double row, then a treble row, then to higher and higher rows of hair. By mid-first century, attached jewels bespeckled the tower of braided hair in gaudy complexity.[134]

The fashionable coiffure became so intense that it necessitated the use of false hairpieces and even full wigs.[135] The names of these "artificial tresses" were *crines*, *galerus*, and *corybium*.[136] The cosmetic market provided various animal, mineral, and vegetable-based concoctions to cater to the prevailing fashionable color and texture. "A woman will dye her hair with the juice of some German herb; and the artificial color becomes her better than the natural one. A woman will appear wearing a mass of hair that she has just purchased. For a little money, she can buy another's tresses."[137] The market of human hair extended throughout the empire, with blond hair coming from Gaul and Germany, while black hair came from far-away India.[138]

The driving force behind the coiffure was vanity. "In ancient Rome hair was a major determinant of a women's physical attractiveness and was thus deemed worthy of considerable exertions to create a flattering appearance."[139] The extent of Roman hairstyling is evident on coins, statues, fresco paintings, and intricate mosaics of the period. A common feature of the period was for the rich to have marble statues of their own likeness displayed in their home or atrium. Several female statues of the period exist with modifications and interchangeable coiffure hairpieces to keep up with the latest fashion. "A woman's age, social status, and public role"[140] defined the extent of her dedication to hairdressing opulence. The process of hairstyling in the Greco-Roman world was considerably more labor intensive than it is today. The Roman author Juvenal penned poetic lines that are valid even today: "To deck her person such the pains they take; / As if her life and honor were at stake! / With curls on curls, like diff'rent stories, rise / Her towering locks, a structure to the skies."[141]

Every wealthy woman possessed a considerable display of cosmetic products to sustain the daily transformation. The final act of the day for a woman was the removal of the cosmetic transformation. All applied compounds were wiped and washed away prior to retiring for the night. The writer Martial penned the following reproach to displayed beauty, "You lie stored away in a hundred caskets, and your face does not sleep with you."[142]

Finally, we must also mention the professional hairdresser or tire-woman—called *ornatrix* in Latin.[143] The *onatrix* was either a hired professional or a trained slave.[144] "The skills of the tire-woman were indispensable for erecting these elaborate scaffoldings, and the epitaphs of many *ornitrices* tell us the dates of their death and the families by whom they were employed."[145]

[2:10] But [what] (which becometh women professing [fear of God][146] godliness) [by means of][147] with good works.

Paul indicates that there is godliness in the Church with good works instead of braided hair and expensive garments.[148]

[2:11] Let the woman learn in [stillness] silence with all [submissiveness][149] subjection.

Silence (Greek *hesychia* ἡσυχία) means "*stillness*, i.e. desistance from bustle or language."[150] When the translators elected to use *silence*, they did not realize the difficulty they generated across the following centuries. It is obvious Jerome influenced them with the Latin translation *silentio* meaning *silence*.[151]

Subjection (Greek *hypotage* ὑποταγή) also means subordination. Paul here means *submissiveness* in the sense of reverent decorum and not usurping priesthood authority as indicated in the next verse. The word *subjection* implies imposition, whereas, *submissiveness* conveys choice.

The declarations of this verse have reference to "behavior in Church assemblies."[152] There is no intention for this statement to curtail women from contributing and taking a primary role in some areas of Church programs.[153] Paul "appeals to the original order and course of things."[154] This is not the first time that Paul penned this teaching. Many years earlier, he wrote the same with greater clarity to the Corinthians: "Let your women keep [still] ~~silence~~ in the [congregations] ~~churches~~: for it is not permitted unto them to [preside][155] ~~speak~~; but ~~they are commanded~~[156] to be under obedience, as also saith the law. And if they will learn any thing, let them ask their husbands at home: for it is [an embarrassment] ~~a shame~~ for women to [be outspoken][157] ~~speak~~ in the church" (1 Corinthians 14:34–35).

[2:12] [For][158] ~~But~~ I [do not permit] ~~suffer not~~ a woman to [give instruction] ~~teach~~, nor to usurp authority over the man, but to be in [stillness] silence.

I suffer not (Greek *epitrepo* ἐπιτρέπω) means to transfer authority. The intended use of this word receives emphasis by the addition of another word in this verse. **To teach** (Greek *didasko* διδάσκω) "denotes to cause to learn" in the sense of "to give instruction."[159] This is an epistle of instruction from an apostle to another Church leader, teaching him about the priesthood authority. From the wording of this section, it is obvious that Paul is responding to some information previously received from Timothy concerning local conditions in the Church. As with incidents in the Corinthian epistles, these statements are in response to local issues. Unfortunately, we do not possess the information Paul had when he dictated this letter. The verses in this section point to some woman or women usurping authority from the ordained leadership of a congregation. One way or the other, Paul was instructing Timothy to end it before it undermined the whole congregation.

[2:13] For Adam was first formed, then Eve.

[2:14] And Adam was not [deluded] ~~deceived~~, but the woman being [deluded] ~~deceived~~ was[160] in [violation] ~~the transgression~~.

These final verses (12–15) are difficult for us to recognize as a conclusion to the subject matter of the past verses. These sentiments would seem to indicate a Jewish answer to the situation. Adam "was not beguiled in comparison with the complete direct beguiling of Eve."[161] If only we knew something about the woman or women to whom Paul was referring. There is no need to play the apologist and impose a supposed sanitized interpretation to these verses. Paul was upset and vented his verbal displeasure in this letter.

[2:15] Notwithstanding [they][162] ~~she shall be~~ [preserved through the bearing of children][163] ~~saved in childbearing,~~[164] if they [remain] ~~continue~~ in faith and charity and holiness with [demureness] ~~sobriety~~.

Sobriety (Greek *sophrosune* σωφροσύνη) "refers to having complete control over the passions and desires so that they are lawful and reasonable."[165] This meaning has since become redundant in the English use of the word. In English, *sobriety* now refers to the period of abstinence in addiction recovery.[166] A German version translated this word to *Sittsamkeit*,[167] meaning "demureness" or "good manners."[168]

The traditional target audience of verses 14–15 is women. However, the inclusion of the term "they remain" (Greek *meinosin* μείνωσιν) in this verse means to *hold good* to something.[169] Of particular importance is the observation that Paul shifts the onus of responsibility from *the woman* in the previous verse to *they* in this verse. It is refreshing to see that the Inspired Version also endorsed this concept with the change from *she* to *they* at the beginning of this

verse. Therefore, the target audience of this verse is not only the women, but also the husbands. Paul declares certain criteria, [*If they* comply] "with the spiritual provisions and requirements of the plan of God: in *faith*, implicitly resting upon God's word of promise; in *love*, yielding themselves heartily to the duties of their special calling, as well as consenting to live and act within its appointed limits; in *holiness*, wakeful, and striving against occasions of sin; and all tempered and controlled by that spirit of meek and wise *discretion* which instinctively shrinks from whatever is unbecoming, heady, or high-minded."[170]

THE CHARACTER OF THE BISHOP (1 TIMOTHY 3:1–7)

In this passage, we see great similarity with Titus 1:7–9. The characteristics and qualities defined in both instances describe individuals who will assume authoritative leadership positions in the everyday affairs of local Church government. Paul well realized the influential position held by a bishop; no other Church leader works so closely with the problems that beset the membership. Timothy was himself an ecclesiastical leader. Through the course of the centuries, the office of bishop distanced itself from its intended position close to the congregation. A bishop who does not know each one of his flock cannot fulfill his calling effectively.

[3:1] [Trustworthy] ~~This~~ is [the word] ~~a true saying~~, **If a man desire the office of a bishop, he desireth a good work.**

A true saying (Greek *logos* λόγος) conveys an expression of thought and, in this instance, equates with the Old Testament context of "hear the word [Hebrew *davar* דָּבָר] of [Jehovah] the Lord" (Ezekiel 6:2).

The office of a bishop (Greek *episkope* ἐπισκοπή) literally means *inspection*, and by implication *superintendence* or, the Christian designation, *episcopate*.[171] The New Testament generally interprets this word in the exclusive sense of *bishop*; however, it may also be applicable to other offices of priesthood leadership. Psalms 109:8[172] reads, "Let his days be few; and let another take his *office*." Prior to the New Testament era, Jewish translators prepared the Septuagint Greek version of the Old Testament. They used the word *episkope*[173] that we have as *bishop* in English. The original Hebrew word *pequddah* (פְּקֻדָּה) conveys the meaning of an official visitation. The Greek word *presbyteros* (πρεσβύτερος) meant it "was of Jewish origin" and referred to the presiding elders (*zeqenim* זְקֵנִים) "of the synagogal community in the first instance, and then of the Christian church."[174] This Hebrew word for *elders* simply transliterated to Greek as *presbyteros* (πρεσβύτερος).[175] The interchange of "the terms [*episkopos*] ἐπίσκοπος and [*presbyteros*] πρεσβύτερος" in the Timothy and Titus epistles makes it clear that the

two designations are interchangeable.[176] Congregations where the converts were predominantly Jewish designated the *bishop* as the *presbyter*. Congregations composed of ethnic Greeks (non-Jewish) designated the *bishop* as the *episkopos* (ἐπίσκοπος), meaning *overseer*. This word had "specific or official designation among the Athenians of whom they sent forth to take the oversight of their subject cities . . . so that, by an easy transference from the civil to the spiritual sphere, the *episcopoi* of the church were those who had the pastoral oversight of the several churches."[177]

[3:2] **A bishop then must be [irreproachable]**[178] ~~blameless~~, **the husband of one wife, vigilant, [prudent]** ~~sober~~, **[well-ordered]**[179] ~~of good behaviour~~, **given to hospitality, [an] apt [teacher]** ~~to teach~~;

Blameless (Greek *anepileptos* ἀνεπίληπτος) means "not arrested, i.e. by implication inculpable,"[180] as in "not open to attack."[181] The intent seems to be that a man called to serve in the office of bishop should not have a criminal record or tendency toward crime.

In this verse, Paul specifically directs that one of the qualifications for ordination to the office of bishop is marriage to *one* wife.[182] The declaration of Paul "is *not* to make *laws* of a 'higher life' for ministers than for people, but to expect the same laws kept in a way to serve for ensample to the flock."[183] Remember that Paul also declared, "marriage is honorable in all"

(Hebrews 13:4). Another author wisely observed, "A bishop is to be a man who neither lives nor has lived in sexual intercourse with any other woman than the one to whom he is married."[184]

Considerable insight is required to interpret such passages without personal, religious, cultural, or traditional bias. Once again, we have Paul responding to a condition that we endeavor to reconstruct from the answer without recourse to the original query. The wise interpretation of the following author is refreshing.

> "In the corrupt facility of divorce allowed by both the Greek and Roman law, it was very common for man and wife to separate, and marry other parties, during the life of one another. Thus, a man might have three or four living wives; or, rather, women who had all successively been his wives. . . . We believe it is this kind of successive polygamy, rather than simultaneous polygamy, which is here spoken of as disqualifying for the Presbyterate."[185]

Sober (Greek *sophron* σώφρων) means "*safe (sound)* in *mind, i.e. self-controlled (moderate* as to opinion or passion)."[186] The translation of *sober* implies sober from alcohol; however, the first word in the next verse deals with alcohol. Therefore, Paul did not convey this meaning; he must have intended *self-control* in the sense of *self-disciplined*. "Properly, a man of a sound mind; [is] one who follows sound reason, and who is not under the control of passion. The idea is that he

should have his desires and passions well regulated. Perhaps the word *prudent* would come nearer to the meaning of the apostle than any single word which we have."[187]

Of good behaviour (Greek *kosmios* κόσμιος) primarily means *orderly, regular, moderate*.[188] Considering the catalog of attributes in these verses, Paul seems to imply a sense of being able to order and organize things. The first word in this verse meant *irreproachable*; therefore, this word should not impose upon the earlier word. Paul is looking for a man with a good sense for business, who keeps his affairs in order, and who is sensible in the extent of his risk-taking.

Apt to teach (Greek *didaktos* διδακτός) means capable of learning and then teaching[189] (in the sense of implementing) what was taught to others. The man must possess a motivational leadership style to convey instruction to others.[190] "We all need to be touched and nurtured by the Spirit, and effective teaching is one of the most important ways this can happen. We often do vigorous enlistment work to get members to come to church but then do not adequately watch over what they receive when they do come."[191]

[3:3] Not [a hard drinker[192] or quarrelsome][193] ~~given to wine, no striker,~~ not [profiteering] ~~greedy of filthy lucre;~~ but patient, not [contentious][194] ~~a brawler,~~ [unavaricious] ~~not covetous;~~

Given to wine (Greek *paroinos* πάροινος) means, "tarrying at wine"; alternatively interpreted to imply not "drunk and disorderly."[195] However, the word here "does not mean simply *drunken* but *imprudent, arrogant in intoxication*."[196] This can be explained further that "one who is in the *habit* of drinking wine, or who is accustomed to sit with those who indulge in it, should not be admitted to the ministry."[197] There is an invariable link between this word and the following word **striker** (Greek *plektes* πλήκτης). Together, the two terms convey one concept, "not a hard drinker nor given to blows."[198]

Greedy of filthy lucre (Greek *aischro-kerdes* αἰσχροκερδής) means *sordid* as "pertaining to or actuated by a low desire for gain."[199] The translation of *profiteering* comes from the similar use of this word in Titus 1:7. Though not specifically indicated, we presume that Paul was referring to the collection of tithing and other contributions and to the disbursement of Church funds in maintenance and care of the poor. "It seems worth stressing that taking private profit from public office was built into the Roman system of provincial administration."[200] A sordid individual may abuse the position of bishop to engage in profiteering from Church funds. Further emphasis on this qualification appears with the use of the word *unavaricious* in this same verse below.

Not a brawler (Greek *amachos* ἄμαχος) means "without battle," in the sense of a person "with whom no one fights."[201] Applications of this word in Greek point to attraction as opposed to repulsion. In this verse, Paul could have chosen a positive word to express the desired characteristic, but he elected to use a negative word and prefix it with the word *not*.

Not covetous (Greek *aphilargyros* ἀφιλάργυρος) means "unavaricious [or] free from the love of money."[202] A modern translation has rendered this term as "free from the love of money."[203] Two French translations are interesting: *non avare*[204] meaning "not miserly"; and *exempt d'avarice*[205] meaning "without avarice." The English word *avarice* means that a person has a passion for riches,[206] and *avaritious*, that a person is greedy for gain.[207] With profiteering institutionalized in the Roman Empire, "both governor and tax-farmer were usually interested in making a private profit."[208] Paul, therefore, sought to counter the Greco-Roman acceptability of avarice in church office from gaining acceptance within the Church. The damage that a bishop who engages in defalcation of Church funds can cause to the spiritual welfare of others is enormous.

[3:4] [Leading] ~~One that ruleth~~ well his own house, [with] ~~having~~ his children [obeying in a manner of proper respect] ~~in subjection with all gravity;~~[209]

One that ruleth (Greek *proistemi* προΐστημι) means "to *stand before* . . . [or] to *preside*"[210] in the sense of *leading*. This portion of the verse speaks of the entire Greco-Roman household, and includes the servants and slaves. If a man "does not know how to preside over his own house, how will he take charge of God's Church."[211] If a bishop is to lead "well his own house with children," it implies the fact that he has a family. A celibate ministry is contrary to the doctrines of biblical Christianity.[212]

[3:5] ([But] ~~For~~ if a man know not how to [manage][213] ~~rule~~ **his own house, how [will] ~~shall~~ he take care of the Church of God?)**[214]

"A church [i.e. congregation] resembles a family. It is, indeed, larger and therefore is a greater variety of dispositions in it than there is in a family. The authority of a minister is less absolute than that of a father. But still there is a striking resemblance. The church is made up of an assemblage of brothers and sisters. They are banded together for the same purposes, and have a common object to aim at. They have common feelings and common wants. They have sympathy, like a family, with each other in their distresses and afflictions. The government of the church is designed to *paternal*. It should be felt that he who presides over it has the feelings of a father; that he loves all the members of the great family; that he has no prejudices, no partialities, no selfish aims to gratify."[215]

[3:6] [And] not a [new convert] ~~novice~~, lest [becoming conceited] ~~being lifted up with pride~~ he fall into the [same]

condemnation [as] ~~of~~ the Devil.[216]

It is not desirable to have a new convert preside over a congregation.[217] The new convert is unlearned in the doctrines of the Church and therefore can inadvertently be the cause of much harm among the membership of the congregation. In this particular verse, Paul also warns of the increased exposure with which such a man may be tempted.

[3:7] Moreover he must have a good [reputation with those outside][218] ~~report of them which are without~~; **lest he fall into reproach and the [noose] ~~snare~~ of the Devil.**

The snare (Greek *pagis* παγίς) "a trap (as fastened by a noose or notch) . . . [as] the allurements to evil by which the Devil ensnares."[219] Translated in German as *Schlinge*,[220] meaning slip-knot as used in a hunting snare for rabbits.[221] Compare with 1 Timothy 6:9 where the same Greek word appears in relation to temptation with respect to riches.

THE CHARACTER OF THE DEACON (1 TIMOTHY 3:8–10, 12–13)

We must observe that Paul speaks of a bishop (singular), and of the deacons (plural). Each organized congregation will have one bishop, but several deacons. Rather than define the qualifications for each priesthood office, Paul elects to define the high standards of character for the lowest office, thereby de facto defining the standards for all other offices in the Aaronic or Levitical and even Melchizedek Priesthood. Before ordaining any man to an office in the priesthood, "They must first be tested; and then if there is nothing against them, let them serve as deacons."[222] A man must first qualify himself for the priesthood before ordination—and not the other way around.

———— 🦋 ————

[3:8] [Deacons in like manner] ~~Likewise~~ must ~~the deacons~~ be[223] [honorable][224] ~~grave~~, not [double-dealing] ~~doubletongued~~, not given to much wine, not [profiteering] ~~greedy of filthy lucre~~;

Double-tongued (Greek *dilogos* δίλογος) "primarily means saying the same thing twice, or given to repetition; hence, saying a thing to one person and giving a different view of it to another."[225] In this context, the English word is comparable to the word *duplicity* meaning *double-dealing*. Double-tongued appears in the English translation of a verse from the Old Testament Apocrypha, "Do not be called a slanderer, and do not lie in ambush with your tongue; for shame comes to the thief, and severe condemnation to *the double-tongued*."[226] In non-scriptural use, this unique word appears in the writings of the Greek author Xenophon centuries earlier.[227] He used the form *dilogia* (δίλογία)[228] which is interpreted as *repetition*, in the sense of *gossip* or *hearsay*.

Greedy of filthy lucre (Greek *aischrokerdes* αἰσχροκερδής) means *sordid*[229] as "pertaining to, or actuated by, a low desire for gain."[230] Schlachter translated this word into German as *Wucherer*[231] meaning *profiteering* and *moneylending*.[232]

[3:9] Holding the [ordinances] ~~mystery~~ of the faith in a pure conscience.[233]

Mystery (Greek *mysterion* μυστήριον) relates to *a secret* "through the idea of silence imposed by *initiation* into religious rites."[234] This Greek word comes from established Greek culture going back many centuries—long before Socrates and Plato lectured in Athens.[235] Greek culture was thick with an over abundance of mysteries with initiation rites.[236] Most prominent and ancient among the cults were the Eleusian mysteries.[237] "The buildings at Eleusis . . . consisted of the temple of Demeter and the Mystic House, in which the secret festivals were held."[238] The Eleusian mysteries were "in two degrees," and "the *Initiates* of the lesser mysteries were called *Mystae*, those of the greater mysteries, *Epoptae* (those who have seen)."[239] Performance of the lesser mysteries—or initiation rites—took place without or before, and the greater rites of induction took place within the Mystic or Sacred House.[240]

The Eleusian initiation rites are only one example of the many cult mysteries. Examples were the Orphic Mysteries, Mysteries of Rhea (Cybele-Attis),

Mysteries of Mithras, and Mysteries of Sabazius.[241] Others were the Mysteries of Cabiri on Samothrace Island;[242] Mysteria Dionysia (Mysteries of Dionyus or Bacchus);[243] Mysteria of Asklepios;[244] and the Mysteries of Zeus on Crete Island in which the initiates "enacted the story of the childhood of Zeus."[245] Even apostate Jews in the pre-Christian era became involved in the secrets of strange mysteries.[246] Through the rites of these mysteries, the initiate became filled with *enthusiasm* (Greek *enthoysiasmos* ἐνθουσιασμός).[247] The base form of this Greek word is *enthoysia* (ἐνθουσία) or *enthoysiao* (ἐνθουσιάω), meaning, "*to be inspired or possessed by a god.*"[248] As one author simply expressed it, "he became an *enthusiast*—a man full of the gods."[249]

The legacy of Greek mysteries and initiation rites were in no way a forerunner to Christian ordinances.[250] Only the vocabulary was adapted to Christian use and not the contents.[251] Christian ordinances were Christ-oriented or Christ-centered, and only coincidentally comparable to any form of Greek cult mysteries.[252] The Greek language evolved through the need to express philosophic terms and thereby created a platform to express the Gospel of Jesus Christ. Likewise, Greco-Roman cult mysteries not only created the vocabulary, but also culturally prepared the minds of the people to embrace Christian ordinances.[253] Satan sought to destroy the minds of the people with cultic pollution, yet the wisdom of God was not thereby thwarted but furthered.[254]

The devils ploughed and planted, but God counter-planted and harvested the gospel wheat and supplanted the tares of cult ignorance. Paul declared once before in Athens, "Forasmuch then as we are the offspring of God, we ought not to think that the Godhead is like unto gold, or silver, or stone, graven by art and man's device. And *the times of this ignorance God winked at; but now commandeth all men every where to repent*" (Acts 17:29–30).

Paul made previous reference to Christian mysteries and initiation ceremonies years earlier when he called himself and the other apostles "stewards of the [ordinances] ~~mysteries~~ of God" (1 Corinthians 4:1–2). He also clearly stated, "We speak wisdom among them that are perfect: yet not the wisdom of this world, nor of the princes of this world, that come to nought: *we speak the wisdom of God in [ordinances]* ~~a mystery~~, *even hidden wisdom*, which God ordained before the world unto our glory" (1 Corinthians 2:6–7). The greatest mystery is how God could harvest wheat from a field of tares!

From the verse here in Timothy, we must conclude that Paul is speaking about the initiation rites of baptism, confirmation, ordination, and sacrament (external or open rites). The intent of this verse is not temple ordinances (internal or closed rites), as the subject is qualifications for deacons of the Aaronic Priesthood—as emphasized in the following verse.

[3:10] And let these also first be proved;

then let them use the office of a
deacon, being found [irreproach-
able] ~~blameless~~.

PRIESTHOOD LEADERS' WIVES (1 TIMOTHY 3:11)

This verse is an interesting interlude in the dialog concerning deacons.
Women are also called upon to rise up
to certain of the qualifications defined
for deacons.

[3:11] Even so must their wives be [honor-
able][255] ~~grave~~, not slanderers, [pru-
dent] ~~sober~~, faithful in all things.

Sober (Greek *sophron* σώφρων) means
"sound in mind" or "self-controlled."[256]
Luther translated this word to German as
besonnen, meaning prudent, circumspect,
or discreet.[257]

DEACON QUALIFICATIONS CONTINUED (1 TIMOTHY 3:12–13)

Following the interlude in verse eleven,
Paul returns to the subject matter first
introduced in verse eight above.

[3:12] Let the deacons be the husbands of
one wife, [leading] ~~ruling~~ their children and their own houses well.

[3:13] For [those who have been deacons
acquire] ~~they that have used the
office of a deacon well purchase to~~

[for] themselves a good [standing][258]
~~degree~~, and great [confidence] ~~bold-
ness~~ in the faith [that][259] ~~which~~ is in
Christ Jesus.

They that have used the office of a deacon
(Greek *diakoneo* διακονέω) as a base
word means, "to *be an attendant*," or to
"*wait upon*."[260] In this verse, the form of
the word *diakonesantes* (διακονήσαντες)
cannot be translated into English as one
word.

TIMOTHY IS IN CHARGE (1 TIMOTHY 3:14–15)

The remaining three verses conclude
the teaching of this chapter. Though
Paul expects to come to Ephesus immediately, yet he anticipates that he may
not be in a position to do so. Therefore,
he indicates his confidence in Timothy's
ability to make the necessary decisions
based upon the instruction Paul has just
provided in this chapter.

[3:14] These things write I unto thee,
hoping to [quickly] come unto thee
~~shortly~~:

The forthcoming arrest and transportation to Rome overruled Paul's plan to
return to Timothy at Ephesus. Paul would
never again visit Ephesus in mortality.

[3:15] But if I [am delayed] ~~tarry long~~,
[this will clarify to thee the expected
behavior] ~~that thou mayest know
how thou oughtest to behave thyself~~

in the House of God, which is the Church of the Living God, the pillar and [the foundation] ~~ground~~ of the truth.[261]

The emphasis of this verse should not be on how Timothy is *to behave*, but on what behavior Timothy is to expect in others. Throughout this chapter, Paul has provided instruction on the expected behavior of those called to serve in the Church. Timothy receives counsel respecting others: he is in harmony with the senior Brethren, yet members of the Church in Ephesus are not.[262]

GODLINESS (1 TIMOTHY 3:16)

Just as verse eleven above was an interjection, so is this verse. The content of the verse is not the issue, only its placement here between the qualifications for priesthood leadership given above, and a prophecy of a forthcoming apostasy in the following verses. There is interruption in the dictation of these concepts. Something is distracting Paul—as indicated in the previous verse. This would partially explain the disruptive flow of the record.

————————— ❧ —————————

[3:16] [263](And without controversy, great [are] ~~is~~ the [ordinances] ~~mystery~~ of godliness:) God was manifest[264] in the flesh, justified in the Spirit, seen [by] ~~of~~ angels, preached unto the Gentiles, believed on in the world, received up into glory.

Mystery (Greek *mysterion* μυστήριον) received attention in detail in verse 3:9 above. Never at any time is it appropriate to use the English meaning of "mystery" for this word. In this verse, the application is either the gospel, simplistic *ordinance*, or the more general meaning *initiation*. The interpretation of this word is contained in the whole concept; great are the *ordinances* or *initiations* of godliness.

Of godliness (Greek *eusebeia* εὐσέβεια) may be interpreted as that which is "communicated through the truths of the faith concerning Christ."[265] Translations interpret "the mystery of godliness" in a lower meaning, instead of a higher meaning. Years earlier, Paul wrote to the Romans, "The Spirit itself beareth witness with our spirit, that we are the children of God: and if children, then heirs; *heirs of God, and joint-heirs with Christ*; if so be that we suffer with him, that we may be also *glorified together*" (Romans 8:16–17). *The initiation of godliness* seems to relate to the future exaltation of man with Christ. Peter clarifies this concept, "Whereby are given unto us exceeding great and precious promises: that by these ye might be *partakers of the divine nature*" (2 Peter 1:4). The Greek word *eusebeia* here translated as *godliness*, translated in Scottish Gaelic as *diadhachd*[266] and in Irish Gaelic *diadhacht* (ᵭᵭᵭᵭᵭᵭᵭ)[267] means the Divine Nature[268] in both Gaelic languages. Recalling the words of Paul penned to the Philippians years earlier, "I press toward the mark for *the prize of the high calling of God* in

Christ Jesus. . . . And if in any thing ye be otherwise minded, *God shall reveal even this unto you!*" (Philippians 3:14–15) These are "the words of faith and of good doctrine" mentioned below in 4:6. This verse may be a quote from a hymn or poem about Jesus the Christ.

PROPHECY ON APOSTASY (1 TIMOTHY 4:1–6)

When speaking of apostasy from the true gospel of Jesus Christ it usually alludes to three phases. The first is the apostasy that followed with the death of all the first century apostles. Phase two is the apostasy of the decadent Middle or Dark Ages (AD 500–1500), when that which was termed Christianity descended to its lowest level of repugnance—prior to the Christian Reformation. Finally, phase three "the latter times" of our present day—prior to the Second Coming of Jesus the Christ—alluded to in the next verse. Prophesies may be applicable to one or all of these phases—with multiple application. How grateful we are to all those who labor to live righteously in these latter days, stand firm, and remain unpolluted in these days of human degeneracy.

[4:1] [But] ~~Now~~ the Spirit speaketh [distinctly] ~~expressly~~, that in the latter times some [will apostatize][269] ~~shall depart~~ from the faith, giving [their mind] ~~heed~~ to seducing spirits, and doctrines of devils;

Expressly (Greek *rhetos* ῥητῶς) means simply *outspoken* or *distinctly*. This verse indicates that the Spirit *speaketh*: Paul distinctly heard a divine voice speaking words of prophesy to him, and not just a spiritual prompting.

Latter (Greek *ysteros* ὕστερος) means *later* in the sense of *occur later* as following after something else.[270] This is the only occurrence of this word in the New Testament.

Giving heed (Greek *prosecho* προσέχω) means to *apply the mind, to be inclined*, or *to persist* in listening to what is said.[271] Satan and his minions are artful spirits at seducing the mind of mortal man—once giving devils access to the mind. Satan pollutes the mind with seductive values. Once these pollutions replace sound principles of the conscience, the seduction is complete. Compromising the doors to the conscience occurs when pride and envy replace the scales of truth and righteousness.

[4:2] [As][272] speaking lies in hypocrisy; having [desensitized] their conscience ~~seared with a hot iron~~;

Seared with a hot iron (Greek *kauteriazo* καυτηριάζω) means to *brand* or to *cauterize*, and thereby to *render numb*. The literal translation is *having cauterized their conscience*.[273] See appendix D, "Conscience, Ethics, and Morality." However, Paul is not using the word to identify with the cauterizing process as though it were a branding. In this sentence, the word highlights that respecting the truth of the gospel, "their conscience" is *desensitized.* The desensitized nature of these ministers in a time of apostasy is significantly applicable to the period of the Dark Ages of Christianity. Under a priesthood of tyranny, the populace of Christianity was enslaved. The process of Christian reformation has accomplished much since the days of Luther, Calvin, Wesley, and other alert reformers.

[4:3] Forbidding to marry, [saying] ~~and commanding~~ to abstain from [foods] ~~meats,~~ which God hath created to be received with thanksgiving [by the faithful[274] knowing] ~~of them which believe and know~~ the truth.[275]

Meats (Greek *bromata* βρωματα) means *foods*—literally or figuratively;[276] translated into German as *Speisen* meaning *foods.*[277] The word *broma* can be translated *meats,* yet this is a restrictive interpretation; whereas, *foods* is a more appropriate interpretation. The declarations of this verse are pointing forward to the time of burden when corrupted Christianity teaches the heretical doctrines of institutional celibacy and peculiar food laws.

[4:4] [Because] ~~For~~ every creature of God is good, and nothing to be [rejected] ~~refused,~~ [being][278] ~~if it be~~ received with thanksgiving:

[4:5] ~~For~~ it is sanctified [through][279] ~~by~~ the Word of God and prayer.

[4:6] [Pointing these things to][280] ~~If thou put~~ the brethren ~~in remembrance of these things,~~ thou shalt be a good minister of Jesus Christ, [being] nourished [with][281] ~~up in~~ the words of [the][282] faith and [by the] ~~of~~ good doctrine, [which you have followed][283] ~~whereunto thou hast attained.~~[284]

GODLY LIVING (1 TIMOTHY 4:7–11)

In this section of the epistle, Paul directs Timothy to "exercise thyself" (v.7)—thus actively refusing and not passively ignoring. Paul entreats Timothy to exercise his innate talents to his advantage in *every way* (v.8); to withstand the apostates and to encourage the faithful who have set their hope in the living God (v.10).

[4:7] But [the] ~~refuse~~ profane and old wives' fables [refuse], and exercise thyself ~~rather~~ unto godliness.

Profane (Greek *bebelos* βέβηλος) actually means "accessible (as by *crossing the door-way*), i.e. (by implication of Jewish notions) *heathenish.*"[285] Paul is using a Jewish term in a Greek environment. The connotation is that *profane* has reference to Jewish fables—independent of the old wives' fables.[286] Another author considered these fables "such as old women tell to children."[287] The counsel to Timothy in this verse is "rather than attempt to understand those fables, do not occupy your time and attention with them."[288] Instead, Timothy is to focus on developing the characteristic of *godliness*. We may conjecture that these comments from Paul were in response to comments made by Timothy in earlier correspondence. This will be true of several disjointed comments in all his response epistles.

[4:8] **For bodily exercise [has] ~~profiteth~~ little [advantage]:[289] but godliness is [advantageous] ~~profitable~~ [in every way][290] ~~unto all things~~, having promise of the life that now is, and of that which is to come.**

Bodily exercise in this verse is possibly a reference "to the mortifications of the body by the abstinence and penance" of cultic "devotees," who considered such to be "a part of their religion."[291]

[4:9] **~~This is a~~ Faithful [is the word] ~~saying~~ and worthy of all [acceptance] ~~acceptation~~.[292]**

[4:10] **For [to this also] ~~therefore~~ we ~~both~~ labor and [are reproached][293] ~~suffer reproach~~, because we [have set hope][294] ~~trust~~ in the Living God, who is the Savior of all men, [especially of the faithful][295] ~~specially of those that believe~~.**

[4:11] **~~These things~~ Command and teach [these things].[296]**

[4:12] **Let no [one][297] ~~man~~ despise thy youth; but [become][298] ~~be thou~~ an example of the believers, in word, in [conduct][299] ~~conversation~~, in [love] ~~charity~~, in spirit, in faith, in purity.**

Youth (Greek *neotes* νεότης) means *newness* as respecting *youthfulness*. The Latin translation of this word is *adulescentiam*—from which the English word *adolescence* is derived. The word referred to "grown-up military age, extending to the 40th year."[300] For example, Marcus Tullius Cicero (106–43 BC) used this Latin word to describe himself when he was age twenty-seven; the word is also applied to Gaius Julius Caesar (100–44 BC) when he was age thirty-five.[301] "We may therefore presume that Timothy was now between thirty and forty."[302]

[4:13] **[Until] ~~Till~~ I come, give attendance to [public scripture] reading, to exhortation, [in][303] ~~to~~ [teaching] doctrine.**

To reading (Greek *anagnosis* ἀνάγνωσις) means "the public *reading* of scripture."[304] This word appears in the Acts of the Apostles, with reference to scripture reading in a Jewish synagogue worship service.[305]

[4:14] **Neglect not the gift ~~that is~~ in thee, [that] ~~which~~ was given thee [through][306] ~~by~~ prophecy, with the laying on of the hands of the [elders][307] ~~presbytery~~.**

Of the presbytery (Greek *presbyterion*

πρεσβυτέριον) refers to "the *order of elders*, i.e. (specifically) Israeli *Sanhedrin* or Christian *presbytery*."[308] This is an obvious reference to the setting apart of Timothy to this current ministry. "It was common to lay on the hands in imparting a blessing, or in setting apart to any office."[309] At the time when Timothy was set apart or ordained to his assignment, we have a record that Paul was one of the elders—if not the actual one—who set apart Timothy. Writing to Timothy in the next epistle, Paul declares, "Stir up the gift of God, which is in thee *by the putting on of my hands*" (2 Timothy 1:6).

[4:15] [Attend to] ~~Meditate upon~~ these things; give thyself wholly to them; that [everyone may see thy progress][310] ~~thy profiting may appear to all~~.

[4:16] [Give attention to] ~~Take heed unto~~ thyself, and [to] ~~unto~~ the doctrine; continue in them: for in doing this thou shalt both save thyself, and [those hearing] ~~them that hear~~ thee.

[5:1] Rebuke not an elder, but [exhort] ~~intreat~~ him as a father; [young ones] ~~and the younger men~~ as [brothers] ~~brethren;~~[311]

[5:2] [Older] ~~The elder~~ women as mothers; [young women] ~~the younger~~ as sisters, [in] ~~with~~ all purity.[312]

WIDOWS (1 TIMOTHY 5:3–16)

The following verses deal with issues concerning the distribution of alms to widows. Those who have posterity should assume their responsibility for the maintenance of their parents and grandparents. Those widows who are without living descendants (left alone) are to receive maintenance support from the Church welfare funds. Though not indicated, we must interject, the capacity to extend welfare support is limited to the extent to which other members of the congregation contribute donations to the Church. In v. 7, Paul instructs Timothy to implement these principles as standard practice for the Church—an executive decision of the Apostles.

[5:3] Honor widows that are [really] widows ~~indeed~~.

Honour (Greek *timao* τιμάω) means to *prize* or *revere* those widows "who are bereft of all human support . . . All almsgiving ought to be an honoring of the recipients, not a lowering of their self-respect."[313] Though the translation is correct, the intended meaning is obscure in English. Several of the women who are practically widows, are well capable of providing for themselves, or remarrying. However, there are widows who are in difficult poor conditions and critical circumstances. *Honor* and provide for those *widows that are really in need* of the funds assigned for *widow's* maintenance.[314]

[5:4] But if any widow [has] ~~have~~ **children or [grandchildren]** ~~nephews~~, **let them learn first to [be godly]** ~~shew piety~~ **[as regards their own house]** ~~at home~~, **and to [make recompense to]** ~~requite~~ **their [progenitors]** ~~parents~~: **for that is good and acceptable before God.**

Their parents (Greek *progonos* πρόγονος) means *forefathers* or *ancestors*.[315] In the context of this verse, this word applies to parents and grandparents—or those who are still living—the converse of the children and grandchildren also mentioned here. It is obvious that the context does not refer to departed ancestors. "The Greek word would not, in fact, properly include nephews and nieces. It embraces only those in a direct line."[316]

[5:5] Now she that is a [true] widow ~~indeed~~, **and [left alone]** ~~desolate~~, **[hath hope]** ~~trusteth~~ **in God, and continueth in supplications and prayers night and day.**

Desolate (Greek *monoo* μονόω) means *isolated*, *bereaved*, or *solitary*. "It does not necessarily imply the idea of *discomfort* which we attach to the word desolate. The sense is, that she had no children or other descendants; none on whom she could depend for support."[317]

Trusteth in God (Greek *elpizo* ἐλπίζω) means to *expect* or *confide*. "She has no one else to look to but God. She has no

earthly reliance, and destitute of husband, children, and property, she feels her dependence."[318]

[5:6] But [the one living] ~~she that liveth~~ **in [self-]pleasure[319] is dead while [living]** ~~she liveth~~.[320]

She that liveth in pleasure (Greek *spatalao* σπαταλάω) "properly means to live in luxury, voluptuously; to indulge freely in eating and drinking; to yield to the indulgence of the appetites. It does not indicate grossly criminal pleasures; but the kind of pleasures connected with luxurious living, and with pampering the appetites."[321]

[5:7] And these things give in charge, that they may be [irreproachable] ~~blameless~~.

Blameless (Greek *anepileptos* ἀνεπίληπτος) actually means *not arrested*. The easiest way to explain this concept is to recognize that Paul is expecting implementation of the welfare program to be *without scandal* or *without reproach*. The distribution of alms must be by recognizable rules and conditions that do not attract scandal among the members or Gentile observers in the respective community.

[5:8] But if any provide not for his own, and [especially his family][322] ~~specially for those of his own house~~, **he hath denied the faith, and is worse than an [unbeliever]** ~~infidel~~.

The expectation that one is to provide for the welfare of his parents and grandparents is not meant to be casual. "The meaning is, that the person referred to is to *think beforehand* ([Greek *pronoei*] προνοεῖ) of the probable wants of his own family, and make arrangements to meet them."[323] Paul is indicating the expectation that members are to take a proactive role in the welfare and maintenance of their parents and not a passive abdicating role. "A neglect of any duty is so far a denial of the faith."[324]

[5:9] Let not a widow be [enrolled] ~~taken into the number~~ under [sixty] ~~threescore~~ years old, having been the wife of one man,

Having been the wife of one man appears in Greek grammatical order as, *having become of one husband wife*. The interpretations on this statement are diverse in Bible commentaries and translations. One English version, perhaps discerningly, translated this as, "has been faithful to her husband."[325] We should not misunderstand Paul as instructing Timothy to refuse alms to an elderly woman just because she did not have the blessing of marriage in her lifetime. In many respects, the expectation for any destitute widow in good health is to work for her living.

The conclusion of this expectation is drawn from the opening words of the next verse; she is "well reported of for good works." There is every indication to expect that *being enrolled* is in reference to an already established Church policy that de facto any widow over sixty years of age can receive alms without any restriction or qualifying criteria. The brethren of the early Church apparently defined the policy many years earlier on this matter in respect of "the daily ministration" of alms (Acts 6:1).

[5:10] [Being testified] ~~Well reported~~ of for good works; [such as][326] ~~if she have brought~~ [having raised] up children, if she ~~have~~ lodged strangers, if she ~~have~~ washed [clothes][327] [of] the [saints] ~~saints' feet~~, if she ~~have~~ relieved the afflicted, if she ~~have~~ diligently followed every good work.

Throughout the ages it has not been uncommon for strangers to seek lodging in homes. There can be no expectation of finding an inn or other form of hotel accommodation in every town or village.

[5:11] But the younger widows refuse [to enroll]:[328] for when they [grow lustful][329] ~~have begun to wax wanton~~ against Christ, they [desire to][330] ~~will~~ marry;[331]

Timothy is not specifically instructed to reject younger widows; he is instructed not *to enroll* them with the over sixty widows, as mentioned above in verse nine. The concept of dependence upon social assistance—even from within the Church—was repugnant at the time as it is today.

They have begun to wax wanton against (Greek *katastreniao* καταστρηνιάω) "means to be undisciplined to the vows of widowhood and receiving care from being on the church's support list."[332]

[5:12] Having [a judgment] ~~damnation~~, because they [set aside] ~~have cast off~~ their first faith.

[5:13] And withal they learn to be idle, [going about the houses] ~~wandering about from house to house~~; and not only idle, but ~~tattlers~~ also [gossips] and busybodies, speaking things which they ought not.

When church alms are provided to the younger widows, they will not have an inclination to work and occupy themselves in any productive endeavor. "It may be feared that they will give themselves up to an indolent life."[333] Therefore, they become idle, gossiping, and burdensome, "with an insatiable curiosity . . . and learn all manner of nonsense."[334] The observation seems to be that dependence upon alms undermines the motivation for industry and sustaining productivity. Relieved of the need to work to earn a living, they idle their time in gossip. It would be a gross ignorance on our part to condemn this apparent injustice from this passing counsel. We are endeavoring to understand the content of an epistle without being able to understand the social and cultural conditions that existed in Ephesus almost twenty centuries ago. What was the query or observation raised in Timothy's correspondence that Paul now responds to in this epistle? That is something we will never know. The inhabitants are gone and so is Ephesus. All that remains are foundation walls, façades, and theater seating without a performance to view.

[5:14] ~~I will~~ Therefore [I desire] ~~that~~ the younger women [to] marry, [to] bear children, [to manage]335 ~~guide~~ the house, give none occasion to the adversary [on account of reproach]336 ~~to speak reproachfully~~.

The prescribed counsel to these *younger women* is to marry, raise a family, and avoid reproachful conversation.

[5:15] For [already] some ~~are already~~ [have] turned aside after Satan.

Turned aside (Greek *ektrepo* ἐκτρέπω), in respect of the counsel in verses 11–14, indicates past tense. Therefore, Paul is speaking of incidences that have already happened. "Some of the younger widows who had been placed upon the roll had thus been led astray."[337] Paul is providing counsel—an executive decision—based upon the consequences of actual conditions and not an arbitrary injunction.

[5:16] If any man or woman that believeth have widows, let them relieve them, and let not the church be [burdened] ~~charged~~; that it may relieve them that are widows indeed.

Be charged (Greek *bareo* βαρέω) means *burdened* with "a charge upon material resources."[338] This is "the later Hellenistic form of the strong classical verb *to weigh down, to oppress*."[339] The capacity of the Church to dispense alms to elderly widows is limited. To include those capable of laboring for their own support, or remarrying, dilutes the financial resources. The issue is not that the younger widows are excluded, but rather that the older widows (those who are widows in need) will suffer through the lack of financial resources to cater to the necessities of the impoverished.

[5:17] Let [well] the [ruling] elders ~~that rule well~~ be counted worthy of double honor, especially [the ones laboring] ~~they who labour~~ in the word and doctrine.

[5:18] For the scripture saith, Thou shalt not muzzle the [threshing] ox ~~that treadeth out the corn~~. And, The laborer is worthy of his [pay] ~~reward~~.

Quoting from Deuteronomy 25:4, "*Thou shalt not muzzle [an]* ~~the~~ *ox when he [is threshing]* ~~treadeth out the corn~~."[340] This phrase is intended to condone the humanitarian aspect of the ox eating from the grain that he is laboring to thresh or mill. Paul now transitions the application to condone a laboring ecclesiastical minister partaking of the humanitarian distributions to meet his own welfare needs.

[5:19] Against an elder receive not an accusation, [unless on] ~~but before~~ [*the testimony of*][341] two or three witnesses.

Not so much a quote as a reference to the concept from Deuteronomy 19:15: "One witness shall not rise up against a man for any iniquity, or for any sin, in any sin that he sinneth: at the mouth of *two* witnesses, *or* at the mouth of *three* witnesses, shall the matter be established." Paul, knowing that Timothy already knew the statement and implication, very liberally shortens the quote.

[5:20] [Those] ~~Them~~ that sin [before all] rebuke ~~before all~~, that others also may fear.

The general interpretation of this verse implies public rebuke of the transgressor, with the intent that others will be frightened away from also transgressing. This may be correct; however, the verse also implies that public rebuke is necessary for a publicly known transgression.

[5:21] I [solemnly witness] ~~charge thee~~ before God, and ~~the Lord~~[342] Jesus Christ, and the elect angels, that thou observe these things without [prejudice] ~~preferring one before another~~, doing nothing by [way of] partiality.

Partiality (Greek *prosklisis* πρόσκλισις) means a *leaning toward* or *proclivity*. The word *proclivity* from Latin *proclivitas*, means to *gravitate towards*.

[5:22] Lay hands [quickly] ~~suddenly~~ on no [one] ~~man~~, [nor share in others' sins] ~~neither be partaker of other men's sins~~: keep thyself pure.

The counsel in this statement is to avoid ordaining men too quickly to the priesthood. The "why" of this counsel is simple. Ordination to the priesthood is a covenant with God; therefore, the inability to remain pure brings further condemnation upon a transgressor because of the priesthood ordination.

Verse 5:23 is repositioned after verse 25 below.

[5:24] [The sins of] some [men] ~~men's sins~~ are [manifest][343] ~~open~~ beforehand, going before to judgment; and some men they follow after.

We can interpret this statement to mean some people knowingly plan to sin and then proceed to do so. They have already sinned in their heart and then carry out their intentions. Others find themselves in situations that undermine their resilience and thereby fall into sin, without having had any intention to do so. For those who plan to sin, the sin is already waiting at the judgment to condemn them.

[5:25] Likewise also the good works of some are manifest beforehand; and they that are otherwise cannot be hid.

This statement is the converse of the previous verse on sin. "So also good works are conspicuous; and even when they are not, they cannot remain hidden."[344] In most instances, those who engage in *good works* already planned the undertaking before actually doing the good deed. The judgment will record the disposition to plan and carry out a good deed prior to the actual undertaking.

[5:23][345] ~~Drink~~ No longer [drink] water, but use a little wine [because of your stomach] ~~for thy stomach's sake~~ and [thy frequent] ~~thine often~~ infirmities.

The first thing to recognize here is that Paul directs the counsel to Timothy and not the Ephesian congregation. Apparently, Timothy had a stomach disorder that was aggravated by local water conditions.[346] This is evident from the declaration that Timothy is to cease drinking local water, not reduce consumption, but cease totally! More appropriately translated, "Be no longer a drinker of water."[347] This condition was not an isolated incident. Paul tells us above that Timothy suffered frequently with this infirmity. The following paraphrased translation is insightful: "If your stomach is out of order and your health much enfeebled, take a little wine as medicine, not as indulgence."[348] Whatever the problem was, it only affected Timothy. This would indicate—as we are well aware—that Timothy was from Lystra (Acts 16:1–3), and not a native Ephesian, as the natives did not receive the same counsel. Since the grape contains distilled water by natural process, it is safer for Timothy, whatever his medical condition was.[349] In the first century it was not known that the fermentation process to alcohol killed any bacteria residing in the liquid.

Timothy was instructed to drink "a little wine" because of the affect the water-borne bacteria was having upon his stomach and intestine (1 Timothy 5:23). For some inexplicable reason, this personal addendum interjects the teaching of this chapter on our current Bible versions. Repositioning it after verse 25 restores the intended thought flow.

CHRISTIANITY AND SLAVERY (1 TIMOTHY 6:1–2A)

In every age there are specific and unique challenges facing the Church. One challenge is the integration of a congregation composed of freemen, slaves, and their masters. Some countries have segregated Christian slaves into separate congregations in different chapels. Alternatively, other countries have segregated their congregations with assigned seating sections in the same chapel. The Brethren of the first century assimilated all into one congregation devoid of any apartheid animosity. They managed to practice the Divine mandate among themselves that the Lord revealed to the prophet Peter. Luke recorded the earlier prophetic pronouncement: "Then Peter opened his mouth, and said, Of a truth *I perceive that God is no respecter of persons*: But in every nation *he that feareth him, and worketh righteousness, is accepted* with him" (Acts 10:34–35). If God does not divide, then the Church cannot segregate the congregation, and the believing Christian cannot legitimately segregate in his heart.[350]

———————— ❧ ————————

[6:1] ~~Let~~ As many ~~servants~~ as are [slaves] under [a] ~~the~~ yoke [esteem] ~~count~~ their own masters worthy of all honor, that

the name of God and his doctrine [may not] be not blasphemed.

The yoke (Greek *zygos* ζυγός) implies *submission to authority* in the sense of *bondage*. The *yoke* couples two animals in a team to pull a wagon. In respect of human application, it metaphorically means non-voluntary enslaved servitude. See appendix C, "Slavers (Servus)." The counsel of this verse is to slaves whose masters are not Christian. Those slaves whose masters are Christian receive counsel in the following verse.

[6:2] And [those having] ~~they that have~~ believing masters, let them not despise them, because they are brethren; but rather [let them serve as slaves] ~~do them service~~, because they are faithful and beloved, partakers of the benefit. These things teach and exhort.

When Paul directs his comments to members of the Church who are slaves, he usually refers to those with Gentile masters. However, in this verse he directs his comments to those slaves whose masters are also Christian—and therefore members of the same congregation. It is inappropriate for any slave to be less respectful to his master just because he is also a Christian.[351] To do so shows disrespect and abuse of status toward his master. "To exhort a slave to manifest a Christian spirit under his oppressions and wrongs is not to justify the system that does him wrong, nor does it prohibit us from showing to masters that the system is contrary to the gospel, and that it ought to be abandoned. This passage, therefore, furnishes no real support for slavery."[352] The instructions of Paul "concerning slaves and women thus reflect a serious problem, one faced by any religious group seeking to make converts; how to maintain the distinctive (but, to outsiders, sometimes offensive) theological and social features of the group while building enough bridges to the outside world to make conversions possible."[353]

[6:3] If [anyone] ~~any man~~ teach otherwise, and [assents] ~~consent~~ not to [sound] ~~wholesome~~ words, [those] ~~even the words~~ of our Lord Jesus Christ, and [according] to the doctrine [of] ~~which is according to~~ godliness;

[6:4] He is [self-conceited] ~~proud~~, [understanding] ~~knowing~~ nothing, but [sick concerning doubts][354] ~~doting about questions~~ and [arguments][355] ~~strifes of words~~, [out of which] ~~whereof~~ cometh envy, strife, [malicious talk][356] ~~railings~~, evil [suspicions][357] ~~surmisings~~,

[6:5] [Incessant wrangling] ~~Perverse disputings~~ of men [whose minds have been corrupted] ~~of corrupt minds~~, and [deprived] ~~destitute~~ of the truth, supposing ~~that~~ gain [to be] ~~is~~ godliness: from such withdraw thyself.[358]

[6:6] But godliness with contentment is great gain.

Contentment (Greek *autarkeia* αὐτάρκεια) means being satisfied with the sufficiency of what you have. This expression is somewhat difficult to grasp in the literal wording. However, the following paraphrased rendition is clearer: "But godliness actually is a means of great gain when accompanied by contentment."[359] Verse 8 elucidates the articles of contentment below.

[6:7] For we [have] brought nothing into [the] ~~this~~ world, and it is [plain] ~~certain~~ we can carry nothing out.

This declaration is in reference to temporal possessions and not to the development of our attributes and characteristics we have molded into our personality. Some noble souls will depart this life having considerably expanded the endowment of talents with which they commenced life. Other ignoble souls have imbued their character with wretched or depraved actions. "Godliness" is the eternal legacy of few souls, and the lost paradigm of many once jubilant "morning stars" (Job 38:7; D&C 128:23).

[6:8] ~~And~~ Having [sustenance][360] ~~food~~ and [clothing] ~~raiment~~ [with these things we will] ~~let us~~ be therewith content.

The contentment of this verse is in clarification to the statement made above in verse six.

[6:9] But [those intend to] ~~they that will~~ be rich fall into temptation and a [noose] ~~snare~~, and into many foolish and hurtful [cravings] ~~lusts~~, which [cause men to sink into ruin and destruction] ~~drown men in destruction and perdition.~~

[6:10] For [a] ~~the love of money is the~~ root of all [evils] ~~evil~~ [is avarice]: [of] which ~~while~~ some [lusting] ~~coveted~~ after, [were seduced][361] ~~they have erred~~ from the faith, and [themselves entangled][362] around] ~~pierced themselves through~~ [by] ~~with~~ many [pains] ~~sorrows.~~[363]

The love of money (Greek *philargyria* φιλαργυρία) means *avarice* or *covetousness*.[364] The meaning of the word does not center on spending money; this is about material possessions, owning, hoarding, possessing. Paul "is not praising poverty, nor declaring it a crime to possess property; he is only rebuking avarice, and showing that real contentment is independent of either poverty or wealth."[365] In the Charles Dickens novel, *A Christmas Carol* (1843), there is a character named Scrooge, who is the embodiment of financial avarice—until he was taught to see things differently.

LAY HOLD ON ETERNAL LIFE (1 TIMOTHY 6:11–19)

Timothy is encouraged to pursue godly attributes and endure the remaining mortal sojourn in faith.[366] Paul further charges Timothy to continue to testify of the truthfulness of the gospel of Jesus the Christ—even as Jesus did before Pontius Pilatus. Finally, he preaches temporal charity to those with

the financial means to relieve suffering in others less fortunate.

❧

[6:11] But thou, O man of God, flee these things; and [pursue] ~~follow after~~ righteousness, godliness, faith, love, patience, meekness.

Man of God is an Old Testament Hebrew expression for a prophet of God.[367] Christian doctrine extended the designation to all believing and devoted saints of the Church.[368]

Follow after (Greek *dioko* διώκω) in a positive sense means "*to pursue, chase, follow,* [or] *trace.*"[369] We understand the selection of this word when reading the following verse. This word has military application as seen in connection with the word *fight* in the next verse.

[6:12] Fight the good fight of faith, lay hold on eternal life, whereunto thou art also called, and [testified the] ~~hast professed a~~ good [testimony] ~~profession~~ [in the presence of] ~~before~~ many witnesses.[370]

Paul speaks in the future tense when he declares, "fight the good fight of faith" in this epistle. In just a few months, he will use this phrase again in the final epistle to Timothy—only this time it will be in the past tense: "I have fought a good fight, I have finished my course, I have kept the faith" (2 Timothy 4:7). Though *fight* is the correct translation, the word does not convey the actual meaning of the passage. The *fight* is a *contest* between good and evil. The emphasis of this fact is that there is a prize to *lay hold on*, namely, *eternal life*.[371] The word *fight* (Greek *agonizomai* ἀγωνίζομαι) means "to *struggle*" in the sense of "to *compete* for a prize."[372] "The figure is athletic rather than military, taken from the arena, not the field of battle. The contest is Faith against Unbelief, and the prize is eternal life."[373]

[6:13] I give thee charge in the sight of God, who [preserves][374] ~~quickeneth~~ all things [alive],[375] and ~~before~~ Christ Jesus, who [witnessed the good testimony] before Pontius [Pilatus] ~~Pilate witnessed a good confession;~~

The correct form of **Pontius Pilate** is his Latin name *Pontius Pilatus* or in Greek as *Pontios Pilatos* (Πόντιος Πιλᾶτος) (Luke 3:1). Pilatus was the fifth or sixth man to serve in the office of Prefect[376] of Judea during the period AD 26-36. To receive the appointment as *prefect* would indicate that he was of the Equestrian caste.

[6:14] That thou keep this commandment [unspotted] ~~without spot~~, [and irreproachable] ~~unrebukeable~~, until the [coming][377] ~~appearing~~ of our Lord Jesus Christ:

The appearing (Greek *epiphaneia* ἐπιφάνεια) means "a *manifestation*, i.e. specifically the *advent* of Christ (past or future)."[378] This word is suitably translated *adventum* in Latin,[379] and *l'apparition* in French.[380] Though *appearing* is the general English translation, the reference is to the millennial Second Coming of Jesus the Christ.

[6:15] [Who] ~~Which~~ in [His own time will reveal] ~~his times he shall shew, who is~~ the blessed and only [Sovereign][381] ~~Potentate~~, the King of [reigning] kings, and Lord of [reigning] lords, [to whom be honor and power everlasting];[382]

[6:16] ~~Who only hath immortality, dwelling in the light which no man can approach unto;~~ Whom no man hath seen, nor can see: [unto whom no man can approach, only he who hath the light and the hope of immortality dwelling in him][383] ~~to whom be honour and power everlasting. Amen.~~

Which no man can approach (Greek *aprositos* ἀπρόσιτος) means *inaccessible*, or more clearly, "inhabiting inapproachable light."[384] This concept does not imply that the children of God may not approach their Heavenly Father. On the contrary, those mortals who are called and elected of God may enter into His presence while yet in this mortal condition. However, to do so requires not only divine condescension but also the process of temporary translation of the mortal soul. "Enoch walked with God" (Genesis 5:24); Jacob declared, "I have seen God face to face, and my life is preserved" (Genesis 32:30); and Moses declared, "I saw the Lord, and he stood before my face" (Moses 7:4). In one incidence, Moses spent so long a time in the presence of God that he too temporarily radiated for an extended period of time. "When Moses came down from Mount Sinai . . . [he] wist not that the skin of his face shone while he talked . . . And till Moses had done speaking with them, he put a [veil] ~~vail~~ on his face" (Exodus 34:29, 33). We should also recall that Paul saw the glory of that radiant light and heard the divine voice in an encounter on the road near Damascus (Acts 9:3–9, 12, 17–18).

Immortality (Greek *athanasia* ἀθανασία) means *deathlessness*, or *exemption from death*.[385] "Immortality is about quantity. Eternal life is about quality. . . . If immortality is God's work, then *eternal life* is God's glory. However, eternal life does not come automatically. We must purge our hearts of evil and fill them with the desire to do good continually."[386] The condition of eternal life is addressed above in verse twelve.

[6:17] [Give orders to] ~~Charge~~ them that are rich in [the present] ~~this~~ world, that they be not high-minded, nor [set hope on the uncertainty of][387] ~~trust in uncertain~~ riches, but in the Living God, [offering to] ~~who giveth~~ us richly all things [for our enjoyment] ~~to enjoy;~~[388]

Charge (Greek *paraggello* παραγγέλλω)

is a military word denoting *to give an order* or *command*. The word specifically refers to the order a military commander gives to his soldiers. See appendix B, "The Imperial Roman Army."

[6:18] ~~That~~ They [are to] do good,[389] [to] ~~that they~~ be rich in good works, ready to [impart][390] ~~distribute,~~ [generously] ~~willing to communicate;~~

[6:19] Laying [by] ~~up in store~~ for themselves a good foundation [for the future][391] ~~against the time to come,~~ that they may lay hold on eternal life.[392]

[6:20] O Timothy, keep [the entrusted deposit][393] ~~that which is committed to thy trust,~~ avoiding profane and vain babblings, and oppositions of [false-named knowledge] ~~science falsely so called:~~

That which is committed to thy trust (Greek *parakatatheke* παρακαταθήκη) is actually "a *deposit*, a trust, or thing consigned to one's faithful keeping . . . to be held firmly and faithfully, and to be conscientiously delivered unto others."[394] This unique word appears only twice in the New Testament—once each in the two Timothy epistles penned by Paul (see 2 Timothy 1:14). The application of this word is similar to another Pauline application in his earlier epistles. God gives the promise of eternal life to us at baptism and confirmation with the gift of the Holy Ghost. Paul refers to this gift as "*the earnest* of the Spirit in our hearts" (2 Corinthians 1:22; 5:5), and "*the earnest* of our inheritance" (Ephesians 1:14). This word *earnest* (Greek *arrhabon* ἀῤῥαβών) is "a *pledge*, i.e. part of the purchase-money or property given in advance as *security* for the rest."[395] *Parakatatheke* in the Timothy epistles appears to be yet another reference to the earnest deposit of the Holy Ghost, until we "lay hold on" the full payment of "eternal life."

Falsely so called (Greek *pseudonymos* ψευδώνυμος) was "the knowledge professed by the propagandists of various heretical cults."[396] This Greek word means *under a false name*, and is the source of the English word *pseudonym* for a *fictitious name*.

Science (Greek *gnosis* γνῶσις) appears twenty-nine times in the New Testament and is translated as *knowledge* twenty-eight of those incidences. The translation *science* is a peculiar deviation from all other incidences. Jerome translated the Greek *gnosis* to Latin as *scientiae*, and taken over as *science* in English.

[6:21] [That] ~~Which~~ some [asserting] ~~professing~~ have [missed the mark] ~~erred~~ concerning the faith. Grace be with thee. Amen.

Have erred (Greek *astocheo* ἀστοχέω) means, to take *aim* at a target and then "to *miss* the mark, fail."[397] The analogy is of a bowman taking aim and then, being distracted, misses the target. In a spiritual sense, the message of Paul implies that their aim was to remain on the path of truth, but now they have deviated from that target. This word also appears in 1 Timothy 1:6 and 2 Timothy 2:18.

[postscript] The first to Timothy was written from [Philippi] ~~Laodicea~~, which is the chiefest city of [the First District of Macedonia][398] ~~Phrygia Pacatiana~~.

The postscript of all epistles was never a component part of the actual letter composed by Paul. There is no evidence to suggest that Paul composed this epistle at Laodicea. This epistle commenced with the declaration that Paul departed from Ephesus for Macedonia (1 Timothy 1:3). A primary consideration is Philippi, or alternatively, another city further along the journey through Greece en route to Corinth in the south. Of the three districts in Macedonia, Philippi was capital of the First District. Laodicea is a fanciful aggrandizement and not a logical reality.

1 Timothy

Epilogue

This letter does not include personal greetings from others. Therefore, the letter was probably sent by a courier (*tabellarii*) in the public transport or mail system (*cursus publicus*), or alternatively, by the captain of a ship sailing from Neapolis (Greek Νεάπολις)[399] to Ephesus (Greek *Ephesos* Ἔφεσος). In the meantime, Paul continued on his journeys, traversing the Greco-Roman world as an ambassador for Jesus the Christ. In consideration that we have yet to review a Second Timothy Epistle, we will defer concluding evaluation of Paul and Timothy until the conclusion of the next epistle.

NOTES FOR 1 TIMOTHY

1. Brown, *The Pastoral Epistles*, xiii.

2. We ascertain the time of year when 1 Corinthians was written from what is said in the epistle, indicating that it was Passover time, which would be March or April. Compare also: "I will tarry at Ephesus until Pentecost" (1 Corinthians 16:8)—being fifty days after Passover.

3. The postscript of 1 Corinthians erroneously accredits Timothy as being one of the epistle scribes. "The first epistle to the Corinthians was written from Philippi by Stephanas and Fortunatus and Achaicus and Timotheus" (1 Corinthians postscript). While Timothy and Erastus were enroute through Macedonia and Achaia to Corinth, Paul dispatched the First Corinthian Epistle by courier across the Aegean Sea from Ephesus to Corinth in April or May AD 57. The clear expectation of Paul was that the letter would undoubtedly preceed the arrival of Timothy and Erastus who were coming by the longer land route.

4. *Cassell's Latin Dictionary*, s.v. "epistula, epistola."

5. Douay-Rheims Version.

6. Compare with 1 Timothy 2:3.

7. The word *Lord* does not appear in some versions, including the Nestle Greek text. See The Revised Standard Version Interlinear Greek-English New Testament.

8. Faulring, et al, *Joseph Smith New Translation of the Bible*, Manuscript 2, Folder 4, 529.

9. Jerome, Biblia Sacra Versio Vulgata.

10. The Interlinear Hebrew-Greek-Engish Bible.

11. Salkinson & Ginsburg, *The New Testament in Hebrew* (הברית החדשה).

12. Jesus in Acts 7:45 and Hebrews 4:8 is in reference to the Old Testament prophet Joshua and not Jesus the Christ.

13. There is perpetuation of the Greek name Jesus in the translation of the Book of Mormon—see 2 Nephi 25:19; Mosiah 3:8; and Alma 6:8. The Messiah introduced himself as Jesus on all occasions in the Doctrine & Covenants—see 6:21; 10:57; and 11:28.

14. Liddell & Scott, *Greek-English Lexicon*, 663 ἐωιταγή, s.v. "κατ ἐπιταγὴν."

15. Jerome, Biblia Sacra Versio Vulgata.

16. Pervanoglu, *A Dictionary of the Greek and English Languages*, 771 s.v. "σωτήρ."

17. Ibid., s.v. σώτειρα.

18. Witherington, *Letters and Homilies for Hellenized Christians*, 103.

19. Ibid. 188.

20. Erdman, *The Pastoral Epistles of Paul*, 20.

21. Calvin, *Commentaries on the Epistles to Timothy, Titus, and Philemon*, 20.

22. Possibly applicable also to Luke 1:47.

23. Ellicott, *The Pastoral Epistles*, 2.

24. This is the only epistle written by Paul where he includes "mercy" in the greeting.

   "In all previous letters his salutations have included 'grace and peace'; never before has Paul added the word 'mercy.' 'Grace' denotes the divine favor in its fullest form; it is the source of all spiritual life and enjoyment. 'Peace' is the experience of a soul in harmony with God, which knows that tranquility and blessedness God alone can give. 'Mercy,' however, turns the thoughts [e]specially upon the ill desert of the recipient and upon the compassion of God." See Erdman, 21.

   The pairing of grace and mercy occurs early in Jewish scripture. "Those who trust in him will understand truth, and the faithful will abide with him in love, because grace and mercy are upon his elect, and he watches over his holy ones." See *Old Testament Apocrypha*, "Wisdom of Solomon" 3:9; 4:15. See also Metzger, *The Apocrypha of the Old Testament—Revised Standard Version*, 977.

25. Today's New International Version Bible.

26. Darby Bible Translation.

27. Compare the following interpretation, "That you might *remonstrate with certain persons* because of their erroneous teaching" (Weymouth, *New Testament in Modern Speech*).

28. Darby Bible Translation.

29. Strong, #3853.

30. Liddell & Scott, 1306, s.v. "παραγγελες /παραγγελία."

31. Ibid., 701, s.v. "ἑτεροδῐδασκᾰλέω."

32. Attic ('τερος); Doric (ἄτερος); Aeolean (ἄτερος). See Liddell & Scott, 702, s.v. "ἕτερος."

33. Ἄλλος, Latin *alius*, "another, i.e. one besides what has been mentioned." See Liddell & Scott, 70, s.v. "ἄλλος."

34. Strong, #2085.

35. *Webster's Dictionary*, 593, s.v. "heterodox."

36. Fables (Greek *mythos* μῦθος) appears in 1 Timothy 1:4 and 4:7; 2 Timothy 4:4; Titus 1:14; 2 Peter 1:16; and Old Testament Apocrypha, Sirach [Ecclesiasticus] 20:20: "A proverb from a fool's lips will be rejected, for he does not tell it at its proper time" (See Metzger, *The Apocrypha of the Old Testament— Revised Standard Version*.)

37. Darby Bible Translation.

38. Today's New International Version Bible

39. "Fanciful tales merely tickle the ears and loosen the tongue. They have no relation to the serious business of life. They are received with foolish credulity instead of rational faith. They end in conversation, not in conversion." See Strachan, 203.

40. This verse ends with "in faith"

(Greek *en pistei* ἐν πίστει), and the next verse reemphasizes with "sincere faith" (Greek *pisteos anupokritou* πίστεως ἀνυποκρίτου).

41. Strong, #3454.

42. Liddell & Scott, 1151, s.v. "μῦθος."

43. "Judaism got itself entangled in a new Platonism. Those endless genealogies which had always charmed the Israelite, as he traced his own pedigree from Seth, and Abraham, and David, were now beginning to soar into higher heights of speculation, till at length they dealt with angelic relationships and lost themselves in interminable mazes of celestial emanations." See Vaughan, *The Wholesome Words of Jesus Christ*, 7.

44. Witherington, 192.

45. Weymouth, *New Testament in Modern Speech*. The Greek word for sincere (*anypokritos* ἀνυπόκριτος) implies without hypocrisy—i.e. genuine.

46. Witherington, 193.

47. Revised Standard American Version.

48. "The Law is good, but it is for those who are not good. Its provisions are negative. Its end is the repression of evil rather than the promotion of righteousness." See Strachan, 204. Compare with the statement in 1 Timothy 1:9

49. Erdman, 24.

50. "The Law is Holy, and the commandment Holy, and just, and good . . . The Law is Spiritual . . . I consent unto the Law that it is good" (Romans 7:12, 14, 16); cf. Matthew 5:21–48; Luke 18:20.

51. "Uses it legitimately." New Revised Standard Version.

52. Green's Literal Translation

53. See Exodus 20:3.

54. "Paul teaches . . . that religion was a condition of freedom, and that the main purpose of religion was not to fetter the minds of the righteous with numberless observance and minute regulations, but that it was to restrain the wicked from sin. This is the case with the law. No good man feels himself fettered and manacled by wholesome laws, nor does he feel that the purpose of law is to reduce him to a state of servitude. it is only the wicked who have this feeling—and in this sense the law is made for a man who intends to do wrong" (Barnes, *The Epistles of Paul*, 134).

55. See Exodus 20:12.

56. Ibid.

57. See Exodus 20:13.

58. Liddell & Scott, 255, s.v. "ἀσέβεια."

59. *Webster's Dictionary*, 1373, s.v. "ungodly."

60. Strong, #462.

61. Ibid., #40.

62. Ibid., #952.

63. Groves, *Greek to English Dictionary*, 113, s.v. "βέβηλος."

64. Riddle and Arnold, *English-Latin*

Lexicon, 457, s.v. "matricide."

65. Jerome, *Biblia Sacra Versio Vulgata*.

66. de Reina & de Valera, *Biblia Reina Valera*. The Greek text consists of only four words, *patroloais kai metraloais, androphonois* (παρολῷαις καὶ μητραλῴαις, ἀνδροφόνοις).

67. Smith, *Dictionary of Greek and Roman Antiquities*, 687, s.v. "Leges Corneliae."

68. Ibid.

69. See Exodus 20:14.

70. Ibid.

71. See Exodus 20:15.

72. See Exodus 20:16.

73. Ibid.

74. Sound or, "literally healthful teaching, as opposed to what is sickly" (see Strachan, 205).

75. Translated to Latin as *fornicariis masculorum*.

76. Liddell & Scott, 127, s.v. "ἀωδραπόδεσσι / ἀωδράποδον."

77. New Revised Standard Version with Apocrypha.

78. Humphreys, , 88.

79. Strong, #989.

80. Liddell & Scott, 317, s.v. "βλάσφημέω."

81. "The meaning is, that he reviled the name of Christ, and opposed him and his cause—not believing that he was the Messiah; and in thus opposing he had really been guilty of blasphemy. The true Messiah he

had in fact treated with contempt and reproaches, and he now looked back upon that fact with the deepest mortification, and with wonder that one who had been so treated by him should have been willing to put him into the ministry" (see Barnes, 137–138).

82. Pervanoglu, 824, s.v. "ὑπερπλεονάζω."

83. Humphreys, 88; emphasis added.

84. Compare with 1 Timothy 3:1; 4:9; 2 Timothy 2:11; and Titus 3:8.

85. This is "a slightly modified form of the original announcement made to Joseph, 'Thou shalt call His name Jesus, for He shall save His people from their sins' " (Fairbairn, *The Pastoral Epistles*, 96).

86. *Vornehmste* in German (Luther's *Heilige Schrift des Alten und Neuen Testaments*); *el primero* in Spanish (de Reina & de Valera, *Biblia Reina Valera*).

87. Witherington, 191.

88. New International Version.

89. Webster's, 750 s.v. "longanimity."

90. This conveys the understanding that God "does not die," whereas the earthly "sovereigns" all expire in death (see Barnes, 142).

91. The phrase "forever and ever" is reminiscent of an Old Testament verse: "Hearken, O Lord, to the prayer of thy servants, according to the blessing of Aaron for thy people, and all who are on the

earth will know that thou art the Lord, the God of the ages." (See Sirach [Ecclesiasticus] 36:17 in Metzger, *The Apocrypha of the Old Testament—Revised Standard Version*).

92. Strachan, 207.

93. See Tobit 13:6 in Metzger, *The Apocrypha of the Old Testament*, 10. Originally written in Hebrew, and now preserved in the Septuagint Greek translation. Compare also Revelation 15:3; Psalm 145:13; Exodus 15:18.

94. See Enoch 9:4. in Charles, *The Book of Enoch*.

95. See Enoch 10:3 in Charles, *The Book of Enoch*.

96. Barnes, 143.

97. Smith, *Doctrines of Salvation*, 1:31.

98. New American Standard Bible.

99. "Faith and conscience are like good angels, eloquently pleading, reluctant to depart, and finally so importunate that they are incontinently thrust out of doors" (Strachan, 208).

100. Jannaris, *Dictionary of English and Modern Greek*, 138, s.v. "excommunicate."

101. Smith, *A Smaller Dictionary of the Bible*, 223, s.v. "Hymenaeus."

102. The Interlinear Hebrew–Greek–English Bible. See also Faulring, 529).

103. Faulring, 529.

104. Strachan, 210.

105. Faulring, 529.

106. Ibid.

107. Capitalized to Man, implying title "Son of Man" for Jesus the Christ (see D&C 122:8).

108. Alternatively, "it's own times" (The Interlinear Hebrew–Greek–English Bible; and Darby Bible Translation).

109. Strong, #487.

110. Liddell & Scott, 859, s.v. "καιρός."

111. Liddell & Scott, 158, s.v. "ἀντίλυτρον."

112. Strong, #2540.

113. Strong, #5087.

114. In Greek, *klisien, thronon tithemi tini*, (κλισίην, θρόνον τίθημι τινί). Liddell & Scott, 1790, s.v. "τίθημι."

115. The Standard American Edition.

116. Old Testament occurrences of lifting up hands in prayer: Genesis 14:22; Psalms 28:2; 63:4; 134:2. There is a distinct similarity between the wording in this verse and an earlier expression, "And holding up their hands to heaven, they all made entreaty" (2 Maccabees 3:20 in Metzger, *The Apocrypha of the Old Testament*).

117. "Anger is a perfect alienation of the mind from prayer, and is therefore contrary to that attention which presents our prayers in a right line to God" (Barnes, 151).

118. Jerome, Biblia Sacra Versio

Vulgata. Also, *des mains pures* in French (Segond, *Nouvelle Édition de Genève*).

119. Strong, #3709.

120. Liddell & Scott, 1246, s.v. "ὀργῆς."

121. Mikołajewski, *Biblii Gdańskiej* [Polish 'Danzig Bible'].

122. Behra, *Dokładny Słownik Polsko-Angeilski i Angielsko-Polski* [Polish-English Dictionary], 62, s.v. "gniewu."

123. Strong, #1261.

124. Mikołajewski, *Biblii Gdańskiej*.

125. Behra, 251, s.v. "poswar, poswarek, poswarku."

126. Green's Literary Translation.

127. Humphreys, 98.

128. Riddle, Latin–English Dictionary, 268, s.v. "habitus." See def. 1–2.

129. Strong, #127.

130. Liddell & Scott, 36, s.v. "a″d√q."

131. Strong, #1708.

132. McManus, "The Flavian Coiffure."

133. Smith, Dictionary of Greek and Roman Antiquities, 330, s.v. "coma."

134. "With the addition of costly ornmanets of gold or ivory, the female coiffure connonoted wealth and luxury" (Bartman, "Hair and the Artifice of Roman Female Adornment," *American Journal of Archaeology* 105, 1:27).

135. "Sometimes these head-dresses were raised to a great height by rows of false curls" (Smith, Dictionary of Greek and Roman Antiquities, 330, s.v. "coma."). "False hair, whether 'extender' tesses or full wigs" (Bartman, 25).

136. Carcopino, *Daily Life in Ancient Rome—The People and the City at the Height of the Empire*, 168.

137. Ovid, *De Artis Amatoriae*, 3:158.

138. Carcopino, 168.

139. Bartman, 25.

140. Ibid.

141. Satire 6:4 in Owen, *A Translation of Juvenal and Persius*, 56.

142. Epigrams 9:37 in Kerr, *Martial: Epigrams*, 2:99.

143. *Cassell's Latin Dictionary*, 416, s.v. "ornatrix." There is a record of the Emperor Claudius referring to this slave office. He once said, "This woman was my mother's freedwoman and tire-woman [*matris meae liberta et ornatrix fuit*]" (Claudius 40:2 in *Graves, Suetonius: The Life of the Twelve Caesars*, 209; Roth, *C. Suetoni Tranquilli: De Vita Caesarium*, Divus Claudius 40:167). Also alluded to by Juvenal, "Some master-barber decks your hair" (Satire 6:1 in Owen, *A Translation of Juvenal and Persius*, 42).

144. "Whether crafted by household slaves or the wearer herself, a woman's hairstyle conveyed her individuality" (Bartman, 25).

145. Carcopino, 167.

146. The Interlinear Hebrew-Greek-English Bible.

147. Ibid.

148. "The women are to appear in the meetings with the adornment, not of dress, but of their general good works" (Huther, 112).

149. New American Standard Bible.

150. Strong, #2271.

151. "Mulier in silentio discat cum omni subiectione" (Jerome, Biblia Sacra Versio Vulgata).

152. Huther, 102.

153. "It is not difficult to understand why such statements by Paul have made him unpopular with certain elect ladies of the present day. Yet it should be said in defense of the apostle that his writings, taken as a whole, have done more for the emancipation of women, more to secure her social and civil and political rights, than the productions of any other author who could be named" (Erdman, 36).

154. Humphreys, 99.

155. Joseph Smith changed "speak" to "rule." Considering our current terminology, "preside" is more appropriate (Faulring, 529).

156. Faulring, 507.

157. In the previous verse, Joseph Smith changed "speak" to "rule." Considering the application in this verse, "speak" must be changed to "be outspoken" (Faulring, 507).

158. Ibid., 529

159. Strong, #1321.

160. " 'Was' does not represent properly the perfect, literal is become, used, according to Greek idiom, because the past event is viewed as having a present influence, and continuing in its effects. Here it helps the transition from the particular case of Eve in the past to the general case of women now. This is also aided by the further change to the future in 'shall be saved' " (Humphreys, 99).

161. Ibid.

162. Faulring, 529.

163. Conybeare, *The Life and Epistles of St. Paul*, 814.

164. "Through her childbearing: her childbearing which is her curse may be her highest blessing, as with man's doom, labor; her domestic life and duties, the sphere of woman's mission, St. Paul lays great stress on good works, the performance of the common duties of life, in opposition to the irregularities of the times; and yet adds the necessary previous condition 'if they abode in faith' " (Humphreys, 100).

165. Strong, #4997.

166. This is the meaning in Luther's German translation. "*So sie bleiben im Glauben und in der Liebe und in der Heiligung samt der Zucht*" [addiction] (Luther's Heilige Schrift des Alten und Neuen Testaments).

167. Die Eberfelder Bibel.

168. Cassell's German–English/English–German Dictionary, 559, s.v. "sittsam, Sittsamkeit."

169. Liddell & Scott, 1103, s.v. "μένω," "μείνωσιν." It is unfortunate that the English Douay-Rheims Version alone translated this term to "she continues."

170. Fairbairn, 132.

171. Strong, #1984. In the context of this verse the form is *episkopes* (ἐπισκοπῆς).

172. Septuagint numbering 108:8.

173. In the context of this verse, the form is *episkopen* (ἐπισκοπὴν) (see Brenton, *The Septuagint with Apocrypha: Greek and English*, 766, Psalm 108:8 [109:8]).

174. Fairbairn, 135.

175. Hillard, *The Pastoral Epistles of St. Paul*, 26.

176. Fairbairn, 135.

177. Ibid., 135–136.

178. Darby Bible Translation.

179. Green's Literal Translation.

180. Strong, #423.

181. Liddell & Scott, 134, s.v. "ἀνεπίληπτος."

182. "The precise meaning of this phrase will probably never cease to be discussed" (Plummer, *The Expositor's Bible: The Pastoral Epistles*, 118). Also: "I consider it more than a mere permission that a pastor should be 'the husband of one wife'—to me it seems all but a matter of necessity" (Fairbairn, 140).

183. Humphreys, 102.

184. Huther, 118.

"There was a special propriety in the prohibition, if understood as prohibiting polygamy. It is known that it was extensively practiced, and was not regarded as unlawful. Yet one design of the gospel was to restore the marriage relation to its primitive condition; and, though it might not have seemed absolutely necessary to require of every man who came into the church to divorce his wives, if he had more than one, yet, in order to fix a brand on this irregular practice, it might have been deemed desirable to require of the ministers of the gospel that they should have but one wife" (Barnes, 162).

"Many converts to Christianity would have more than one wife. They are nowhere commanded to put away all but one; but it was not seemly that a man in such a position should be a Christian minister, who ought in all respects to be an ensample to the flock" (Humphreys, 103).

185. Conybeare, 814.

186. Strong, #4998.

187. Barnes, 163.

188. Liddell & Scott, 984, s.v. "κόσμιον."

189. Liddell & Scott, 421, s.v. "διδακέον."

190. Alternatively expressed as "skilled

in teaching" (Conybeare, 814).

191. Kimball, *The Teachings of Spencer W. Kimball*, 524.

192. Luther appropriately translated this word as *Weinsäufer* (Luther's Heilige Schrift des Alten und Neuen Testaments). A *Weinsäufer* is a wine "drunkard, alcoholic, [or] . . . boozer" (Betteridge, 510, s.v. "Säufer").

193. More correctly *pugnatious* in English (New American Standard Bible). "Disposed or inclined to fight; quarrelsome" (*Webster's Dictionary*, 1021, s.v. "pugnatious").

194. "He should not be a man given to contention, or apt to take up a quarrel" (Barnes, 164).

195. Humphreys, 104.

196. Huther, 119.

197. Barnes, 164.

198. The New Testament in Modern Speech.

199. *Webster's Dictionary*, 1198, s.v. "sordid."

200. Hopkins, *Conquerors and Slaves*, 43.

201. Liddell & Scott, 78, s.v. "ἄμαχος."

202. Strong, #866.

203. New American Standard Bible.

204. La Sainte Bible—l'Ancien et le Nouveau Testament.

205. Ostervald, *La Bible.*

206. *Webster's Dictionary*, 99, s.v. "avarice."

207. *Webster's Dictionary*, 99, s.v. "avaricious."

208. Hopkins, 44.

209. "In a manner worthy of full respect." (Today's New International Version Bible).

210. Strong, #4291.

211. Brown, 26.

212. Compare 1 Timothy 4:1–3. "This implies that a minister of the gospel would be, and ought to be, a married man. It is everywhere in the New Testament supposed that he would be a man who could be an example in all the relations of life" (Barnes, 164).

213. New American Standard Bible.

214. "A man that has a disobedient, disorderly, unruly, or riotous family is not a proper man to be a bishop" (Graham, *A Practical and Exegetical Commentary on the Epistle to Titus*, 32–33). This teaching receives endorsement in Titus 1:6.

215. Barnes, 165.

216. The same expression is contained in the following translation: "And not a new convert, so that he will not become conceited and fall into the condemnation incurred by the devil" (New American Standard Bible).

217. "Not a novice, or recent convert ([Greek *neophyton*] νεόφυτον, literally, "newly planted"). Of course such a qualification must be understood relatively—in some a less, in others a longer period of probation being required, according to

circumstances" (Fairbairn, 142–143).

218. "Directly, persons of this description have no right to interfere with the appointment of a Christian pastor; but it is of importance that they have nothing to object" (Fairbairn, 144).

219. Strong, #3803.

220. Die Schlachter Bibel.

221. Betteridge, 526, s.v. "Schlinge."

222. See NIV Bible, 1 Timothy 3:10.

223. Faulring 531.

224. "Ser honestos" (Biblia Reina Valera).

225. Strong, #1351.

226. Sirach [Ecclesiasticus] 5:14 in Metzger, *The Apocrypha of the Old Testament*.

227. Xenophon, De Re Equestri Libellus 8:2 in Cooper, *The Whole Works of Zenophon*, 723.

228. Liddell & Scott, 431, s.v. "δῐλογία."

229. Strong, #146.

230. *Webster's Dictionary*, 1198, s.v. "sordid."

231. Die Schlachter Bibel.

232. Betteridge, 732, s.v. "Wucher, Wucherer." The Dutch language also has a comparable one-word term for this translation, *geenvuil-gewinzoeker* or *vuil-gewinzoeker* (Statenvertaling, *De Ganse Heilige Schrift*).

233. "Purity of conscience is the only atmosphere in which faith can live" (Brown, *The Pastoral Epistles*, 28). See Appendix D: Conscience, Ethics, and Morality.

234. Strong, #3466. "The Greek 'mysteries' were certain religious celebrations or rites (notably those of Demeter at Eleusis), to which only the initiated were admitted" (Hillard, *The Pastoral Epistles of St. Paul*, 33).

235. "The Greek word μυστήριον [*musterion*] does not, of its own force, imply anything, in our sense of the word, mysterious, that is to say, obscure or difficult to comprehend. That which it connotes is rather something which can only be known on being imparted by someone already in possession of it, not by mere reason and research which are common to all" (Cheetham, *The Mysteries Pagan and Christian*, 40–41).

236. "The people were looking for certain things in religion and they found them in these cults. . . . The mystery religions emphasized the idea of personal immortality" (Kirk, *The Religion of Power*, 67–68).

237. Henne am Rhyn, *Mysteria*, 49.

238. Ibid., 50–51.

239. Ibid., 55–56.

240. Ibid., 56.

241. Ibid., 66; Kirk, 63.

242. *Mysteria*, 57–59.

243. Ptolemy IV Philopator (221–221 BC) was so enraged that the Jews

prohibited him from entering the temple at Jerusalem that he decreed the Jews of Egypt must become "initiated into the mysteries" of Dionysus or be reduced to the status of slaves" (3 Maccabees 3:30 in Metzger, *The Apocrypha of the Old Testament*; *Mysteria*, 66.

244. "Rites of an impressive kind were enacted" (Caton, *The Temples and Ritual of Asklepios at Epidauros and Athens*, 31.

245. Henne am Rhyn, 59.

246. "And this became a hidden trap for mankind, because men, in bondage to misfortune or to royal authority, bestowed on objects of stone or wood the name that ought not to be shared. Afterward it was not enough for them to err about the knowledge of God, but they live in great strife due to ignorance, and they call such great evils peace. For whether they kill children in their initiations, or celebrate secret mysteries, or hold frenzied revels with strange customs" (Wisdom of Solomon 14:21–23 in Metzger, *The Apocrypha of the Old Testament*).

247. Jannaris, *A Concise Dictionary of the English and Modern Greek Languages*, 134, s.v. "enthusiasm."

248. Liddell & Scott, 566, s.v. "ἐνθουσία."

249. Kirk, 68.

250. "A 'mystery' in the New Testament, means a truth once concealed but now revealed. 'The mystery of

faith,' therefore, means the knowledge of Christ and his salvation" (Erdman, 43).

251. "We must therefore be cautious in inferring from the mere use of a word that a corresponding institution accompanied it" (Cheetham, 75).

252. "It is very obvious, though it seems sometimes to have been forgotten, that the Church of necessity adopted at any rate the language of those to whom it brought its message. The first preachers of the Gospel must use words familiar to those whom they addressed. In order to be understood of the people they must use popular language, and the New Testament is a witness that they did so. They spoke the Greek language, which they heard around them, as we find it preserved in the works of the philosophers, historians, and comedians both of their own time and of that which went before. . . . Christians of the first days had no scruple whatever in adopting words which had been used in the service of paganism" (Cheetham, 15–18).

253. Ordinances rites in the Old Testament were also known as *mysteries*. "You have been in heaven, but all the *mysteries* had not yet been revealed to you" (1 Enoch 16:3 in Charles, *The Book of Enoch*, 44). "I know the mysteries of the holy ones; for He, the Lord, has showed me and informed me, and I have

read (them) in the heavenly tablets"
(1 Enoch 106:19 in Charles, 152).

254. "These cults also provided a new conception of social relationship.s . . . They were essentially social and democratic. They expressed the feeling of John Wesley that 'people should go to heaven in companies and not one by one.' All men, without regard to their previous condition, became brothers in the temples of the gods. Master and man, freedman and slave, found themselves associated on terms of equality in the daily worship. The brotherhood has a community supper, which symbolized this new relationship. . . . By turning social passion into religious channels these cults made it easier to form Christian communities among peoples already familiar with the form and desirability of such associations" (Kirk, 70–71).

255. "Ser honestos" (Biblia Reina Valera).

256. Strong, #4998.

257. Betteridge, 106, s.v. "besonnen."

258. American Standard Version; "The rare word [*bathmos*] βαθμός is difficult. It seems to have been used for threshold in the [Septuagint Greek Old Testament] (1 Samuel 5:5, also [Old Testament Apocrypha,] Sirach [Ecclesiasticus] 6:36) and for the degrees of a sundial, which were possibly marked by a flight of steps (2 Kings 20). But apart from this there is no instance of its use in the literal sense of step" (Hillard, 34; see also Humphreys, 108).

259. New American Standard Bible.

260. Strong, #1247.

261. Faulring, 531. Joseph Smith moved the words "the pillar and ground of the truth is" from the end of verse fifteen to the start of verse sixteen for clarity.

262. Compare the following translation of this verse. "But if I am long in coming, this will make clear to you what behaviour is right for men in the house of God, which is the church of the living God, the pillar and base of what is true" (Hooke, *Bible in Basic English*).

263. Insertion of the parenthesis indicates that "the pillar and foundation of truth" from the previous verse is Jesus the Christ (see Faulring, 531).

264. "Appeared in the flesh," in the sense of "in human nature" (Barnes, 174).

265. Strong, #2150.

266. British & Foreign Bible Society, *Tiomnadh Nuadh*.

267. Mac Carthaigh [ꝳ&ᴄ ᴄáꞃċ&ᵹ], *An Bíobla Naofa*.

268. Dinneen, Foclór Gaedhilge agus Béarla [ꝼoᴄᵽóꞃ ᵹ&eòᵽᶘᵹe &ᵹuꞃ ᵬéᵽꞃᶘ&], 331, s.v. "Ɗᶥ&òᵭ&ċ."

269. Darby Bible Translation.

270. Liddell & Scott, 1905, s.v. "ἐστερέω" (ἕστερος).

271. Groves, 449, s.v. "Προσέχω."

272. Faulring, 531.

273. This interpretation appears in a Spanish translation, *Teniendo cauterizada la conciencia*" (Biblia Reina Valera).

274. Darby Bible Translation.

275. Compare with this alternative translation, "By those who believe and know the truth" (New Revised Standard Version).

276. Strong, #1033.

277. *Speisen* in all three German translations by Luther, Schlachter, and Brockhaus.

278. Darby Bible Translation.

279. Young's Literal Translation.

280. New International Version Bible.

281. Darby Bible Translation.

282. Ibid.

283. Green's Literal Translation

284. The following translation is a good rendition to grasp the meaning of the verse. "If you point these things out to the brothers, you will be a good minister of Christ Jesus, brought up in the truths of the faith and of the good teaching that you have followed." (New International Version).

285. Strong, #952.

286. Barnes, 188.

287. Lock, *The Pastoral Epistles*, 50. A similar reference appears in Plato's *Republic*. "Take your choice then; either allow me to say as much as I please, or if your prefer asking questions, do so: and I will do with you as we do with old women when they tell us stories: I will say 'good,' and nod my head or shake it, as the occasion requires" (Plato 1:350 in Davies, *The Republic of Plato*, 35).

288. Barnes, 188.

289. "Bodily exercise profiteth . . . for a little time" (Barnes, 188).

290. New Revised Standard Version.

291. Barnes, 188.

292. Young's Literary Translation.

293. Interlinear Hebrew-Greek-English Bible.

294. Interlinear Hebrew-Greek-English Bible.

295. Douay-Rheims Version.

296. New International Version.

297. Darby Bible Translation.

298. Young's Literary Translation.

299. Interlinear Hebrew-Greek-English Bible.

300. Lock, *The Pastoral Epistles*, 52.

301. Simpson, *Cassell's Latin Dictionary*, 22, s.v. "adulescentulus."

302. Hillard, *The Pastoral Epistles of St. Paul*, 45.

303. The word "in" is not in the Greek text; however, this insertion indicates that the exhortation is to be in teaching doctrine.

304. "The context makes clear that the reference is to the care required in reading the scriptures to a company" (Strong, #320).

305. "After the reading of the Law and

the prophets the rulers of the synagogue sent unto them, saying, Ye men and brethren, if ye have any word of exhortation for the people." (Acts 13:15).

306. Interlinear Hebrew-Greek-English Bible.

307. A selection of versions with "elders" in the translation

English:

"elders"	New Revised Standard Version
"elders"	World English Bible
"elders"	Weymouth New Testament in Modern Speech
"eldership"	Young's Literary Translation
"elderhood"	Darby Bible Translation

German:

"Ältesten"	Luther Heilige Schrift
"Ältesten"	Die Schlachter Bibel

French:

"enciens"	Segond Nouvelle Édition de Genève
"enciens"	Martin La Sainte Bible

Swedish:

"Äldste"	Bibeln elder Den Heliga Skrift

Danish:

"Ældste"	Det Danske Bibelselskab

308. Strong, #4244.

309. Barnes, 193.

310. Today's New International Version.

311. Young's Literary Translation.

312. Young's Literary Translation.

313. Brown, 41.

314. "Give proper recognition to those widows who are really in need" (New International Version).

315. Liddell & Scott, 1473, s.v. "προγον-ητκός –ιος, – ος."

316. Barnes, 199.

317. Ibid., 199.

318. Ibid., 199–200.

319. This word also appears in James 5:5.

320. Compare with Revelation 3:1.

321. Barnes, 200.

322. Young's Literary Translation.

323. Barnes, 200.

324. Ibid., 201; "With such alarming results we must remind ourselves that the Church welfare system was never designed or intended to care for the healthy member who, as a result of his poor management or lack of preparation, has found himself in difficulty. It was designed to assist the membership in case of a large, physical disaster, such as an earthquake or a flood. It was designed to assist the ill, the injured, the incapacitated, and to rehabilitate them to a productive life. In far too many cases, members who should be making use of their own preparedness provisions are finding that there is nothing there and that they have to turn to the Church" (L. Tom Perry, "The Need to Teach Personal and Family

Preparedness," *Ensign*, April 1981); "No self-respecting Church member will voluntarily shift the responsibility for his own maintenance to another. Furthermore, a man not only has the responsibility to care for himself; he also has the responsibility to care for his family" (Marion G. Romney, "The Basics of Church Welfare," 2).

325. New International Version.

326. New International Version.

327. Faulring, 531.

328. The words "to enroll" are inserted for clarity; they are not in the the original Greek text.

329. Interlinear Hebrew-Greek-English Bible.

330. Darby Bible Translation.

331. Compare the following translation of this verse: "As for younger widows, do not put them on such a list. For when their sensual desires overcome their dedication to Christ, they want to marry" (New International Version).

332. Strong, #2691.

333. Barnes, 205.

334. Wuest, *Word Studies in the Greek New Testament*, 4:84.

335. New International Version.

336. Young's Literary Translation.

337. Humphreys, 131.

338. Strong, #916.

339. Humphreys, 131.

340. The Hebrew word order reads, "Not you shall muzzle an ox when he is treading out (grain)" (Interlinear Hebrew-Greek-English Bible).

341. The insertion of words "the testimony of," though not in the original text, are implied and included here for clarification.

342. The words "the Lord" do not appear in most manuscripts.

343. Darby Bible Translation.

344. New Revised Standard Edition

345. "Note the 24th and 25th verses in this chapter are to be placed immediately after the 22nd, and the 23rd is the last verse of this chapter" (Faulring, 531).

346. "It would seem obvious that the weak stomach of Timothy should not be used as an argument that modern liquor is needed as a beverage. . . . The very advice which Paul gives to Timothy seems to caution him against any false extremes, and to urge him to use his sanctified common sense" (Erdman, 68).

347. Humphreys, 136.

348. Ibid.

349. Many water-borne parasites infect the intestine of a victim: "After passage through the acid barrier of the stomach, the organisms colonize . . . the small intestine" (World Health Organization, *Guidelines for Drinking-Water Quality*, 120).

350. "Should not the old relations in such a case rather give way? Practically, no doubt, they would in a

great measure do so. But formerly it was not the slave's part to demand this, or to act as if, by reason of his church-fellowship with his master, he could claim civil freedom as his right; for this had been to turn the gospel into a political charter, and give rise to the greatest confusion. The change in that direction must be wrought for the slave, not asserted by him, and should only be brought about by the gradual diffusion of right views respecting men's relation to God, and, growing out of this, their relation one to another. Meanwhile, the most effectual way to secure a partial amelioration, and untimately a general abolition, of the evil, was by the Christian slaves themselves bearing their burden and doing their part with Christian meekness and generosity" (Fairbairn, 231–232).

351. Compare with the teaching of Jesus in Luke 22:25–27.

352. Barnes, 224.

353. Bassler, *1 Timothy, 2 Timothy, Titus*, 107.

354. Interlinear Hebrew-Greek-English Bible.

355. Green's Literal Translation

356. New International Version.

357. Darby Bible Translation.

358. "It is the mark of a base disposition to cultivate godliness for the sake merely of the temporal gain it may yield; but there is, at the same time, a real and more important temporal gain connected with it" (Fairbairn, 235).

359. New American Standard Bible

360. Darby Bible Translation.

361. "The notion of deception or delusion is in the word, and the sense, that, deceived by the promises held out by the prospect of wealth, they have apostatized from the faith" (Barnes, 227).

362. Douay-Rheims Version.

363. "With such sorrows as remorse, and painful reflections on their folly, and the apprehension of the future" (Barnes, 227).

364. Pervanoglu, 855, s.v. "φιλαργυρία."

365. Erdman, 73.

366. "The supreme concern of the Christian pastor must ever be that of the purity and sanctity of his own motives" (Ibid., 74).

367. "Moses the **man of God** (Deuteronomy 33:1; Joshua 14:6); "A **man of God** came unto me, and his countenance was like the countenance of an angel of God" (Judges 13:6); "there came a **man of God** unto Eli" (1 Samuel 2:27); "there is in this city a **man of God**, and he is an honourable man; all that he saith cometh surely to pass" (1 Samuel 9:6); "the word of God came unto Shemaiah the **man of God**" (1 Kings 12:22); "to the sign which the **man of God** had given by the word of [Jehovah] the Lord" (1 Kings 13:5); "I know that thou

art a **man of God**, and that the word of [Jehovah] the Lord in thy mouth is truth" (1 Kings 17:24); "I perceive that this [Elisha] is an holy **man of God**" (2 Kings 4:9).

368. The term "man of God" appears here and also in 2 Timothy 3:17.

369. Groves, Greek and English Dictionary, s.v. "διώκω." The dictionary also defines the word with a negative sense, "to drive away, put to flight, expel, [or] banish." However, it is clear from the content of this verse that Paul used the word in a positive application.

370. New Revised Standard Edition

371. Fairbairn, 240–241.

372. Strong, #75.

373. Strachan, *The Captivity and the Pastoral Epistles*, 232.

374. Darby Bible Translation.

375. Green's Literal Translation

376. Though generally referred to as *procurator*, this title did not come into use in Judaea until after the death of King Herod Agrippa in AD 44. In the period when governors ruled, prior to the appointment of Agrippa as king by the Emperor Claudius, the Judaean governor was a *prefect*. The 1961 discovery at Caesarea of the "Pilate Stone" refers to Pilate as "Prefect of Judæa"—*Pontivs Pilatvs Praefectvs Iudæa* (Vardaman, *Journal of Biblical Literature*, 81:70–71).

377. Douay-Rheims Version.

378. Strong, #2015.

379. Jerome, Biblia Sacra Versio Vulgata.

380. Nouvelle Édition de Genève.

381. Weymouth, *New Testament in Modern Speech*; see also New Revised Standard Edition

382. Faulring, 531.

383. Ibid.

384. Barnes, The Epistles of Paul, 230.

385. Ibid., 229.

386. Jospeh B. Wirthlin, "What is the Difference Between Immortality and Eternal Life," *The New Era*, November 2006.

387. Young's Literary Translation.

388. "Pride of purse is 'not merely vulgar, it is sinful" (Erdman, 79).

389. New Revised Standard Edition

390. Interlinear Hebrew-Greek-English Bible.

391. Darby Bible Translation.

392. "The life in God is real on both sides of the grave" (Strachan, *The Captivity and the Pastoral Epistles*, 234); compare also Doctrine & Covenants 6:7; 11:7; 14:7; 29:43.

393. Darby Bible Translation.

394. Strong, #3872.

395. Strong, #728.

396. Strong, #5581.

397. Strong, #795.

398. "Philippi, which is the [first] chief city of [the] that part of Macedonia, and a colony" (Acts 16:12). Part

(Greek *meris*) denotes a portion of a province known as a district.

399. Neapolis is now the city of Kavala (Greek *Kabala* Καβάλα).

Part Two

2 TIMOTHY

2 Timothy

PROLOGUE

The Second Epistle of Paul to Timothy is the last known letter that Paul wrote prior to his death. There may well have been others written in the final winter months after Second Timothy, however, they did not survive the ravages of time. Few people recognize the future potential worth of letters they receive from friends, relatives, and decision makers of the future.

From the content of this letter, we learn that Paul is in his present situation because of a 'Judas' by the name of "Alexander the coppersmith," of whom Paul says, "did me much evil" (2 Timothy 4:14). This Alexander was a former member of the Church, excommunicated for apostasy, and obviously held a determined vendetta against Paul, who probably imposed the disciplinary action. He mentions Alexander again in this epistle in association with another apostate, "Hymenæus and Alexander," of whom Paul declared, "I have delivered unto Satan that they may learn not to blaspheme" (2 Timothy 1:20). We contrast the sentiments of Paul for Alexander with the compassionate recollections that he has for Timothy. "[Recalling] ~~When I call to remembrance~~ the unfeigned faith that is in thee, [that] ~~which~~ dwelt first in thy grandmother Lois, and thy mother Eunice; and I am persuaded that in thee also" (2 Timothy 1:5).

In this epistle, Paul declares that he knows the end of his ministry and execution is forthcoming. "I have fought the good

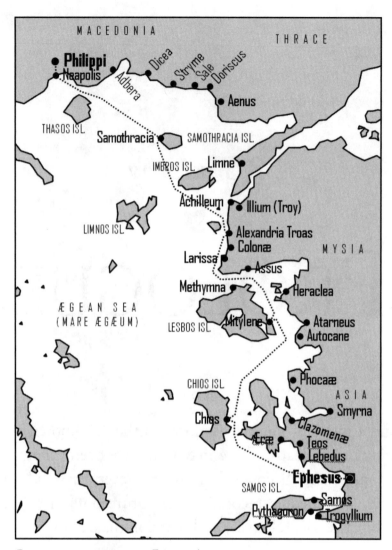

PHILIPPI IN RELATION TO EPHESUS[1]

fight, I have finished the race, I have kept the faith" (2 Timothy 4:7). This is the oft-quoted verse from this epistle; however, the next verse answers the question, why? The answer is contained in a usually overlooked verse, "[There remains,] ~~Henceforth there is laid up for me~~ [the] ~~a~~ crown of righteousness [laid up for me], which the Lord, the righteous judge, shall [award] ~~give~~ me at that day; and not to me only, but unto all [who have longed for] ~~them also that love~~ his appearing" (2 Timothy 4:8).

It is somewhat peculiar that the epilogue epistle of the apostle Paul is not chronologically placed at the end of his compilation of epistles. Tradition through the centuries has dictated the order of compilation, and we reluctantly inherit that legacy. The order of the books in the New Testament is actually irrelevant to the intended value of teaching and testimonial to the truths of the Gospel of Jesus the Christ as a collective witness. Let us proceed with a study of this epistle and glean all that we can from the words of an apostle of the Lord Jesus the Christ.

2 Timothy

❧

COMMENTARY

This is the second of two surviving epistles written by Paul to Timotheus. This is also the last known epistle written by Paul prior to his execution at Rome to survive the ravages of the centuries.

SALUTATION (2 TIMOTHY 1:1–5)

There are several points of interest in the opening of this epistle. Verse 1 opens with a declaration of faith in the will of God, and of hope in the promise of eternal life. Then verse 2 indicates his acceptance of his circumstances with a declaration of mercy and peace. In verse 3, he simply indicates his tranquil state of a pure conscience. There is a tearful recollection of Timothy expressed in verses 4 and 5 and how he has progressed from humble circumstances back home in remote Lystra.

[1:1] Paul, an apostle of Jesus Christ [through]² ~~by~~ the will of God, according to the promise of life [that] ~~which~~ is in Christ Jesus,

The will (Greek *thelema* θέλημα) indicates determination, specifically a purpose, or decree; "what one wishes or has determined shall be done."³

The promise (Greek *epaggelia* ἐπαγγελία) is an announcement conveying a sense of "assent or pledge; especially a divine assurance . . . except in Acts 23:21, it is used only of the promises of God."⁴

Paul reiterates the assurance of God that eternal life is promised to all those who remain true and faithful in this life. In an earlier epistle, Paul wrote to the Hebrews, "God, willing more abundantly to shew unto the heirs of promise the immutability of his counsel, confirmed it by an oath" (Hebrews 6:17). New Testament scripture is clear as to who gave the divine assurance, "the promise of my Father" (Luke 24:49),[5] declared Jesus. Paul further elucidated the concept, "For this cause he is the mediator of the new [covenant] ~~testament~~, that by means of death, for the redemption of the transgressions that were under the first testament, they which are called might receive the promise of eternal inheritance" (Hebrews 9:15).

Of life (Greek *zoe* ζωή) simply means life in a literal or a figurative sense. This and the previous word complete the term, "the promise of life." Though not stated in this verse, it is clear that eternal life is implied. This promise is asserted by the apostle John, "This is the promise that he hath promised us, even eternal life" (1 John 2:25). Even Paul conveyed this concept with greater clarity in First Timothy than he did in Second Timothy, "Godliness is profitable unto all things, having promise of the life that now is, and of that which is to come" (1 Timothy 4:8). Paul mandates all Christians to seek after this divine inheritance: "Let us therefore fear, lest, a promise being left us of entering into his rest, any of you should seem to come short of it" (Hebrews 4:1). There is a reiteration of the Christian inheritance later in a simple decree, "Inherit the promise" (Hebrews 6:12).

[1:2] To Timothy, [and]⁶ ~~my dearly~~⁷ beloved son; Grace, mercy, and peace, from God the Father and Christ Jesus our Lord.

Grace (Greek *charis* χάρις) can simply mean graciousness. However, in a theological sense, "Grace indicates favor on the part of the giver, thanks on the part of the receiver."[8] "Because grace is the principle of transformation and action, it calls for constant collaboration"[9] between both parties—the giver and the receiver. In this verse, we note that Paul clearly recognizes the distinction between grace and mercy. Some readers inadvertently equate grace with mercy.[10]

[1:3] [Grateful¹¹ I am to] ~~I thank~~ God, whom I serve from my forefathers with pure conscience, that without ceasing I have [mention] ~~remembrance~~ of thee in my prayers night and day;

I serve (Greek *latreuo* λατρεύω), in a basic sense, means "to work for hire," however, in a religious application it means to minister or to render to God.[12] For a Jew, the word "was specially used to render the worship of Jehovah by the covenant people."[13] Jesus used this word in his encounter with Satan, "Get thee hence, Satan: for it is written, Thou shalt worship the Lord thy God, and him only shalt thou serve [*latreuesis* λατρεύσεις]" (see Matthew 4:10 and Luke 4:8). See appendix D, "Conscience, Ethics, and Morality." There is a covenant implication in this context; you cannot serve or worship a God with whom you have not a covenant commitment. His Jewish parents nurtured the principles of courage, dedication, and faith in Paul (see Acts 26:4–5 and Philippians 3:4–6). "Christianity never seemed to . . . Paul to be a different religion from Judaism, but its natural and legitimate development."[14] He had faith in the Jehovah of his forefathers, embraced the same truths, and had the same hope in the resurrection of the faithful.[15]

Remembrance (Greek *mneia* μνεία) is a different word than the two other Greek words also translated remembrance in the following two verses. Mneia "is always used in connection with prayer."[16] This particular word translates easily as thought or mention (Romans 1:9; Ephesians 1:16; 1 Thessalonians 1:2; Philemon 1:4).

[1:4] Greatly desiring to see thee, being mindful of thy tears, that I may be filled with joy;

This verse is cumbersome in its English translation. Compare the following rendition: "Recalling your tears, I long to see you, so that I may be filled with joy."[17] Rearranging the three phrases so that the second appears first makes the verse clear.

[1:5] [Recalling] ~~When I call to remembrance~~ **the unfeigned faith that is**

in thee, which dwelt first in thy grandmother Lois, and thy mother Eunice; and I am persuaded that in thee also.

Unfeigned (Greek *anypokritos* ἀνυπόκρῐτος) means without dissimulation[8] or without hypocrisy (James 3:17). This word is generally "peculiar to religious language"[19]—particularly in English, where it conveys the sense of not pretended.

ACTIVE AND FEARLESS FAITH (2 TIMOTHY 1:6–14)

In the following verses, Paul makes an unusual but inspiring analogy. He charges Timothy to "fan the flame of the gift of God" (2 Timothy 1:6) that is in him. In essence, Paul says, "Be not ashamed to fan the flames of your gospel testimony in the holy calling you have received. God did not give you a 'timid spirit' (2 Timothy 1:7) when you were ordained; or, in other words, received your 'vocation' (2 Timothy 1:9). Keep the commandment of God and achieve a sound mind with power and love." Paul speaks of his own spiritual witness, "I know him in whom I have faith" (2 Timothy 1:12)

[1:6] Wherefore, I put thee in remembrance that thou [fan the flame[20] of] ~~stir up~~ **the gift of God, which is in thee [through]** ~~by~~ **the [laying]**[21] ~~putting~~ **on of my hands.**[22]

Stir up (Greek *anazopyreo* ἀναζωπυρέω) means to rekindle, in the sense of to fan the flame.[23] "The original word [*anazopyrein* ἀναζωπυρεῖν] used here denotes the kindling of a fire, as by bellows."[24] This word is interpreted as "Stir (the embers) into a flame."[25] Plutarch used this Greek word in his biography of Pompey, "That inveterate enemy, who was again kindling the flames of war."[26] Paul is now a prisoner at Rome, and the term may be inspired by the duties of the Vestalis Maxima priestess whose "chief office was to watch by turns, night and day, the everlasting fire which blazed upon the altar of Vesta."[27] Paul is here instructing Timothy "to use all proper means to keep the flame of pure religion in the soul burning."[28]

The gift (Greek *charisma* χάρισμα) has reference to "a (divine) gratuity," in the sense of "a (spiritual) endowment."[29] This word appears seventeen times in the New Testament, nigh on exclusively by Paul—with one exception by Peter (see 1 Peter 4:10).

Putting on (Greek *epithesis* ἐπίθεσις), in an official sense, means an imposition of hands.[30] This Greek word appears four times in the New Testament.[31]

[1:7] For God hath not given us the spirit of [timidity][32] ~~fear~~; but of power, and of love, and of a sound mind.

Fear (Greek *deilia* δειλία) "denotes cowardice, unmanliness, and timidity."[33] The word fear is "an emotion excited by threatening evil or impending pain,

accompanied by a desire to avoid or escape it"[34]; whereas the word *timid* is a "shrinking from danger or publicity," found in a person who is "easily frightened," in the sense of being "shy" or "lacking self-confidence."[35]

During the crucifixion there was a short dialog between Jesus and the two thieves. One of the thieves rebukes his companion in crime and says, "Dost not thou fear God, seeing thou art in the same condemnation? And we indeed justly; for we receive the due reward of our deeds" (Luke 23:40–41). The fear that man must have before God is with respect to the judgment He justifiably must execute upon sinful man at the Great Day when we stand before Him. This is reiterated in the Book of Revelation: "Fear God, and give glory to him; for the hour of his judgment is come" (Revelation 14:7). Those who live in righteousness repent and make restitution, need not have fear of the judgment of God. The translation of *fear* in this verse distorts the context.

Of a sound mind (Greek *sophronismos* σωφρονισμός) suggests the teaching of morality[36] and enabling "the exercise of that self-restraint that governs all passions and desires, enabling the believer to be conformed to the mind of Christ."[37] This is the only incidence of this word in the Greek New Testament. The following statement provides further perception on this unique word. "The state referred to here is that in which the mind is well balanced, and under right influences; in which it sees things in their just proportions and relations."[38]

[1:8] Be not thou therefore ashamed of the testimony of our Lord, nor of me his prisoner; but be thou [a partner with the gospel in its afflictions][39] ~~partaker of the afflictions of the gospel~~ **according to the power of God;**

Partaker of the afflictions of (Greek *sygkakopatheo* συγκακοπαθέω) conveys the understanding "to suffer hardship in company with" someone.[40] Paul is perhaps creating a personification of the Gospel with Jesus the Christ; for Paul, "it is all one and the same."[41] Of necessity, we must change "of the gospel" to "with the gospel."

[1:9] Who hath saved us, and called us with an[42] **holy [vocation]** ~~calling~~**, not according to our works, but according to his own purpose and grace, which was given us in Christ Jesus before [times eternal]** ~~the world began,~~

Hath saved us (Greek *sozo* σῴζω), "The Christian use of the word [*sozo*] . . . had its origin in the Jewish use. To a Jew it implied being saved from 'the wrath' and being made a participator in the Messianic Kingdom."[43] Theologically, *saved* means "rescued from the consequences of sin and subsequent otherwise impending damnation."[44]

In this verse, Paul places together two words of related meaning, causing confusion of understanding in English translations. First, **called** (Greek *kaleo* καλέω) in the sense of "to call someone by name."

Second, **calling** (Greek *klesis* κλῆσις) indicating a calling into court or, in a religious sense, an invitation. This word "is always used in the New Testament of that 'calling' the origin, nature and destiny of which are heavenly (the idea of invitation being implied)."[45] The confusion is resolved by translating to vocation instead of calling.[46]

[1:10] But is now [revealed through] ~~made manifest~~ **by the [manifestation]** ~~appearing~~ **of our Savior Jesus Christ, who hath abolished death, and hath brought life and immortality to light through the gospel:**

Who hath abolished (Greek *katargeo* καταργέω) means "to be (render) entirely idle (useless),"[47] or "to render powerless."[48] The statement about the abolition of death is a reiteration of First Corinthians, "The last enemy death shall be destroyed."[49] Consider this phrase in conjunction with the remainder of the verse. Though darkness is not mentioned, it is nonetheless implied: death and darkness are replaced and contrasted by life and light.

Having brought to light (Greek *photizo* φωτίζω) metaphorically means spiritual enlightenment. The implication being "that these things were before obscure or unknown, and that they have been disclosed to us by the gospel, [and] that all ambiguity and doubt are removed."[50] This concept relates to more than just the physical incarnation of Jesus in mortality. Paul is referring to "the whole work of redemption."[51]

[1:11] Whereunto I am appointed a [herald][52] ~~preacher~~, and an apostle, and a teacher of [nations] ~~the Gentiles~~.

Am appointed (Greek *tithemi* τίθημι)[53] denotes an appointment to serve. The appointment of Paul and Barnabas occurred at the time of their ordination to the office of apostle at Antioch early in AD 43 (Acts 13:2–3). This word is particularly used by Jesus in reference to his apostles during his ministry, "Ye have not chosen me, but I have chosen you, and ordained [*etheka* ἔθηκα] you" (John 15:16). However, this word does not specifically mean the actual ordination but the ordained appointment or calling. Compare with another example, "I will put [*theso* θήσω] my spirit upon him" (Matthew 12:18). This example is a quote from Isaiah, "I have put [*natati* נָתַתִּי] my spirit on him" (Isaiah 42:1). This Hebrew word *nathan* (נָתַן) means to give something, commit to their care, hand something over, or to transfer something.[54] In Spanish, this word is translated *puesto*[55] meaning "an assigned post," an "employment, dignity, [or] office."[56]

THE "DEPOSIT" OF THE SPIRIT (2 TIMOTHY 1:12, 14)

The Confirmation of the Holy Ghost is a "deposit" and promise we have from God that we shall receive Eternal Life—if we prove faithful.

———— 🕊 ————

[1:12] For the which cause I also suffer these things; nevertheless I am not ashamed; for I know [him in][57] whom I have [faith] ~~believed~~, and [I] am persuaded that he is able to [guard my deposit until] ~~keep that which I have committed unto him against~~ that day.

Have committed unto him (Greek *paratheke* παραθήκη) simply means a deposit. "The word signifies money or other precious things deposited in a bank or treasury, to be returned when demanded."[58] Though this is the only occurrence of this word in the Greek New Testament, *paratheken* (παραθήκην—in the verse context) is another form of *parakatatheken* (παρακαταθήκην—also in verse context) used in verse 14 below and also in 1 Timothy 6:20. The same word also appears in the Greek Septuagint Old Testament translation,[59] and also in the deuterocanonical Greek Second Book of Maccabees.[60] See verse 14 below for an explanation of the significance and meaning of this word used here by Paul.

The designation that **day** (Greek *ten Emeran*, τὴν Ἡμέραν) is in respect of the Judgment Day at the end of the world. Paul retains his hope in a time deposit with God to the Day of Judgment. Redemption of the matured deposit with eternal interest equivalent will qualify for eternal life in the kingdom of God.

[1:13] [Retain] ~~Hold fast~~ [a pattern][61]

~~the form~~ of [healthy] ~~sound~~ words, which thou hast heard of me, in faith and love which is in Christ Jesus.

The form (Greek *hypotyposis* ὑποτύπωσις) means an outline sketch, or "a sketch (figuratively) for imitation."[62] This is the "first draft of a thing, as painters do when they begin a picture."[63] Paul uses this word here and in 1 Timothy 1:16—both epistles to Timothy. Peter used a similar analogy in one of his epistles, "Christ also suffered for us, leaving us an example [Greek *hypogrammos* ὑπογραμμός], that ye should follow his steps" (1 Peter 2:21).

[1:14] That good [entrusted deposit][64] ~~thing~~ **which was committed unto thee keep by the Holy Ghost which dwelleth in us.**

Thing (Greek *parakararheke* παρακαταθήκη) means "something put down alongside, i.e. a deposit (sacred trust)."[65] The application of this word is similar to another Pauline application in his earlier epistles. God gives the promise of eternal life to us at baptism and confirmation with the gift of the Holy Ghost. Paul refers to this gift as "the earnest of the Spirit in our hearts" (2 Corinthians 1:22; 5:5), and "the earnest of our inheritance" (Ephesians 1:14). This word *earnest* (Greek *arrhabon* ἀρραβών) is "a pledge, i.e. part of the purchase-money or property given in advance as security for the rest."[66] *Parakatatheke* in the Timothy epistles appears to be yet

another reference to the earnest deposit of the Holy Ghost, until we "lay hold on" the full-payment of "eternal life."

CHALLENGING TIMES (2 TIMOTHY 1:15–18)

The apostasy and treason of the former converts Phygellus and Hermogenes was a great disappointment to Paul (1:15). In contrast, he reiterates the merciful ministration of Onesiphorus while he was at Ephesus and now also at Rome (1:16–18).

[1:15] This thou knowest, that all they which are in Asia [*Province*][67] ~~be~~[68] **turned away from me; of whom are Phygellus and Hermogenes.**

Asia (Greek *Asia* Ἀσία) refers to the Roman province of Asia Minor, composing the districts of "Lydia, Mysia, Caria, and Phrygia"[69]—equivalent to present-day west Turkey.

Be turned away (Greek *apostrepho* ἀποστρέφω) means to turn away or to turn back. In the context of this verse, the word means to revoke "allegiance," or "to defect."[70] Pilate uses this word in relation to the unsubstantiated accusation against Jesus. "Ye have brought this man unto me, as one that perverteth [*apostrephonta* ἀποστρέφοντα] the people."[71]

[1:16] The Lord give mercy unto the house of Onesiphorus; for he [often] ~~oft~~

refreshed me, and was not ashamed of my chain:

Give mercy (Greek *eleos* ἔλεος) means "compassion (human or divine)," and conveys the understanding of an "outward manifestation of pity; it assumes need on the part of him who receives it and resources adequate to meet the need on the part of him who shows it."[72] This word appears twenty-seven times in the Greek New Testament and is consistently translated "mercy."

He oft refreshed (Greek *anapsycho* ἀναψύχω) "means to cool again, to cool off, recover from the affects of heat; to refresh one's spirit."[73] This is the only occurrence of this word in the Greek New Testament.

[1:17] But, when he was in Rome, he sought me out very diligently, and found me.

[1:18] [May][74] the Lord grant unto him [to][75] ~~that he may~~ find mercy [from] ~~of~~ the Lord in that day; and in how many things he ministered ~~unto me~~ at Ephesus, thou knowest very well.

REMAIN FAITHFUL IN TRIALS (2 TIMOTHY 2:1–7)

This section of the letter presents three analogies or descriptive images portraying faithfulness in challenging circumstances. "Timothy is exhorted to suffer like a soldier, to strive like an athlete, [and] to labor like a husbandman."[76]

First, an enlisted or drafted soldier (2:3–4); second, a participant in the Greek athletic games (2:5); and third, an agrarian husbandman (2:6–7). The analogies provide three different paradigms on faithful endurance in the difficult circumstances that each committed Christian witness encounters.

[2:1] Thou therefore, my son, be [empowered] ~~strong~~ in the grace that is in Christ Jesus.

Strong (Greek *endynamoo* ἐνδυναμόω) means to empower in the sense of "to make strong."[77] The word *strong* usually implies human effort, whereas *empower* connotes authorization to conduct the affairs of another. Therefore, regardless of the physical and mental capabilities of Timothy—his own strength—he is still empowered through Jesus the Christ in the office of his ministry.

[2:2] And [what][78] ~~the~~ things ~~that~~ thou hast heard of me [through] ~~among~~ many witnesses, the same [entrust] ~~commit~~ thou to faithful men, [such as will] ~~who shall~~ be [competent][79] ~~able~~ [also] to teach others ~~also~~.

Among (Greek *dia* διά) means "the channel of an act . . . in very wide applications, local, casual, or occasional."[80] "*Dia* intimates that the witnesses were present to confirm the apostle's word."[81] Timothy heard Paul teach with a Spirit-confirmed witness of the divinity of the gospel. He saw Paul perform miracles by priesthood authority and power. Yet, additionally, Timothy heard further witness from many others who also heard and saw manifold witness of Paul in his ministry. Timothy received both direct and indirect witnesses of the Gospel of Jesus the Christ. Having received so many witnesses,[82] conveys the same to others, just as much as you also received, that you may "be able to teach others also."[83]

Witnesses (Greek *martys* μάρτυς) means a judicial witness. In the Greek New Testament, it is usually in reference to "one who bears witness by his death"; however, in this verse, the word implies "in a historical sense."[84] This Greek word is the source of the English word martyr.

THE ANALOGY OF THE ROMAN SOLDIER (2 TIMOTHY 2:3–4)

[2:3] Thou therefore endure [hardship][85] ~~hardness~~, **as a good soldier of Jesus Christ.**

Endure hardness (Greek *kakopatheo* κακοπαθέω) is compounded from *kakos* meaning evil, and *pathos* meaning suffering.[86] The same word also appears in verse nine of this chapter. Compare the following paraphrased rendition, "Be ready to do without the comforts of life, as one of the army of Christ Jesus."[87]

In this military metaphor, Paul indicates that Timothy is a soldier in the army of Jesus Christ, as opposed to a soldier in the Roman army. Timothy is fighting in a dirty war, which causes him to "suffer hardship." Likewise, Paul is also suffering in this dirty war, as indicated by the prison "chain" restricting his movement (1 Timothy 1:16). "[Paul] compares profane warfare with the spiritual and Christian warfare in this sense. The condition of military discipline is such, that as soon as a soldier has enrolled himself under a general, he leaves his house and all his affairs, and thinks of nothing but war; and in like manner, in order that we may be wholly devoted to Christ, we must be free from all the entanglements of this world."[88] See appendix B, "The Imperial Roman Army." The metaphor continues in the following verse.

[2:4] No man [serving as a soldier entangles] ~~that warreth entangleth~~ **himself with the affairs of this life, that he may please [the One]** ~~him~~ **who hath [enlisted]** ~~chosen~~ **him** ~~to be a soldier.~~

With the affairs of life (Greek *tais tou biou pragmateiais*, ταῖς τοῦ βίου πραγματείαις) "means the care of governing his family, and ordinary occupations; as farmers leave their agriculture, and merchants their ships and merchandise, till they have completed the time that they agreed to serve in war."[89] This verse is a continuation of the soldier concept introduced in the previous verse.

Hath chosen him (Greek *stratologeo* στρατολογέω) is a compounded word meaning to gather as one would conscript or enlist recruits to the army. Comparable to the Latin phrase *milites conscribere* (military conscription).[90]

To be a soldier (Greek *strateuomai* στρατεύομαι) refers to military service in the army. The Authorized Version misplaced this word in translation. The Greek word appears at the beginning of this verse, and not the end.

THE ANALOGY OF THE GREEK ATHLETE (2 TIMOTHY 2:5)

[2:5] [Again, also] ~~And~~ if [an athlete] ~~a man also~~ [competes] ~~strive~~ for masteries, [he][91] ~~yet~~ is ~~he~~ not crowned, except he [compete] ~~strive~~ lawfully.

A man (Greek *athleo* ἀθλέω) means a contestant in the public lists of the competitive games. This word appears twice in this verse in two different forms: first, a *man* (Greek *athle* ἀθλῇ), referring to the participating competitor, and the *strive* (Greek *athlese* ἀθλήσῃ), referring to the competition. The ancient Olympian Games were conducted every fourth year at the first full moon following the summer solstice

from 776 BC to AD 394.[92] "The combatants were called athletes."[93]

Strive (Greek *athleo* ἀθλέω) is the second instance of this word in this verse, and here means "to contend in public games."[94] This word refers to the disciplined athletic training required to qualify and participate. Athletes "were obliged to obey the directions of a public trainer, and if they disobeyed they were liable to be excluded."[95] A practical example was the Olympic Games, whereby an athlete "had to swear before the statue of Zeus that they had undergone training for ten months. To 'contend [*nomimos*] νομίμως' would therefore mean that this rule and oath had been fulfilled."[96] The process of compliance for the contest "taxed to the upmost the endurance and strength of the contestant, alike in the preparation and the struggle."[97] Calvin pointed out that Paul probably implied "that no man may think that he has done enough when he had been engaged in one or two conflicts."[98] In this verse, strive also means to endure—to the end.

He [not] crowned (Greek *stephanoo* στεφανόω) means to crown as a "reward of victory in the games"[99]—the negative inverses the meaning. This is the crowning of the winner in an athletic competition and not the crowning of a monarch. "The difference is to be noted; men may receive a kingly crown out of favor or by descent, they cannot receive a victor's crown unless they have actually won the victory."[100]

Strive lawfully (Greek *nomimos athlese*, νομίμως ἀθλήσῃ) means "lawfully he competes,"[101] according to the rules laid down for the contest. There were "rules of training, diet, exercise, etc., without observing which no one could hope to win a victory, so also must the Christian life be one of self-discipline."[102] The force of this verse emphasizes that the athlete must compete in an active, not passive, preparation and participation in the games.[103]

THE ANALOGY OF THE HUSBAND-MAN/FARMER (2 TIMOTHY 2:6–7)

[2:6] The [hard-working farmer]104 ~~husbandman that laboureth~~ [should]105 ~~must~~ be first partaker of the fruits.106

That laboureth (Greek *kopiao* κοπιάω) means "to feel fatigue; by implication to work hard; to grow weary, tired, exhausted with toil or burdens of grief;"[107] "toil to weariness."[108] There is a contrast between this analogy and the two previous analogies of the soldier and athlete. This hard-working farmer analogy speaks of a farmer whose efforts are not through winning a battle or race but through patience in the time between planting and harvesting. Collectively, these three analogies come from the daily life of the Greco-Roman first century. If the farmer works diligently, then he will reap the reward of his labor. "How much more unreasonable will it be for us to refuse the labors which Christ enjoins upon us, while he holds out so great a reward?"[109]

[2:7] [Reflect on]110 ~~Consider~~ what I say,[111] and the Lord give thee understanding112 in all things.

IDENTIFY WITH CHRIST (2 TIMOTHY 2:8–13)

The witness that Paul received when he both saw and conversed with the resurrected Jesus the Christ on the Damascus road is his unchanging witness that Christ lives (2 Timothy 2:8). Paul indicates that he has endured much hardship only because of concern for the eternal welfare of others (2 Timothy 2:9–10). Just as Jesus was raised from death, so shall we be raised from the dead (2 Timothy 2:11) and reign with Jesus (2 Timothy 2:12) in the eternal kingdom. This is the promise of eternal glory, and God is "faithful" to his promises, for "he cannot deny himself" (2 Timothy 2:13).

[2:8] Remember that Jesus Christ of the seed of David was raised from the dead, according to [the]113 ~~my~~ gospel;

According to my gospel (Greek *euaggelion* εὐαγγέλιον) "originally denoted a reward for good tidings;" however, "later the idea of reward dropped, and the word stood for 'the good news' itself."[114]

[2:9] Wherein I suffer [hardship] ~~trouble~~, ~~as an evil doer~~, **even [in chains as a criminal]** ~~unto bonds~~; **but the Word of God is not [chained]** ~~bound~~.[115]

An evil doer (Greek *kakourgos* κακοῦργος) means a wrong-doer, by implication a criminal. This word appears four times in the New Testament: the gospel according to Luke renders the other three occurrences as malefactor in connection with the crucifixion (Luke 23:32–33, 39). Paul may have selected this word to place himself in the image of one under execution with Christ—as were the two criminals crucified with Jesus. The imprisonment of Paul as a criminal will not stop the spread of the gospel—the Word of God is not bound—it is free (Compare with 1 Corinthians 15:31).

In the first imprisonment of Paul at Rome, he enjoyed considerable liberty, dwelling "two whole years in his own hired house" under house arrest (Acts 28:30). The circumstances of this second imprisonment of Paul at Rome are significantly different. He is now a criminal retained on imperial charges. "Paul was accused, and ultimately condemned, not as a Christian, but as a disturber of the peace, an evil-doer. To be a Christian was not in itself a crime till the days of Domatian (AD 81–96)."[116] Under this charge, he would also not have been confined "in any 'guard house' of the Prætorium; or any minor state prison, such as that of Appius Claudius, if it still existed. Neither would he have been interred at the 'Stone Quarry Prison,' Lautumiæ, at the furthest northwest corner of the Forum, but (we may believe) in the Carcer itself, the Tullianum [in the upper floors] or [the] 'Well-Dungeon,' at the foot of the Capitol. This last, with its chill vault and oozing spring, was the worst."[117] The *Tullianum* (or *Carcer*)—also known by the medieval Latin name *Carcere Mamertino*, or the Mamertine Prison[118]—was located at the Forum Romanum on the northeast slope of the Capitoline Hill. Construction of the Tulliainum (640–616 BC) occurred during the reign of Ancus Marcius King of Rome.[119]

Traditional legend conveys that both Paul and Peter were concurrently interred in the Tullianum. However, this Second Epistle of Paul to Timothy is silent respecting the legendary presence of Peter. If Peter were present with Paul in the Tullianum, he would not have declared, "Only Luke is with me" (1 Timothy 4:11). We must therefore conclude that either the internment of Peter is elsewhere within Rome, or his internment in the Tullianum was not concurrent with Paul.

[2:10] [Because of this,][120] ~~Therefore~~ **I endure all things [on account of]**[121] **for the [elect]** ~~elect's sakes~~, **that they may also obtain the salvation which is in Christ Jesus with eternal glory.**

The elect's (Greek *eklektos* ἐκλεκτός) means more than just "select"; it also means to be picked out,[122] or chosen out, in the sense of a favorite. Paul is referring to the doctrine of election introduced by Jesus during his ministry, "Ye have not chosen [*exelexasthe* ἐξελέξασθε] me, but I have chosen [*exelexamen* ἐξελεξάμην] you, and ordained you" (John 15:16). For the benefit and blessing of others, Paul is willing to endure hardship in the gospel ministry, that they may also obtain a like salvation.[123]

Eternal (Greek *aionios* αἰώνιος) means perpetual with respect to past, present, or future. The word can mean "either undefined but not endless," or "undefined because [it is] endless."[124] In the Greek New Testament, the word appears in context of the endless nature of God—power, glory, redemption, salvation, or resurrection.

[2:11] [For this][125] ~~It~~ is a faithful saying:[126] ~~For~~[127] if we [died] ~~be dead~~ with him, we shall also live with him;[128]

[2:12] If we [endure also][129] ~~suffer~~, we shall ~~also~~ [co-]reign ~~reign~~ with him; if we deny him, he also will deny us;

We shall also reign with him (Greek *symbasileuo* συμβασιλεύω) means "to be co-regent" in the context of "to reign together with" someone in the future.[130] The other incidence is in First Corinthians, "I would to God ye did reign, that we also might reign with [*symbasileusomen* συμβασιλεύσωμεν] you" (1 Corinthians

4:8).[131] In Latin, Jerome expressed the correct meaning with the word *conregnabimus*.[132] The only simple English word to express the Greek meaning is co-reign, rather than reign.[133]

[2:13] If we believe not, yet he abideth faithful; he cannot deny himself.

[2:14] [Remind them] of these things ~~put them in remembrance~~, charging them before the Lord that they strive not about words to no profit, but to the subverting of [those hearing][134] ~~the hearers~~.[135]

Charging (Greek *diamartyromai* διαμαρτύρομαι) means to "call gods and men to witness, protest solemny, especially in case of falsehood or wrong."[136] In a gospel sense, the purest meaning is "to bear solemn witness."[137] Translating the Old Testament from Hebrew to Greek, the Septuagint version uses *diamartyromai* (διαμαρτύρομαι) for the Hebrew word *ud* (עוּד): "Set your hearts unto all the words which I [have testified] ~~testify~~ [*meid* מֵעִיד] among you this day" (Deuteronomy 32:46). In English this word means "to take as witness" or "to bear witness."[138]

[2:15] [Be eager to present][139] ~~Study to shew~~ thyself [proven][140] ~~approved~~ unto God, a workman that [doth not blush][141] ~~needeth not to be ashamed~~, rightly dividing the Word of Truth.

Study (Greek *spoudazo* σπουδάζω) "signifies to hasten to do a thing, to exert oneself, endeavor, give diligence."[142] There is a certain sense of enthusiasm involving eagerness to accomplish the objective. No amount of study will attain approval from God; active implementation is essential. "If we have only the Holy Scriptures, it is not enough that each of us read it in private. But the doctrine drawn from it must be preached to us in order that we may be well informed."[143] Paul counsels Timothy to be eager and not embarrassed about his testimony of the gospel message—"who is not ashamed, because he has nothing to be ashamed of."[144] In modern days, we are encouraged to share our gospel conviction with eager enthusiasm.

Rightly dividing (Greek *orthotomeo* ὀρθοτομέω) means "to make a straight cut, i.e. (figuratively) to dissect (expound) correctly. . . . The meaning passed from the idea of cutting or 'dividing' to the more general sense of 'rightly dealing with a thing.' "[145] "Literally, who rightly cutteth up the word; an allusion to the action of the priest who opened and divided the sacrifice; or rather, of one who carves at table and distributes meat to the guests, according to their ages and their state of health."[146] "Paul assigns to teachers the duty of dividing or cutting, as a father, in giving food to his children, were dividing the bread by cutting it into small pieces."[147]

Word (Greek *logos* λόγος) simply means thought. However, in several instances—including this verse—*Logos* is a designation for Jesus the Christ, and therefore

capitalized as Word. The expression of this meaning appears in the opening verse of the Gospel of John. There is every reason to accept that Paul meant Word of Truth (*Logon tes Aletheias*, Λόγον τῆς Ἀληθείας)[148] to be a title for Jesus the Christ. English translations rarely express this interpretation, yet such is common in other languages.[149] The Word of Truth in this verse is part of a play on words by Paul with "their word" in verse seventeen below.

Jesus, as the Messiah, is the incarnation of the Word of God. Christians of Jewish origin would understand this concept from several Jewish scriptural statements:

1. "By the Word of [Jehovah] [*bidvar Yahweh*, בִּדְבַר יְהוָה the Lord] were the heavens made; and all the host of them by the breath of his mouth" (Psalm 33:6).

2. "He sendeth forth his commandment upon earth: his Word [*bidvar Yahweh*, יְהוָה בִּדְבַר] runneth very swiftly" (Psalm 147:15).

3. "O God of my fathers and Lord of mercy, who hast made all things with thy Word [*Logo* Λόγῳ]."[150]

4. "The Word [*elohenu udavar*, אֱלֹהֵינוּ־וּדְבַר][151] of our God shall stand for ever" (Isaiah 40:8).

The word of the Lord is a well recognized Old Testament phrase.

"The word of God indicates God's thoughts and will. This should be contrasted with His name, which indicates His person and presence."[152] Early Christianity equated the Hebrew word *davar* (דָּבָר) with the Greek word *logos* [λόγος]. This was not merely a translation, logos was also theologically comparable to the philosophical legacy of Socrates, Plato, and Aristotle. *Logos* [Λόγος] therefore, enabled the unification of two opposing theological cultures—Jewish and Greco-Roman.

[2:16] But shun [godless chatter][153] ~~profane~~ and vain babblings; for they will [advance][154] ~~increase~~ unto more ungodliness.[155]

Profane (Greek *bebelos* βέβηλος) literally means a threshold, or the accessibility of crossing the doorway. "This word suggests a trodden and trampled spot that is open to the casual step of every intruder or careless passer-by. This word means, primarily, 'permitted to be trodden, accessible;' hence, 'unhallowed, profane.' "[156] The profanity that is implied is in respect of "the absence of any divine or sacred character, [which] leads on to positive impiety."[157] In a religious context, the word came to designate someone who is "unfit to take part in holy things."[158] We would attribute this to someone who professes a hollow piety, "without any solid substance of good works by the hand."[159] There is more meaning in English to translate this word as *godless* to complement the word *ungodliness* at the end of the verse.

[2:17] And their word will [grow][160] ~~eat~~ as doth [gangrene][161] ~~a canker~~; of whom is Hymenaeus and Philetus;

Paul creates a play on "the word" between verse 15 and this verse. Above, in verse 15, he says "the Word of Truth" (*ton Logon tes Aletheias*, τὸν Λόγον τῆς ἀληθείας),[162] and here he uses "their word" (*o logos auton* ὁ λόγος αὐτῶν).[163] In both instances, the Greek word *logos* (λόγος) literally means mental reasoning. However, *Logos* in verse 15 refers to God as compared to the Gospel of John 1:1, "In the beginning was the Word [*Logos Λόγος*], and the Word [*Logos Λόγος*] was with God, and the Word [*Logos Λόγος*] was God." In this verse, Paul would have used *mythos* (μῦθος)[164] meaning mythical, as diametrically opposed to *logos* (λόγος). For the reason of a pun, he elected to write *logos* to highlight their deceptive reasoning of the apostates that will eventually turn to spiritual gangrene.

Doth a canker (Greek *gaggraina* γάγγραινα) "is 'an eating sore,' spreading corruption," as an analogy to apostates who "produce spiritual gangrene."[165] This is the only occurrence of this word in the New Testament.

[2:18] Who concerning the truth have [missed the mark] ~~erred~~, saying that the resurrection is past already; and overthrow the faith of some.

Have erred (Greek *astocheo* ἀστοχέω) refers to taking aim at a target but missing the mark, implying failure.[166] When an archer is distracted when taking aim, he misses the target. In a spiritual sense, Paul's message implies they well understood the truth of the doctrine of the resurrection. Their *aim* was to remain on the path of truth, but now they have deviated from that target and veered away from the truth, "claiming that the resurrection has already taken place."[167]

Unfortunately, the Hellenistic philosophy that purports there is no physical resurrection has assimilated into traditional Christian theology. "According to the Greek concept, the soul of man, which is incorruptible by nature, enters into divine immortality after death [and severs] its bodily ties."[168]

"They affirmed that the only resurrection Christ promised was a spiritual resurrection from ignorance and error by believing the gospel. And that the resurrection having already happened, no other is to be expected. . . . By explaining the doctrine of the resurrection in a figurative sense, Hymeneus and Philetus endeavored to recommend the gospel to the Greek philosophers, who considered the resurrection of the body, not only as impossible in itself, but as a thing highly disadvantageous, had it been possible."[169]

Another example of Hellenistic rejection of the concept of resurrection is contained in the encounter of Paul with the city leaders at Athens. "He [God] hath given assurance unto all men, in that he [God] hath raised him [Christ] from the dead. And when they heard of the resurrection of the dead, some mocked: and others said, We will hear thee again of this matter" (Acts 17:31–32). This response can be understood as, don't call us, we might call you! "The Resurrection appears to have been a doctrine particularly distasteful to the Greek mind."[170]

A GREAT HOUSE (2 TIMOTHY 2:19–22)

The Church is compared to a Great House containing items made of precious materials (gold and silver) and other items of common manufacture (wood and clay). Regardless of the product material, the items are either functional or useless. Therefore, can we fulfill the purpose that God knows we can accomplish? Let us take upon us the name of Christ and depart from iniquity that we may have the sure seal of acceptance before God.

[2:19] [However,] ~~Nevertheless~~ the foundation of God standeth [firm] ~~sure~~, having this seal, The Lord knoweth them [who] ~~that~~ are his. And, Let every one that nameth the name of Christ depart from iniquity.

Quoting from Numbers 16:5, "And he spake unto Korah and unto all his company, saying, Even to morrow the Lord will shew who are his, and who is holy; and will cause him to come near unto him: even him whom he hath chosen will he cause to come near unto him." Paul's quote comes from the Greek Septuagint version of the Old Testament. Paul may also have based the latter part of this verse upon Numbers 16:26, "Depart, I pray you, from the tents of these wicked men, and touch nothing of theirs, lest ye be consumed in all their sins." Considering both concepts are from the same chapter in Numbers, we conclude they are of uniform source.

Seal (Greek *sphragis* σφραγίς) is usually the seal "affixed to the foundation"[171] of a property, boundary post or stone. In many cultures, a series of boundary posts identify a property; each post bears an insignia, inscription, or engraving of the owner. In a different example, the branding of cattle with an insignia identifies to which cattle ranch or owner they belong. In each instance, the seal identifies ownership. Paul indicates that he is speaking of the saints in the Church. These saints are engraved with the signet or seal of Christ. Paul is apparently referring to a specific Old Testament directive given to Moses, "Thou shalt make a plate of pure gold, and [engrave] grave [*ufittachta* וּפִתַּחְתָּ] *upon* it, like the engravings [*pittuchei y* פִּתּוּחֵי] of a signet [*chotam* חֹתָם], HOLINESS [BELONGS] TO [JEHOVAH] THE LORD" (Exodus 28:36). Instead of the name of Jehovah, Paul declares for the name of Christ.[172]

[2:20] But in a great house there are not only vessels of gold and of silver, but also of wood and [earthenware][173] **of earth; and some to [honorable]**[174] **honour, and some to [common use]**[175] **dishonour.**

Of earth (Greek *ostrakinos* ὀστράκινος) means earthenware made from baked clay; derived from *oyster* (Greek *ostrakon* ὄστρακον)—"because being burnt in the fire, they are hard like shells."[176]

"A vessel once made by the artificer cannot change itself. It cannot become of any other material than that of which it was originally made. But here St. Paul represents vessels as changing themselves. This is absolutely incompatible with the idea that God has made a certain number of souls to be saved and a certain number to be destroyed. It is, on the contrary, the most surprising assertion of the freedom of the human will in scripture: for a man is not only supposed to be able, but is responsible for changing himself from that which is typified by an earthen vessel into that which is typified by a golden one. Hymenæus and Philetus had fallen from being golden vessels (for they had faith, and some faith, or at least some spiritual discernment, is necessary for men to profess a spiritual resurrection) into earthen ones, but if they repented they might become gold or silver ones; that is, if they purged themselves from the error in question, and abstained from associating with those who held it."[177]

[2:21] If a man therefore purge himself from these, he shall be a vessel unto honor, sanctified, and [made

useful][178] ~~meet for the~~ [master] ~~master's use~~, and [having been][179] prepared unto every good work.

Meet (Greek *euchrestos* εὔχρηστος) means useful[180] or serviceable.[181] "If the true believer is to be a vessel fit for the Master's use he must purge himself individually."[182]

[2:22] Flee also youthful lusts;[183] but follow [after][184] righteousness, faith, charity, peace, with them that call on the Lord out of a pure heart.

Youthful lusts (Greek *neoterikas epithymias*, νεωτερικὰς ἐπιθυμίας) identifies juvenile cravings. This term emphasizes the "longing, or desire for what is usually forbidden. It refers to the whole world of active lusts and desires . . . [which] the natural appetite impels."[185] There is a temptation to interpret this to mean only sexual immorality. However, he "does not mean sensual lusts only, but ambition, pride, love of power, rashness, and obstinacy; vices which some teachers who are free from sensual lusts are at little pains to avoid."[186] The message of this verse regards the fleeting mortal lusts of this world; pursue the ennobling attributes of (1) righteousness, (2) faith, (3) charity, and (4) peace. The foundation upon which these characteristics are acquired "out of a pure heart."

[2:23] But [refuse][187] foolish and [senseless controversies][188] ~~unlearned questions avoid~~, knowing that they

[beget contentions][189] ~~do gender strifes~~.

Unlearned (Greek *apaideutos* ἀπαίδευτος) means uninstructed. The word stems from *apaideysia* (ἀπαιδευσία), meaning for want of education.[190] Timothy possesses the theological training and induction of a gospel matured leader. These unlearned individuals seek a theological joust with Timothy, and Paul commends Timothy to ignore the gauntlet of the theologically immature. The unlearned element confronting Timothy seeks not theological learning and understanding but rather the victory of contentious debate. This is the only occurrence of this unusual Greek word in the New Testament. The sentiment of this verse continues in the following three verses.

[2:24] And the servant of the Lord must not strive; but be gentle unto all men, [an] apt [teacher] ~~to teach~~, [forbearing] ~~patient~~;

Apt to teach (Greek *didaktikos* δῐδακτικός) means capable of learning and then teaching[191] (in the sense of *implementing*) what was taught to others. A person must possess a motivational leadership style to convey instruction to others.

Patient (Greek *anexikakos* ἀνεξίκακος) means "enduring of ill, i.e. forbearing," as in "patiently forbearing evil"[192]— "here referring specifically to the flouts of opponents."[193] This word conveys more than just the patient endurance of the circumstances but also the enduring pain or evil that necessitates the forbearance.[194] The same word also appears in the Old Testament Apocrypha, "make trial of his forbearance (*anexikakian* ἀνεξικακίαν)."[195]

[2:25] In meekness instructing those [who have opposed,] ~~that oppose themselves~~**; if [perhaps] God** ~~peradventure will~~ **[may] give them [a change of mind]** ~~repentance~~ **[for a full knowledge]** ~~to the acknowledging of the truth;~~[196]

Peradventure (Greek *mepote* μήποτε) literally means "not ever" or "if ever." The choice of this Greek word "points out the difficulty of the case, as being nearly desperate or beyond hope."[197] It is as though Paul were expressing a hopeless situation to Timothy: "Do your best to win back those who are only in the first stage of opposition."[198]

[2:26] And ~~that~~ **they [regaining senses]**[199] ~~may recover themselves~~ **out of the snare of the devil, who are taken captive by him at his will.**

May recover themselves (Greek *ananepho* ἀνανήφω) literally means "to become sober again, i.e. figuratively [to] regain (one's) senses . . . to return to soberness as from a state of delirium or drunkenness;"[200] as in a return "to a state of former sobriety."[201] This is the only occurrence of this word in the New Testament.

"The word [*ananepsosin*] ἀνανήψωσιν properly signifies to awake out of a deep sleep occasioned by drunkenness. In this passage, wicked men are represented as asleep, or deprived of the use of their faculties through the intoxication of sensuality. During this sleep of their reason, they are caught in the toils of error by the Devil. However, being laid hold upon by the servant of the Lord, they are taken alive out of that snare, by his representing to them the dangers of their state, and are at length roused to do the will of God.[202]

Snare (Greek *pagis* παγίς) "a trap (as fastened by a noose or notch) . . . [as] the allurements to evil by which the Devil ensnares."[203] The word *pagis* refers to the rope or wire used in a trap to snare rabbits and other small animals. This meaning is captured in a German translation as *Schlinge*,[204] implying the slipknot used in a snare for rabbits.[205] Paul's metaphor alludes to the ease by which the devil places the slipknot over the unwary members of the Church who apostatize. The slipknot pulls tight, and only then do they realize they are in the noose and have become an ensnared victim, exerting a futile effort to become free. Alternatively translated, "And being caught alive by him out of the snare of the devil, they may awake to do the will of God."[206]

The Forthcoming Great Apostasy (2 Timothy 3:1–9)

Prophetic view of the social, ethical,

and moral corruptions in the last times (3:1). The ascent of selfish narcissism and profanity (3:2); intransigence and cruelty (2:3); conceit (3:4), godlessness (3:5) and lustfulness (3:6). "This chapter describes the way in which evil principle and evil conduct will spread in the last days."[207]

————————— ❧ —————————

[3:1] This know also, that in the last days [grievous] ~~perilous~~ times [are imminent] ~~shall come.~~

Perilous (Greek *chalepos* χαλεπός) means "hard to do or deal with."[208] This word only appears twice in the New Testament, in this verse and in Matthew 8:28, where the two possessed with devils were difficult to deal with. "There met him two possessed with devils, coming out of the tombs, exceeding fierce [*chalepoi* χαλεποὶ], so that no man could pass by that way."[209] The peril of any age comes when humanity is egotistical. Society dilutes and disintegrates as egoism concentrates and asserts.

[3:2] For men shall be [egotistical][210] ~~lovers of their own selves~~, [avaricious] ~~covetous~~, boasters, [uplifted in pride][211] ~~proud~~, blasphemers, disobedient to parents, unthankful, [profane][212] ~~unholy,~~

Lovers of their own selves (Greek *philautos* φίλαυτος) means fond of self in the sense of selfishness. This is the only occurrence of this word in the New

Testament. "One of the characteristics of those [forthcoming] times [is] that men shall be eminently selfish."[213] This condition "is described by Aristotle[214] as denoting one who 'assigns to himself the larger share in wealth, honors and bodily pleasures,' and is distinguished from the true self-lover who seeks the highest good both for himself and others."[215] A French translation captures the true sense of *philautos*; "*Car les hommes seront égoïstes,*"[216] meaning *egotist* in English. The following dictionary clarification expresses the emphasis: "Egoism is giving the 'I' undue supremacy in thought; egotism is giving the 'I' undue prominence in speech and action."[217]

Covetous (Greek *philargyros* φιλάργυρος) means "fond of silver (money), i.e. avaricious . . . literally money-loving."[218]

Avaricious is the choice of several language translations: *avaros* in Spanish;[219] *avarentos* in Portuguese;[220] *geldgierig* in German;[221] and *geldgierig* in Dutch.[222] We all need money to provide for our needs; therefore, money is a means to an end. That changes when money becomes the objective itself, when unnecessary wants become the passionate intent—regardless of damage, distress, or injustice to others. "The necessities of life compel us to make money, and the point at which it becomes avarice is not easily recognizable."[223]

Boasters (Greek *alazon* ἀλαζών) "primarily signifies 'a wanderer about the country, a vagabond: hence, an imposter;

one who is full of empty and boastful professions and only while in the company of others.' "[224] We can define a boaster as one who is a legend in his own mind, and is the principal subject of his own dialog and hero worship.

Proud (Greek *huperephanos* ὑπερήφανος) means "one who compares himself (secretly or openly) with others and lifts himself above them. His arrogance consists in claiming honor for himself. His comparing himself is not the sin; it is his sin that causes him to compare. This word is always used in the evil sense of arrogant."[225]

Any one of these foregoing words would have been enough, but not all together; on the first reading it seems to be overkill. However, on further deliberation, we recognize that collectively these descriptive words illustrate progressive degeneracy of human character. Lest we forget, Paul is not speaking of conditions in his own time. As indicated in 3:1, he speaks prophetically of our time—"in the last days." Doubtless, the iterated characteristics prevailed in the Greco-Roman period of Paul, and in all probability have existed in all ages since then. We live "in the last days" and these characteristics do predominate in our culture. The polluted ego has resulted in personal elevation, the exclusion of gratitude for God, and the eventual blasphemous rejection of God. The catalog of indulgences continues in the following verses.

Disobedient to parents (Greek *goneusin apeitheis*, γονεῦσιν ἀπειθεῖς) means "disowning what among all races has been regarded as the most binding human claim."[226] Parental obligation stabilizes each generation of society. The thankless ingratitude of children to parents is more pronounced when they are "unwilling to be persuaded, spurning belief"[227] and parental advice. Parents observe and recognize the hazards of reckless choices in their children, and these children reject the wisdom to discipline their own avaricious and lustful cravings. Their hearts become hardened toward the legacy of righteous living, and stability in society is undermined.

[3:3] [hard-hearted] ~~Without natural affection,~~ [unyielding][228] ~~trucebreakers,~~ [slanderers][229] ~~false accusers,~~ [without self-control] ~~incontinent,~~ [cruel][230] ~~fierce,~~ [hostile to those that are virtuous] ~~despisers of those that are good,~~

Without natural affection (Greek *astorgos* ἄστοργος) means to be hard-hearted toward their own kindred.[231] This word "seems to denote one who does not abide by the contracts into which he has entered."[232] The inverse of this word "denotes primarily and properly the love between parents and children and thence between those connected by similar or parallel relations."[233]

Trucebreakers (Greek *aspondos* ἄσπονδος) literally means "without libation (which usually accompanied a treaty), i.e. (by implication) truceless."[234] Jerome translated this word to *sine pace*[235] in Latin—meaning without peace: however, *implacabilis* would have been a better choice. Though acceptable in translation, the understanding of the word is no longer relative to our modern culture. In most ancient cultures of the Greco-Roman world, a libation was the pouring out of a small quantity of liquid as a ceremonial act to the gods. Libations were part of the daily ritual of home and public life. In the context of this use by Paul, a libation seals a treaty between warring parties or seals a reconciliation following a disputation or argument. The Greek word for a libation is *spendo* (σπένδω), meaning, to pour out.[236] Paul uses the inverse of *spendo* with the word *aspondos* meaning "without libation."

"The idea is of people who forgive nothing and give up nothing in order to render amity possible."[237] In this verse, Paul is referring to people who hold a grudge, will not forgive (even in minor issues), intransigent, or implacable.

False accusers (Greek *diabolos* διάβολος) literally means traducers, slanderers, or backbiters[238]; someone who willfully causes defamation of character with slander by misrepresenting the truth. When Jesus was tempted by the devil, Matthew referred to him with this word *diabolos* (Matthew 4:1, 5).

Fierce (Greek *anemeros* ἀνήμερος) actually means untamed or savage, as applicable to "living in or belonging to the most primitive and rude condition of human life and society."[239] Unfortunately, the word savage is not conducive in an English translation of this verse.

The alternative is to translate this word to cruel, defining those who are "disposed to inflict suffering, indifferent to others' suffering."[240]

Despisers of those that are good (Greek *aphilagathos* ἀφιλάγαθος) means hostile to virtue, as in opposed to goodness.[241] To despise the good is a subdued translation for the actual hate or aggression intended in the Greek word. A German translation reads, *dem Guten feind*— "the enemy of the good."[242] The hate is hostility towards the righteous; that is, righteous with respect to the characteristic of virtue in keeping the commandments of God.

[3:4] [Betrayers]243 ~~Traitors~~, [reckless]244 ~~heady~~, [conceited]245 ~~highminded~~, [pleasure-lovers] ~~lovers of pleasures~~ [rather]246 ~~more~~ than [God-lovers] ~~lovers of God~~;

Traitors (Greek *prodotes* προδότης)[247] means to betray in "the sense of giving forward into another's (the enemy's) hands."[248] This is not treason to the state, but treason to others. Therefore, they are betrayers having deceived others[249]— "false to their friends."[250] While most translations use traitors, the closer English alternative word is usually treacherous.[251]

Heady (Greek *propetes* προπετής) means falling forward; in other words, "rushing headlong precipitate."[252] "Headstrong is the appropriate understanding."[253] This designation seems to signify "swelling and puffed up, like smoke issuing from a fire, and dilating himself with a vain-glorious and empty cloud of spiritual pride, which makes a great show, but is nothing but misty and murky vapor."[254]

High-minded (Greek *typhoo* τυφόω) actually means "to wrap in smoke" and is a metaphor for conceit,[255] as in overwhelming self-esteem.

Lovers of pleasures (Greek *philedonos* φιλήδονος) means fond of pleasure, "sensual pleasures, or vain amusements."[256] This is the only occurrence of this word in the New Testament.

[3:5] **Having a form of godliness, but [having denied]**[257] ~~denying~~ **the power thereof; ~~from such~~ turn away [from these].**[258]

[3:6] **For [these]**[259] ~~of this sort~~ **are they [creeping]**[260] ~~which creep~~ **into houses, and [leading]**[261] ~~lead~~ **captive silly women [overwhelmed by their]**[262] ~~laden with~~ **sins, led away [by] ~~with~~ divers lusts,**

Silly women (Greek *gynaikarion* γυναικάριον) means little women, deriving from the diminutive form of *gune* (γυνή) and is contemptuously intended.[263] This concept is alternatively translated "weak-willed women"[264] to emphasize that the weakness is of mind (spiritual) and not of body (physical).[265]

Laden (Greek *soreuo* σωρεύω) means "to heap one thing on another, [and is] . . . used metaphorically of women . . . overwhelmed with sins."[266]

Laden is alternatively translated as *heaped*, in the sense of burdened down. "The metaphor suggests the idea of being so covered that they cannot struggle out."[267]

Led away (Greek *ago* ἄγω) means to lead. "Being properly applied to beasts who are led in halters whithersoever their owners please, it signifies that these women were slaves to their lusts."[268]

[3:7] **[Always] ~~Ever~~ learning, and never able to come to [a full]**[269] ~~the~~ **knowledge of the truth.**[270]

[3:8] **Now as Jannes and Jambres withstood Moses, so do these also [withstand]**[271] ~~resist~~ **the truth; men of corrupt minds, [counterfeit]**[272] ~~reprobate~~ **concerning the faith.**

Jannes (Greek *Iannes* Ἰαννῆς) and **Jambres** (Greek *Iambres* Ἰαμβρῆς) were the magicians at the court of Pharaoh who copied the miracle by Moses and Aaron of turning the rod into a snake (Exodus 7:8–12). The historian Eusebius mentions these magicians and alludes to their superior skills in magic: "Jannes and Jambres, Egyptian sacred scribes, men judged to have no superiors in the practice of magic, at the time when the Jews were being driven out of Egypt."[273] A record of the activities of Jannes and Jambres is contained in an Old Testament Apocryphal book:

> Pharaoh sent for Balaam the magician and to Jannes and Jambres his sons, and to all the magicians and conjurors and counselors

[that] ~~which~~ belonged to the king, and they all came and sat before the king. And the king told them all the words which Moses and his brother Aaron had spoken to him, and the magicians said to the king, But how came the men to thee, on account of the lions which were confined at the gate? And the king said, because they lifted up their rod against the lions and loosed them, and came to me, and the lions also rejoiced at them as a dog rejoices to meet his master. And Balaam the son of Beor the magician answered the king, saying, these are none else than magicians like ourselves.[274]

The "men" referred to above in verse 2 are now accused of "imitating and pretending to surpass the truth as taught by St. Paul."[275] "The point of the remark of the apostle here, is that they resisted Moses by attempting to imitate his miracles, thus neutralizing the evidence that he was sent from God."[276]

[3:9] But they shall [not make further advance]²⁷⁷ ~~proceed no further~~; for their folly, [as the other two,]²⁷⁸ shall be manifest unto all men, ~~as theirs also was~~.²⁷⁹

The Greek sentence structure used by Paul does not lend itself well to translation in many western languages. This problem—in part—occurs because of biblical parsing of the sentences into numbered verses. A difficulty of verses is taking thoughts out of context, and the other difficulty is losing the link with previous verses, rendering incomplete statements.

[3:10] But thou hast [been thoroughly acquainted with]²⁸⁰ ~~fully known~~ my²⁸¹ [teaching] ~~doctrine~~, [the conduct]²⁸² ~~manner of life~~, [the] purpose, [the] faith, [the] longsuffering, [the] charity, [the] patience,

[3:11] Persecutions, afflictions, which came unto me at Antioch [*in Pisidia*],²⁸³ at Iconium, at Lystra; what persecutions I endured; but out of them all the Lord delivered me.

Paul first came to "Antioch in Pisidia" in company with Barnabas (Acts 13:14). They preached openly in the synagogue, and many accepted the gospel teaching—especially the Gentiles (Acts 13:48). "But when the Jews saw the multitudes, they were filled with envy, and spake against those things which were spoken by Paul" (Acts 13:45). Unfortunately, the apostolic successes in the capital city of Galatia incurred substantial animosity. "The Jews stirred up the devout and honorable women, and the chief men of the city, and raised persecution against Paul and Barnabas, and expelled them out of their coasts" (Acts 13:50). Departing from Antioch in Pisidia, they came east to Iconium, and in "the synagogue" they preached to "a great multitude" of Jews and gentiles (Acts 14:1). Some time later, "the unbelieving Jews stirred up the Gentiles" (Acts 14:2) which caused division among the population (Acts 14:4). The public disturbance escalated until "there was an assault made both of the Gentiles, and also of the Jews with their rulers" (Acts 14:5).

This public disturbance necessitated a clandestine departure from Iconium, and they "fled unto Lystra and Derbe," in the Galatian "region" of "Lycaonia" (Acts 14:6). While at Lystra, they were first received with jubilation for the miraculous healing of a cripple "impotent in his feet, being a cripple from his mother's womb, who never had walked" (Acts 14:8). Zealots from Antioch and Iconium learned that Paul and Barnabas were preaching in the hinterland villages of Lystra and Derbe, and they came thither and "persuaded the people" against Paul and Barnabas (Acts 14:19). On this occasion, Paul did not manage a clandestine escape. The vigilantes "drew him out of the city" and "stoned Paul," leaving him for dead (Acts 14:19).

Seemingly, Barnabas ministered a priesthood blessing unto Paul, "as the disciples stood round about him, [and] he rose up [alive], and came [again] into the city" (Acts 14:20). Luke then curtly records that they "departed" from Lystra "the next day" and went "to Derbe" (Acts 14:20). In this epistle to Timothy, Paul summarized the Galatian experience with the words in this verse, "but out of them all the Lord delivered me."

[3:12] [And indeed,][284] Yea, and all [desiring to][285] that will live godly in Christ Jesus [will be persecuted] shall suffer persecution.

Unfortunately for the early Church,

before the first century of the Christian era (*Anno Domini*) was over, martyrdom befell many in the first Christian Holocaust.

[3:13] [For][286] But evil men and [imposters][287] seducers shall [grow][288] wax worse and worse,[289] [leading astray] deceiving, and being [led astray] deceived.[290]

Seducers (Greek *goes* γόης) means "to wail" in respect of "a wizard (as muttering spells)."[291] "This word was properly applied to the chanters of spells."[292] Paul is speaking of apostasy from within the Church. These apostates, pretending to be legitimate ministers of the gospel, are ecclesiastical imposters and traducers, who "misrepresent willfully the conduct or character" of the Church.[293]

Deceiving and being deceived (Greek *planontes kai planomenoi*, πλανῶντες καὶ πλανώμενοι), with greater clarity, leading astray, and being led astray. "Observe the order: A man may be deceived first and then deceive others, but the reverse is possible. He keeps repeating the claims or teachings by which he hopes to impose on others (e.g., for purposes of gain or influence) until he comes at last to believe in his own claims and teaching."[294]

[3:14] But continue thou in [what][295] the things which thou hast learned and hast been assured of, knowing [from] of whom thou hast learned them;

THE WISE USE OF SCRIPTURE (2 TIMOTHY 3:15–17)

Study of "the Sacred Scriptures" will "make the wise unto salvation" (2 Timothy 3:15). The study of scripture is "profitable" as one learns "doctrine" with "instruction in righteousness" (2 Timothy 3:16). Through this endeavor, we will each become a "man of God," who thoroughly equips himself for the work to which he is assigned (2 Timothy 3:17).

[3:15] And that from [infancy]²⁹⁶ a child thou hast known the [Sacred] holy Scriptures, which are able to make thee wise unto salvation through faith which is in Christ Jesus.

Holy (Greek *hieros* ἱερός) literally "means sacred, consecrated to deity, pertaining to God."²⁹⁷ Scriptures (Greek *graphe* γραφή) in this context specifically means "a document, i.e. holy writ."²⁹⁸ Scriptures is short for the full term, Sacred Scriptures (Greek *iera grammata,* ἱερὰ γράμματα) or sacred writings, in the sense of scriptural learning (Latin *sacras literas*).²⁹⁹ From an early age, children received teaching in Jewish families to study and memorize scriptural passages. Jewish children commenced learning the Mosaic Law at "the age of five years."³⁰⁰ The Holy Scriptures include those writings regarded by the Jews as canonical and composed of the Law, the Prophets, and the Hagiographa; collectively referred to by Hellenistic Jews as the Holy or Sacred Scriptures (Greek *ta iera grammata,* τὰ ἱερὰ γράμματα).³⁰¹ Here, Paul uses the word as "a technical phrase" for "education."³⁰² Though Hellenistic Jews coined this term, we must understand that the early Church leaders expanded the application of the term to include the new scripture the early apostles were then writing. Over time, this included gospel accounts and an array of doctrinal epistles were designated as *Canonized* (Greek *Graphai* Γραφαὶ).³⁰³ Those who choose to limit the application of the term to only the Mosaic canon must accept that the established canonized scripture was sufficient "to make thee wise unto salvation through faith which is in Christ Jesus," as Paul indicated above. From this paradigm, Old Testament or New Testament thereby becomes a superfluous argument.

[3:16] [And]³⁰⁴ All [God-inspired] scripture is given by inspiration of God, and³⁰⁵ is profitable for doctrine, for reproof, for correction, for instruction in righteousness;

Reproof (Greek *elegchos* ἔλεγχος) means proof, or conviction of sin.³⁰⁶ Before sacred scripture commences the process of change in the human soul, it must awaken the conscience with reproof in the form of recognition that the individual has transgressed. When King David recognized his sinful relationship with Bathsheba, he declared, "I acknowledge my transgressions: and my sin is ever before me" (Psalm 51:3).

Correction (Greek *epanorthosis* ἐπανόρθωσις) means "a straightening up again, i.e. (figuratively) rectification (reformation),"[307] in the sense of "recreation of character."[308] Sacred scripture has the power to reform a soul that recognizes its sinful state, and seeks reconciliation.

[3:17] That the man of God may be perfect, thoroughly [equipped][309] ~~furnished~~ [for every] ~~unto all~~ good [work] ~~works~~.

Be Faithful in the Ministry (2 Timothy 4:1–5)

Paul emphasizes the need for diligence in proclaiming the the Word of God (4:1). Teach the doctrines and reprove, rebuke, and exhort with patience (4:2). A time will come when the world, as well as many members in the Church, "will not endure sound doctrine" (4:3–4). Paul reminds

Timothy to be alert and be strong in enduring the hardships ahead (4:5).

[4:1] I [solemnly witness][310] ~~charge thee~~ therefore before God, and the Lord Jesus Christ, who [is about to][311] ~~shall~~ judge the [living] ~~quick~~ and the dead at his appearing and [in][312] his Kingdom;

[4:2] [Proclaim] ~~Preach~~ the Word; be [urgent] ~~instant~~ in season; [those who are][313] out of season, reprove, rebuke, exhort with all longsuffering and doctrine.

In season (Greek *eukairos* εὐκαίρως) means opportunity and is the inverse of out of season (Greek *akairos* ἀκαίρος), meaning inopportuneness, and "as an adverb denotes . . . unseasonably."[315] This word does not occur elsewhere in the New Testament. "It is the opposite of the former, and means that a minister is to seek opportunities to preach the gospel even at such

Greek	Latin	English	KJV
kerysso (κηρύσσω)	*praedicatio*	proclaim	preach
ephistemi (ἐφίστημι)	*instantia*	stand ready	be instant
elegcho (ἐλέγχω)	*arguo*	declare | prove	reprove
epitimao (ἐπιτιμάω)	*obsecro*	rebuke | warn	rebuke
parakaleo (παρακαλέω)	*increpo*	exhort	exhort

(2 Tim. 4:2) With a brisk statement, Paul summarizes his instructions to Timothy in military fashion. This verse contains "five short, sharp, military words of command."[314]

periods as might be inconvenient to himself, or when there might be hindrances and embarrassments, or when there was no stated appointment for preaching."[316]

[4:3] For [a] ~~the~~ time will come[317] when they will not endure sound doctrine; but [having itching ears, they will accumulate for] ~~after their own lusts shall they heap to~~ themselves teachers, [to suit their own desires] ~~having itching ears;~~[318]

Shall they heap (Greek *episoreuo* ἐπισωρεύω) means to accumulate further, in the sense of "appropriating a number of teachers to suit the liking of those who do the gathering."[319] "The madness of men will be so great, that they will not be satisfied with a few deceivers, but will desire to have a vast multitude."[320] Unfortunately, most translations structure this verse to imply that the teachers had the itching ears rather than the hearers. The teachers had itching tongues, but the digressing members of the Church had the itching ears. This interpretation receives validation in the content of the next verse. These members rejected the apostolic teachers, and instead gathered "round them a rabble of teachers,"[321] who anesthetized the Christian mind with centuries of Hellenistic philosophy.

[4:4] **And they shall turn away their ears from the truth, and shall be turned unto [myths]**[322] ~~fables.~~[323]

[4:5] But ~~watch~~ thou [be sober-minded] in all things, endure [hardships][324] ~~afflictions~~, do the work of an evangelist, [carry out] ~~make full proof of~~ thy ministry.

THE MINISTRY OF PAUL IS CONCLUDING (2 TIMOTHY 4:6–8)

In this concluding chapter, Paul utters his final declaration of faith: "I have fought the good fight, I have finished the race, I have kept the faith" (2 Timothy 4:7). Of all the words of Paul, these words are perhaps the most oft quoted. In verse eight, Paul articulates in what he has hope—to achieve exaltation and receive the "crown of righteousness" in the kingdom of God following the Day of Judgment (2 Timothy 4:8).

[4:6] **For I am [already being poured out]** ~~now ready to be offered~~, **and the time of my [dissolution]** ~~departure~~ **is [come]**[325] ~~at hand.~~

Ready to be offered (Greek *spendo* σπένδω) means to pour out, in the sense of "a libation or drink-offering to [a] God."[326] The analogy of Paul is "to devote one's life or blood, as a sacrifice."[327] This word appears only twice in the New Testament. The other occurrence reads, "If I be offered upon the sacrifice and service of your faith" (Philippians 2:17). A Mosaic animal sacrifice included a drink offering.[328] The Hebrew word *nesech* (נֶסֶךְ) also means a libation in the same sense as the Greek word.

The forthcoming execution of Paul will result in his life's blood literally being spilled on the ground. Thus, the analogy, his mortal death will be a libation of his own blood and life.[329] "The shedding of blood is analogous to the pouring out of the drink-offering; and as the libation formed the conclusion of the sacrifice, the apostle's martyrdom closed his apostolic service, which to him was the same as a service of sacrifice (Romans 10:16; Philippians 2:17)."[330] Isaiah uses the analogy of the spilling of life's blood as a libation in reference to the atoning sacrifice of Jesus the Christ, "he hath poured out [Hebrew *heerah* הֶעֱרָה] his soul unto death: and he was numbered with the transgressors; and he bare the sin of many" (Isaiah 53:12). Again, "Until the spirit be poured upon [Hebrew *yeareh* יֵעָרֶה] us from on high" (Isaiah 32:15).

Departure (Greek *analysis* ἀνάλυσις) does mean "departure"; however, the word also means to "unravel" in the sense of the threads in a woven fabric. In the context of this verse, *analuseos* (ἀναλύσεώς) has two interpretations: (1) In the nautical sense of a ship "casting off,"[331] or "loosening from [its] moorings"; and (2) in the military sense of an army "breaking up an encampment."[332] Paul "had been bound to the present world, like a ship to its moorings, and [his] death would be a release. He would

"weigh anchor, [and] depart."[333] He would now spread his sails on the broad ocean of eternity."[334]

Paul specifically does not use the word *death*, which would imply an end or termination. Instead, he uses the word *departure/dissolution*, conveying an understanding of the separation of the spirit and the body. He will exit from the mortal condition, and proceed to live in another dimension as a disembodied spirit to await the resurrection. There is further endorsement of this interpretation in verse 8 below, not only for Paul, but for all who do likewise.

[4:7] I have fought [the] a good fight,[335] I have finished [the] my [race] course, I have kept the faith;

Fight (Greek *agon* ἀγών) means "a place of assembly . . . by implication a contest . . . figuratively an effort or anxiety. . . . It implies a contest against spiritual foes as well as human adversaries."[336] In a further clarification, "The language is not restricted to a fight, but may denote any form of contest . . . [Alternative translation:] 'I have maintained the noble contest.' "[337] This verse is in continuation of the military metaphor in the previous verse.

[4:8] [There remains,][338] Henceforth there is laid up for me [the] a crown of righteousness [laid up for me], which the Lord, the righteous judge, shall [award] give me at that day; and not

to me only, but unto all [who have longed for]³³⁹ ~~them also that love~~ his appearing.

Henceforth (Greek *loipon* λοιπόν) means "something remaining" or "for the rest." In this verse, Paul conveys an analogy with the Greek games—or to our understanding, the modern Olympics. In verse 7, he indicated that he has finished his course; that is, the race is over, and he won.

There is laid up (Greek *apokeimai* ἀπόκειμαι) commonly means reserved. All that remains is to receive a crown from the judge of the games—the Lord Jesus the Christ. However, in this race there is more than just one winner—"not to me only, but to all."

"No one is excluded because another is successful; no one fails of the reward because another obtains it. Who then would not make an effort to win the immortal crown?"³⁴⁰

Crown of righteousness (Greek *dikaiosynes stephanos*, δικαιοσύνης στέφανος), compare with "crown of life" (James 1:12; Revelation 2:10), and "the crown of glory" (1 Peter 5:4)—"the righteousness which is of God by faith" (Philippians 3:9). The winner of an Olympic athletic competition received a crown of leaves to signify his accomplishment. This Olympic crown is perishable; however, those who win the race of life receive a crown of righteousness—a crown that is imperishable: "The crown of righteousness is not the kingly crown, but the victor's crown."³⁴¹

THE STATE OF AFFAIRS (2 TIMOTHY 4:9–15)

Timothy is entreated to come to Rome with all haste (2 Timothy 4:9). Several of the brethren have departed (2 Timothy 4:10, 12), and currently only "Luke is with me" (2 Timothy 4:11). On the way to Rome, Timothy is to call in at Alexandria Troas and collect the document portfolio that Paul left with Carpus (2 Timothy 4:13). Timothy is advised of the "evils" of "Alexander the coppersmith" (2 Timothy 4:14–15).

[4:9] [Make haste]³⁴² ~~Do thy diligence~~ to come ~~shortly~~ unto me [quickly];³⁴³

[4:10] **For Demas [forsook]** ~~hath forsaken~~ **me, having loved this present world, and is departed unto Thessalonica; Crescens to Galatia, Titus unto Dalmatia.**

Titus (Greek *Titos* Τίτος) is possibly the brother of Luke.³⁴⁴ We draw this conclusion from two particular references made by Paul. First: "And we have sent with him [Titus] the brother [by implication, to Luke], whose praise is in the gospel throughout all the churches" (2 Corinthians 8:18) Second: "I desired Titus, and with him I sent a brother [by implication, Luke]" (2 Corinthians 12:18). In both incidences, the word *brother* (Greek *adelphos* ἀδελφός) in the literal sense means a brother of the womb, as in "male children of the same parents."³⁴⁵

Galatia (Greek *Galatia* Γαλατία) in most manuscripts; however, other manuscripts read **Gaul** (*Gallian* Γαλλίαν),[346] "the current Greek name for Gaul in 1st and 2nd centuries AD."[347]

Dalmatia (Greek *Dalmatia* Δαλματία) was a region of Illyricum and equates to present-day southern Bosnia-Herzegovina, Montenegro, and north Albania.

[4:11] Only Luke is with me. Take Mark, and bring him with thee: for he is [serviceable] ~~profitable~~ to me for the ministry.

Luke or **Lucas** (Greek *Loukas* Λουκᾶς) is a contracted form of *Loukanos* (Λουκανός),[348] and is a translated from the Latin name Lucanus.

Mark (Greek *Markos* Μάρκος) is equivalent to **Marcus** in Latin. His full name is John Mark (*Johanan Marcus*) (See Acts 12:12, 25; 15:36–38).[349] He was nephew to the apostle Barnabas (Colossians 4:10; Acts 12:12).

[4:12] And Tychicus have I sent to Ephesus.

Tychicus (Greek *Tychikos* Τυχικός) means fortuitous.[350] There is mention of Tychicus being a native of Asia Minor Province (Acts 20:4)—traditionally believed to be from Ephesus. He is further considered as one of the Seventy disciples (Luke 10:1–24) or senior Church leaders after the Twelve Apostles. There are profuse unsubstantiated claims to Tychicus being "bishop" in several Greek cities.[351]

[4:13] The [portfolio] ~~cloke~~ that I left at [*Alexandria*] Troas with Carpus, when thou comest, bring with thee, and the books, but especially the parchments.

The content of this verse is complicated and unclear. There are three Greek words of particular interest: first, **cloke** (*phelonen* φελόνην); second, **but especially** (*malista* μάλιστα), and third, **parchments** (*membranas* μεμβράνας). On the first reading, we interpret that Paul entreated Timothy to bring three things—cloak, books, and parchments. However, the inclusion of "but especially" implies reiterated emphasis for priority of something that was mentioned earlier. The second item, books or scrolls, is clear; yet the third item, parchments, would then be a reemphasis of the first item, cloak or coat.

Cloke (Greek *phelones* φελόνης) "is a cloak with long sleeves, especially for winter use."[352] We ask ourselves why Paul would request Timothy to collect a winter coat and suffer the inconvenience of carrying it from northwest Turkey, traversing Greece and Italy to Rome.[353] If Paul were discomfited in prison, then Luke would have procured a cloak or blanket at Rome, such being a generic article. The translation to cloak is therefore suspect.

There is the distinct probability that this unique Greek word meant *a portfolio*[354]—"a chest or box for containing books,"[355] or *scrolls*. In some instances, the papyrus or parchment document rolls were contained in a "vellum wrapper" so that the document "was encased to protect it. This "was called a [*phainoles*] φαινόλης [in Greek] or *pænula* [in Latin]."[356] This hypothesis is substantiated by the literal rendering of the Syriac Peshitta Version (Aramaic New Testament written in the Syriac alphabet) manuscript of this epistle. A literal translation from the Syriac Bible of this verse reads, "And when thou comest, bring the bookcase, which I left at Troas with Carpus, and the books, but especially the roll of parchments"[357]—i.e. that which is contained in the bookcase.[358] The word *bookcase* in Syriac is *bsheeta* (ܒܫܝܬ̈ܐ),[359] a case for writings (ܕܟ̈ܬܒܐ),[360] or *book-carrier* (ܢܣܒ ܟܬ̈ܒܐ).[361] "The parchments were costly, and doubtless were writings of high importance."[362] In all probability, this contained "the diploma of Paul's Roman citizenship."[363] The meaning of a chest or document pouch containing important parchments clarifies why Paul was specific in requesting the portfolio containing the parchments—which were not procurable at Rome.[364] An 1849 translation from Western Peshitta reads, "The case (for) books[365] which I left at Troas with Karpos, when thou comest bring, and the books, and especially the roll of parchments."[366] The roll of parchments was contained in the bookcase, therefore mentioned first and reiterated again at the last.

Troas (Greek *Troas* Τρῳάς) is properly Alexandria Troas[367]—located some distance south of ancient Troy. Paul visited here several times (Acts 16:8, 11; 20:5–6; 2 Corinthians 2:12). The town "was first built by Antigonus, under the name of Antigoneia Troas . . . Afterwards it was embellished by Lysimachus, and named Alexandria Troas."[368]

The books (Greek *biblion* βιβλίον) "means primarily a small book, a scroll, or any sheet on which something has been written."[369] The portfolio or chest contained these papyrus rolls in addition to the more valuable parchment documents.

The parchments (Greek *memvrana* μεμβράνα) means a written sheepskin. "Membrana is a Latin word . . . from membrum, 'a limb,' but denoting 'skin, parchment.' The English word 'parchment' is a form of *pergamena* . . . signifying 'of Pergamum,' the city in Asia Minor where 'parchment' was either invented or brought into use."[370] This is the only occurrence of this word in the New Testament. The books probably refer to documents written on papyrus, while the parchments refer to documents written in animal skin. Only precious and important documents were committed to parchment.[371]

The execution of both Peter and Paul occurred at Rome. Peter died by painful crucifixion, not being a Roman citizen. They beheaded Paul swiftly by the sword—a privilege of citizenship.[372] The open question is: How was Paul able to prove that he was a freeborn Roman citizen?

The answer is that those who possessed such citizenship[373] possessed documents of identification.[374]

Roman citizenship was a privileged social status with respect to laws, property, and governance. Citizenship was affected by legislation—specifically the Lex Iulia de Civitate Latinis Danda (enacted by Lucius Julius Caesar in 90 BC).[375] For a Roman, documents of citizenship consisted of at least three parchments. The first parchment contained a notarized declaration of entitlement to the honor of Roman citizenship—issued at the time of his birth in his hometown.[376] A second parchment contained an official notarized pedigree chart called a stemma,[377] detailing how, from, and through whom the Roman citizenship was first granted. Usually a third parchment included a notarized declaration of political, military,[378] civil offices,[379] and service rendered in the city of Tarsus, province of Cilitia, or the Imperial State.

These documents or parchments were for all practical purposes an Imperial Roman passport. Collectively they were termed his *dignitas*—documents of his dignity and prestige.[380] Normally the holder of such parchments deposited these valuable documents in a safe place. We therefore conclude that Paul did not carry them about with him. The abrupt transportation of Paul to Imperial Roman custody hindered him from procuring the documents earlier.

[4:14] Alexander the coppersmith did me
much evil; the Lord [will][381] reward him according to his works;[382]

The term "reward him according to his works" is not in contradiction to "Let your light so shine before men, that they may see your good works, and glorify your Father which is in heaven" (Matthew 5:16). This man was engaged in "the works of darkness" (Romans 13:12) and not the "works of Christ" (Matthew 11:2). The works of this Alexander were destructive and not constructive. When "the Son of man shall come in the glory of his Father with his angels." At that time, "he shall reward every man according to his works" (Matthew 16:27). In a comparative sense, Alexander became a Judas to Paul with a vendetta of "much evil."

[4:15] [You too should be on your guard against him][383] ~~Of whom be thou ware also~~; **for he** ~~hath~~ **greatly [opposed]** ~~withstood~~ **our words.**

[4:16] At my first [defense] ~~answer~~ **no [one]** ~~man~~ **stood with me, but all [deserted]** ~~men forsook~~ **me;** ~~I pray God that it~~[384] **may [it] not be laid to their charge.**

Answer (Greek *apologia* ἀπολογία) means apology, specifically "to give a cogent explanation for one's beliefs."[385] In respect of this first charge, "the allusion is apparently to what was called in Roman law the *prima actio*. While this was being heard, no man stood forward for him, whether in friendly sympathy, or (more probably) as his official *patronius* or *advocatus* [English advocate]. The Greek word *symparegeneto* (συμπαρεγένετο)[386] can mean no one "stood forward with me"—as witness (*advocati*) or counsel for the defense (*advocatus*).[387] Paul had to plead his case alone."[388] Paul apparently faced two separate charges. "Here the defense was on the first count, and on this he seems to have been acquitted."[389]

Though Paul was arraigned before the imperial court at the time of this first case, the Emperor Nero was not at Rome; he was in Greece, attending the Isthmian Games near Corinth and attempting to construct a canal across the Corinth Isthmus.[390] Since Nero was not presiding at the imperial court, "we must therefore conclude that Paul was arraigned before the City Prefect—Prefectus Urbi."[391] That Paul was acquitted, and yet remanded in prison, indicates that there was at least one other charge yet to be prosecuted. Nero wanted each charge presented separately and not collectively.[392]

[4:17] **[But]** ~~Notwithstanding~~ **the Lord stood with me, and [empowered]** ~~strengthened~~ **me; that [through]** ~~by~~ **me the preaching might be fully [proclaimed]** ~~known~~**, and that all the Gentiles might hear [it]; and I was delivered[393] out of the mouth of the lion.**

Quoting from Psalm 22:21, "Save me from the lion's mouth: for thou hast heard me from the horns of the unicorns."

[4:18] **And the Lord shall deliver[394] me from every evil work, and will preserve me unto his Heavenly Kingdom; to whom be glory for ever and ever. Amen.**

SALUTATIONS (2 TIMOTHY 4:19–22)

Paul includes greetings to his old friends, Aquila and his wife, Prisca (4:19) whom he first met in Corinth many years ago (AD 52–53) during his second missionary tour.[395] He includes personal greetings from Bishop Linus at Rome and his parents, Prudens and Claudia (2 Timothy 4:21).

[4:19] **Salute Prisca and Aquila, and the household of Onesiphorus.**

Prisca (Greek *Priska* Πρίσκα) or *Priscilla* (Greek *Priskilla* Πρίσκιλλα). The name Priscilla, meaning "little Prisca," is a diminutive of Prisca. The name Prisca derives from Latin *priscus*, meaning ancient. This woman is the wife of Aquila—also mentioned in this verse.[396]

Aquila (Greek *Akylas* Ἀκύλας), though a Greek name, is probably derived from the Latin word *aquila* meaning an eagle. Luke took the trouble to record that Aquila was "born in Pontus," had also been resident at Rome (Italia), Corinth, Ephesus, and Antioch-on-the-Orontes (Syria) (Acts 18:1–2, 17–18, 24–26; Romans 16:3; 1 Corinthians 16:19). In each instance, the mention of Aquila is always in tandem with his wife Priscilla.

Onesiphorus (Greek *Onesiphoros* Ὀνησίφορος) derives from two other Greek words and means profit-bearer. Onesiphorous receives a mention twice in this epistle (2 Timothy 1:16; 4:19).

[4:20] Erastus [remained][397] ~~abode~~ **at Corinth; but Trophimus have I left at Miletum sick.**

Erastus (Greek *Erastos* Ἔραστος) is derived from *erao* (ἐράω) meaning to love.[398] He was a missionary companion with Tromphimus dispatched to Macedonia (Acts 19:22). It is most likely that Erastus was formerly a city chamberlain or treasurer (Romans 16:23).

Trophimus (Greek *Trophimos* Τρόφιμος) though here used as a given name; the word means "a slave's young master."[399] Trophimos came from Asia Minor (Acts 20:4), and identified as an Ephesian (Acts 21:29). He accompanied Paul on one of his return journeys to Jerusalem (Acts 20:4; 21:9). Legendary records indicate that during Nero's Christian persecution, Trophimus died by beheading.[400]

[4:21] Do thy diligence to come before winter.[401] **Eubulus greeteth thee, and Pudens, and Linus, and Claudia, and all the brethren.**

Linus (Greek Linos Λῖνος) is a male name, probably drawn from *linon* (λίνον), meaning flax and, by implication, linen.[402] There is every indication that Linus was bishop of the first organized congregation at Rome.[403] Early documents were transcribed into a codex dated 1056 at Constantinople. This codex includes the following statement: "Of the church of Rome, Linus the son of Claudia was the first, ordained by Paul; and Clemens after Linus' death, the second, ordained by me Peter."[404] The early Christian historian Eusebius recorded "the first man to be appointed Bishop of Rome was Linus. He is mentioned by Paul when writing to Timothy from Rome, in the salutation at the end of the epistle."[405]

Claudia (Greek *Klaudia* Κλαυδία) is the female form of the male name *Klaudios* (Κλαύδιος), or Claudius. Prudens and Claudia in this verse are possibly husband and wife, and Linus their son.[406]

[4:22] The Lord Jesus Christ be with [you, and][407] ~~thy spirit~~ **grace be with you [all].**[408] **Amen.**

[postscript] The second epistle unto Timotheus, ordained the first bishop of the church of the Ephesians, was written from Rome, when Paul was brought before Nero the second time.

The postscript of all epistles never was a component part of the actual letter composed by Paul.

2 Timothy

EPILOGUE

An epilogue to the Second Epistle of Paul to Timothy is also the eulogy for the Apostle Paul. The arrangement of the epistles of Paul in the New Testament is not in chronological order. The Bible compilers elected to arrange the books in size order—from the largest to the smallest.[409] Therefore, the eulogy for Paul appears here in conjunction with the last known letter penned by Paul, and not at the conclusion of the compilation of his letters.

TIMOTHY AND MARK JOURNEY TO ROME

There is no indication as to who undertook the task of courier for this epistle from Rome to Ephesus. The most likely candidate is at least one, if not two, energetic young men from the Roman congregation. We have no doubt that upon receipt of this letter at Ephesus, Timothy commenced preparations for the journey to Rome as requested by Paul.[410] Timothy likely informed John Mark of the specific request from Paul for his presence at Rome.[411] Mark and Timothy then accompanied the Roman courier(s) and traveled by ship from Ephesus north to Alexandria Troas[412] to visit Carpus and collect the portfolio of books and parchments (2 Timothy 4:13). Departing from Alexandria Troas, they sailed to the Macedonian mainland and probably docked at Neapolis, near Philippi. They traversed the Roman provinces of Greece and Illycrium on the Roman highway Via Egnatia,[413] passing through Thessalonica, all the way west to the Adriatic port of Dyrrachium.[414] Again by ship, they likely traversed the Adriatic Sea to the port of Brindisi (Brundisium) on the Italian mainland. Once in Italy, they crossed the Via Appia[415] all the way north-west to Rome.

Timothy and Mark probably first went to Luke to learn of the status concerning Paul in prison. Luke likely related the circumstances surrounding the first trial (Acts 4:16) and of the "Judas" threat from Alexander the coppersmith. Eventually they would apply to visit Paul in prison and deliver the portfolio of books and parchments. Thereafter, all continued to wait for Paul to receive information concerning a date for his second trial.

THE SECOND TRIAL AND EXECUTION

Eventually, the Emperor Nero returned from his escapades in Greece. He attended the Isthmian Games[416] in AD 67 and attempted to excavate a canal across the Isthmus of Corinth.[417] There is no historical record of the timing of the second trial. However, we do know the decision of the Imperial Court of last instance was to sentence Paul to death by decapitation. The saints of Rome recoiled in horror. Prayers ascended unto the Throne of Grace over the following days in behalf of a condemned apostle.[418]

In general, public executions took place within the city of Rome. If the authorities considered an execution might provoke public unrest, they relocated the execution

to the south at the Salvian Marsh. This policy limited the threat of reprisal within the city. Tradition indicates that the City Prefect (*Præfectus Urbi*),[419] or the cruel Praetorian Prefect (*Præfectus Prætorii*), Gaius Ofonius Tigellinus,[420] remanded Paul in the Tullianum prison.[421] On a morning in the early spring of the year AD 68, Prætorian soldiers and legal lictors marched the condemned Paul to execution. They left the city of Rome through "the Porta Trigemina [in the old Servian Wall] past the Pyramid of Cestius."[422] This execution party made their out of the city on the Via Ostiensa. Then they "turned off on the Via Laurentiana and after about half an hour they came to the Salvian Marsh (Aquæ Salviæ)."[423]

Since 507 BC, the Roman constitution laid down the form of execution for criminals of Roman citizenship. "The condemned criminals were bound to the stake. . . . [Then] consuls took their seats on the tribunal; the lictors were ordered to carry out the sentence. The prisoners were stripped, flogged, and beheaded."[424] The executioner's blade waited as the approaching warmth of the new day dispelled the chill of the morn. Paul knelt before the executioner and, in a moment, passed from one world into another.

THE MORTAL REMAINS OF PAUL

While the spirit finds that state of peace and rest from mortal cares, the earthly tabernacle is laid to rest in the arms of mother earth. It is conjectured that Prudens, Claudia, Linus, and others, having retrieved the body of Paul, interred it in a local cemetery on the Via Ostiensa. The mortal remains of Paul reposed here until exhumed by order of the Emperor Constantine. The remains were reinterred in a sarcophagus and placed under the high altar of a new church in AD 324.[425] Sixty-years later in AD 386, the church was demolished and the larger Basilica di San Paolo fuori le Mura opened in AD 395. A careless fire in 1823 destroyed the basilica. In 1840, the reconstructed basilica opened.[426] The public is not generally aware that the sovereign state of the Holy See composes several enclaves within and around Rome, in addition to the Vatican. The Basilica of Saint Paul's Outside the Walls is one of these enclaves of the state of the Holy See under the terms of the Lateran Treaty of 1929.[427] Therefore, the basilica is not a territorial component of the Republic of Italy.

The original location of the execution of Paul was in the Salvian Marsh—a centuries-old, malaria-infested marsh. Eventually the marsh was drained and cleaned, and an abbey was constructed, the Abbazia delle Tre Fontane, known in English as the Three Fountains Abbey.[428]

From 2002 to 2006, the Holy See conducted an extensive evaluation of the sarcophagus beneath the altar, and the interred human remains were revealed on 11 December 2006.[429] A few years later, on 29 June 2009, Pope Benedict XVI announced that carbon-14 dating of bone fragments in the sarcophagus confirmed the remains were from the first or second centuries.[430]

We have no doubt that Peter, John the Revelator, John the Baptist, Paul, and indeed all the other prophets of the early Christian era were resurrected in the intervening centuries since then. The remains of some faithful Christians from the early era are indeed interred at Rome. However, those of the apostolic commission continue their ministry and holy stewardship beyond the portal we call physical death. We worship not before the bones or sarcophagus of any departed saints, but before the Throne of Grace of the Living God. Paul, the man, saint, and apostle,[431] led a life of service worthy of emulation by any people, in any age—especially the present!

NOTES FOR 2 TIMOTHY

1. Map by the author William V. Blacoe, 2009.

2. Green's Literal Translation; The Interlinear Hebrew-Greek-English Bible; Young's Literal Translation; Revised Standard American Version; Luther's Heilige Schrift des Alten und Neuen Testaments; Die Schlachter Bibel; Die Eberfelder Bibel.

3. Strong, #2307.

4. Strong, #1860.

5. Compare Acts 1:4. Also "the promise [witness] of the Holy Ghost" (Acts 2:33); confirmed in "That we might receive the promise of the Spirit through faith" (Galatians 3:14).

6. Faulring, 533.

7. The word "dearly" is not in the Greek.

8. Strong, #5485.

9. Léon-Dufour, 20.

10. "The mercy of God might be defined as His compassion or forbearance. God displays or extends His mercy by granting grace to His children. This grace is an extension of divine help or enabling power" (Golden, "Grace," Ensign, October 2003, 48).

11. Preserved in the modern Latin-based languages—French: "grâces" (Nouvelle Édition de Genève); Portuguese: "graças" (Bíblia Sagrada); Spanish: "gracias" (Biblia Reina-Valera); and Italian: "grazie" (Riveduta Bibba).

12. Strong, #3000.

13. Humphreys , 154.

14. Brown, The Pastoral Epistles, 56.

15. Barnes, The Epistles of Paul, 240.

16. Strong, #3417.

17. New International Version.

18. Liddell & Scott, 168, s.v. "ἀνυπόκρῐτος."

19. Hillard, The Pastoral Epistles of St. Paul, 71.

20. New International Version; Green's Literal Translation.

21. New Revised Standard Version; Green's Literal Translation; New Testament in Modern Speech.

22. "Moses ordained Joshua as his successor by the laying on of hands (Numbers 27:18, 23; Deutronomy 34:9). Jesus's apostles used this procedure in authorizing seven men to manage practical economic matters in the early church (Acts 6:1–6). Paul and Barnabas were ordained to a missionary journey by the laying on of hands of the 'prophets and teachers at Antioch'" (Ludlow, Encyclopedia of Mormonism, 1:814, "Laying on of Hands").

23. The Interlinear Hebrew-Greek-English Bible.

24. Barnes, 241.

25. Strachan, The Captivity and the Pastoral Epistles, 238.

26. Plutarch, Pompey 41:2; Perrin, Plutarch's Lives, 220–21 (anazopurounta ἀναζωπυροῦντα).

27. Smith, Dictionary of Greek and Roman Antiquities, s.v. "Vestales."

28. Barnes, 241.

29. Strong, #5486.

30. Strong, #1936.

31. "And when Simon saw that through laying on of the apostles' hands the Holy Ghost was given, he offered them money" (Acts 8:18); "The laying on of the hands of the presbytery" (1 Timothy 4:14); "The doctrine of baptisms, and of laying on of hands" (Hebrews 6:2).

32. New International Version.

33. Strong, #1167.

34. *Webster's Dictionary*, 462, s.v. "fear."

35. Ibid., s.v. "timid."

36. Liddell & Scott, s.v. "σωφρονισμός."

37. Strong, #4995.

38. Barnes, 242.

39. Wordsworth, *The New Testament of Our Lord and Saviour Jesus Christ*, 459.

40. Strong, #4777.

41. Humphreys, 159.

42. Faulring, 533.

43. Hillard, 73.

44. "To be saved is to be taken out of a dangerous situation in which one risked perishing. According to the nature of the danger, the act of saving manifests itself in protection, liberation, ransom, cure and health, victory, [and] life peace" (Léon-Dufour, 518–19).

45. Strong, #2821.

46. Other comparative languages: *vocação* in Portuguese; *vocación* in Spanish; and *vocation* in French.

47. Strong, #2673.

48. Hillard, 74.

49. Faulring, 509; 1 Corinthians 15:26.

50. Barnes, 244; "To bring into light that which before was hidden" (Hillard, 74); "More exactly, abolishing death, as he did, and bringing into light instead life and immortality" (Humphreys, 160).

51. Ellicott, *The Pastoral Epistles*, 108.

52. New Revised Standard Version; New International Version.

53. In the context of this verse *etethen* (ἐτέθην).

54. Strong, #5414.

55. Biblia Reina-Valera.

56. Veláquez, 524, s.v. "puesto."

57. Humphreys, 161.

58. Brown, 62.

59. For example, in Leviticus 6:2, *paratheke* παραθήκῃ, and 6:4, *paretethe* παρετέθη (Brenton, *The Septuagint with Apocrypha: Greek and English*, 131–32).

60. "The high priest explained that there were some deposits (*parathekas* παραθήκας) belonging to widows and orphans. . . . The priests prostrated themselves before the altar in their priestly garments and called toward heaven upon him who had given the law about deposits (*parathekes* παραθήκης), that he should keep them safe for

those who had deposited them" (2 Maccabees 3:10, 15 in Metzger, *The Apocrypha of the Old Testament*; Brenton, 187).

61. Green's Literal Translation.

62. Strong, #5296; "This word properly means a sketch or outline, giving the main points of a subject" (Hillard, 75); "This word literally means an under-writing, to trace letters for copying by scholars; hence, a writing-copy, including all the letters of the alphabet, given to beginners as an aid in learning to draw them" (Strong, #5261).

63. MacKnight, *Apostolical Epistles*, 237; "The compound signifies the first roughly modeled block in the sculptor's art; just as in the sister art the similarly formed compound hypogrammos is the pencil drawing to be traced over in ink, or the outline to be filled in and colored" (Humphreys, 162).

64. Compare with 1 Timothy 6:20.

65. Strong, #3872; "From its use in 1 Timothy 6:20 it is plain that the words 'guard the deposit' had been often on St. Paul's lips, and that Timothy well understood them" (Hillard, 76).

66. Strong, #728.

67. Though Province is not in the original, it is nonetheless implied, and therefore included for clarification (New International Version).

68. "Omit 'be,' the tense describes a definite act, not a continuing state" (Humphreys, 163).

69. Humphreys, 163.

70. Strong, #654.

71. The Interlinear Hebrew-Greek-English Bible, Luke 23:14.

72. Strong, #1656.

73. Strong, #404.

74. The Interlinear Hebrew-Greek-English Bible.

75. Ibid.

76. Strachan, 242.

77. Strong, #1743.

78. The Interlinear Hebrew-Greek-English Bible.

79. "Competent to instruct" (Darby Bible Translation).

80. Strong, #1223.

81. Huther, *Critical and Exegitical Handbook to the Epistles of Saint Paul to Timothy and Titus*, 267.

82. This concept of witnesses is well expressed by Paul earlier in his Epistle to the Hebrews, "so great a cloud of witnesses" (Hebrews 12:1).

83. The Interlinear Hebrew-Greek-English Bible.

84. Strong, #3144.

85. New American Standard Bible.

86. Strong, #2553.

87. Bible in Basic English.

88. Calvin, *Commentaries on the Epistles to Timothy, Titus, and Philemon*, 210; Respecting the soldier, another author wrote: "His readiness to

endure hardship and the readiness with which he breaks away from all ties that are inconsistent with the life of a soldier" (Hillard, 79).

89. Ibid; "Legionary soldiers among the Romans were not suffered to engage in agriculture, merchandise, mechanical employments, or any business which might divert them from their profession. The apostle, by applying the Roman law respecting soldiers to the ministers of the gospel, hath established a scripture canon, whereby all who undertake the office of the ministry, are prohibited from following such secular businesses, as engross their attention and require much time to execute" (MacKnight, 244).

90. Ellicott, 115.

91. The word he comes before is, and the word yet is omitted (Faulring, 533).

92. Humphreys, 167.

93. MacKnight, 244.

94. Strong, #118.

95. Sadler, The Epistles of St. Paul to the Colossians, Thessalonians, and Timothy, 273–74.

96. Hillard, 80; "The following were among the regulations of the athletic contests. Every candidate was required to be of pure Hellenic descent. He was disqualified by certain moral and political offenses. He was obliged to take an oath that he had been ten months in training, and that he would violate none of the regulations. Bribery was punished by a fine. The candidate was obliged to practice again in the gymnasium immediately before the games, under the direction of judges or umpires, who were themselves required to be instructed for ten months in the details of the games" (Conybeare, *The Life and Epistles of Saint Paul*, 539, fn. 3. Compare also Hebrews 12:1–2).

97. Harvey, *Commentary on the Pastoral Epistles*, 95; "They who transgressed the laws of the Ancient Games were fined: the six statues of Jupeter at Olympia, called [Zanes] Ζᾶνες, were made from the fines levied on Athletes who had not contended lawfully" (Wordsworth, 460). There is clear record of Callippus of Athens bribing other athletes in the penthathlum (penthathlon) in the Olympic Games in 332 B.C. From this fine, the six statues were made in honor of Zeus (*Pausanias* [Παυσανίας], Description of Greece [Ἑλλάδος περιήγησις]; Jones, *Pausanias: Description of Greece*, 504–5).

98. Calvin, 211.

99. Strong, #4737.

100. Sadler, 274.

101. The Interlinear Hebrew-Greek-English Bible.

102. Brown, 66.

103. "No one could obtain the prize unless he had complied with all the laws of the games, and had thus given to those with whom he contended, a

fair opportunity to succeed" (Barnes, 252).

104. New International Version.

105. New International Version. In the Authorized Version this word is generally translated ought. Therefore, the verse can read, "It is the farmer who does the work who ought to have the first share of the crops" (New Revised Standard Version).

106. Compare with 1 Corinthians 3:6–9.

107. Strong, #2872.

108. Hillard, 80.

109. Calvin, 212.

110. New International Version.

111. Consider the following two similarities, "Whereby, when ye read" (Ephesians 3:4); "Take heed therefore how ye hear" (Luke 8:18).

112. Alternatively translated "insight" (New International Version).

113. Faulring, 533.

114. Strong, #2098.

115. New Revised Standard Version.

116. Strachan, 244.

117. Humphreys, 164.

118. The Tullianum is now located beneath the church of San Giuseppe dei Falegnami (St. Joseph of the Carpenters), Rome.

119. Livius, 1.33:8; de Sélincourt, *Livy— The Early History of Ancient Rome*, 72.

120. The Interlinear Hebrew-Greek-English Bible.

121. Ibid.

122. Liddell & Scott, 512, s.v. "ἐκλεκτέος."

123. "It is clear that people do not all have the same talent for recognizing truth and believing the doctrines of salvation. Some heed the warning voice and believe the gospel; others do not. . . . Every person stands alone in choosing his beliefs and electing the course he will pursue. No two persons are born with the same talents and capacities; no two are rooted in the same soil of circumstances; each is unique . . . we all lived as spirit beings, as children of the Eternal Father, for an infinitely long period of time in the pre-mortal existence. There we developed talents, gifts, and aptitudes; there our capacities and abilities took form; there, by obedience to law, we were endowed with the power, in one degree or another, to believe the truth and follow the promptings of the Spirit. And the talent of greatest worth was that of spirituality" (McConkie, *A New Witness for the Articles of Faith*, 33).

124. Strong, #166.

125. Faulring, 533.

126. Compare with 1 Timothy 1:15; 3:1; 4:9; Titus 3:8.

127. Faulring, 533.

128. Compare with Colossians 2:20.

129. "Those who faithfully adhere to Christ and to his truths and ways, whatever it costs them, will certainly have the advantage of it in another world. . . . If we be faithful to Christ,

he will certainly be faithful to us. If we be false to him, he will be faithful to his threatenings: he cannot deny himself, he cannot recede from any word that he hath spoken" (Henry, *An Exposition of the Old and New Testament*, 477).

130. Strong, #4821.

131. The Greek historian Plutarch used this word on one occasion. "The man who held the largest share in all the undertakings of Lycurgus and co-operated [*sumbasileuonta* συμβασιλεύοντα] with him in the enactment of his laws" (Plutarch, 5:4; Perrin, 218–19).

132. Biblia Sacra Versio Vulgata.

133. German translations capture this correctly with the word with *mith-errschen* (Luther's Heilige Schrift des Alten und Neuen Testaments; Die Eberfelder Bibel; Die Schlachter Bibel).

134. Green's Literal Translation.

135. Liberally, yet more comprehendible to understand in the following translation. "Keep reminding them of these things. Warn them before God against quarrelling about words; it is of no value, and only ruins those who listen" (New International Version).

136. Liddell & Scott, 403, s.v. "διαμαρτύρομαι."

137. Humphreys, 173.

138. Compare also Isaiah 8:2, "And I took unto me faithful witnesses to record, Uriah the priest, and Zechariah the son of Jeberechiah." The concept is split in the Authorized King James Version. Literally translated to, "And I took to record [*veaidah* וְאָעִידָה] for me witnesses faithful."

139. The Interlinear Hebrew-Greek-English Bible.

140. Translated in German as *bewährt* (Die Eberfelder Bibel; Die Schlachter Bibel), meaning "proven" or "established."

141. Calvin, 221.

142. Strong, #4704.

143. Calvin, 222.

144. Huther, 280.

145. Strong, #3718.

146. MacKnight, 247.

147. Calvin, 222–23.

148. The Interlinear Hebrew-Greek-English Bible.

149. In German, *das Wort der Wahrheit* means "the Word of Truth" (Luther's Heilige Schrift des Alten und Neuen Testaments; Die Eberfelder Bibel). In Dutch, *het Woord der waarheid* means "the Word of truth" (De ganse Heilige Schrift—het Oude en Nieuwe Testament).

150. Wisdom of Solomon 9:1; Brenton, *The Septuagint with Apocrypha: Greek and English.*

151. The Interlinear Hebrew-Greek-English Bible.

152. Strong, #1697.

153. Beautifully expressed in a modern English translation, "Avoid godless

chatter, because those who indulge in it will become more and more ungodly" (New International Version). Perhaps the TNIV translation was inspired from an older German translation, "Die ungöttlichen [ungodly] eitlen Geschwätze aber vermeide; denn sie werden zu weiterer Gottlosigkeit [ungodliness] fortschreiten" (Die Eberfelder Bibel).

154. The Interlinear Hebrew-Greek-English Bible.

155. The Greek word *asebeias* (ἀσεβείας) is also effectively translated "impiety" (Darby Bible Translation).

156. Strong, #952.

157. Brown, 71.

158. Hillard, 84.

159. Wordsworth, 461.

160. The Interlinear Hebrew-Greek-English Bible.

161. Calvin, 223.

162. The Interlinear Hebrew-Greek-English Bible.

163. Ibid.

164. The Greek word *muthos* (μῦθος) is used five times in the New Testament (1 Timothy 1:4; 4:7; 2 Timothy 4:4; Titus 1:14; and 2 Peter 1:16).

165. Strong, #1044.

166. Liddell & Scott, 262 s.v. "στόχαστος/-έω"; Strong, #795.

167. New Revised Standard Version.

168. Léon-Dufour, 494.

169. MacKnight, 248.

170. Sadler, 281.

171. Barnes, 257.

172. "The solid foundation of God's spiritual house, the Church (1 Timothy 3:15), has these two mottos inscribed upon it: 'The Lord knoweth them that are His' (Numbers 16:5; Nahum 1:7; John 10:14, 27). He seeth, loveth, and will preserve them from all peril. Here is a comfortable assurance of His favor to us. And, 'Let all who name the name of the Lord (. . .) depart from iniquity' (Numbers 16:26; Isaiah 52:11) (Wordsworth, 461).

173. New Testament in Modern Speech.

174. Ibid.

175. Ibid.

176. MacKnight, 249.

177. Sadler, 283–84.

178. The Interlinear Hebrew-Greek-English Bible.

179. Greek *etoimasmenon* (ἡτοιμασμένον) (The Interlinear Hebrew-Greek-English Bible); "zubereitet" (Die Schlachter Bibel). Other New Testament occurrences: "thou hast prepared [*etoimasas* ἡτοίμαστας]" (Luke 2:31); "the things which God hath prepared [*etoimasen* ἡτοίμασεν] for them that love him" (1 Corinthians 2:9); "which were prepared [*etoimasmenoi* ἡτοιμασμένοι] for" (Revelation 9:15).

180. The Interlinear Hebrew-Greek-English Bible.

181. Gibbons & Challoner, 1582–1899,

Douay-Rheims Version.

182. The Annotated Bible, 191.

183. "Be a different man yourself, flee the lusts of the younger men" (Humphreys, 177).

184. "Add 'after,' in order to give the proper force of active pursuit" (Humphreys, 177).

185. Strong, #1939.

186. MacKnight, 250; "Paul means all desires that make the special temptation of youth, not only sensual desires. He would include all the temptations of luxury and pleasure, pride in physical prowess, love of notoriety and position, the desire to display one's intellectual acuteness, love of variety and impatience of monotony. . . . Several passages in the Epistle suggest a warning against compromise" (Hillard, 87).

187. Green's Literal Translation.

188. New Revised Standard Version. This term is alternatively translated in a modern version, "ignorant speculations" (New American Standard Bible).

189. Darby Bible Translation.

190. Liddell & Scott, 174, s.v. "ἀπαιδευσία."

191. Liddell & Scott, 421, s.v. "διδακτέον."

192. Strong, #420.

193. Hillard, 88.

194. Liddell & Scott, 133, s.v. "ἀνεξῐκᾰκ-έω – ία – ος."

195. Wisdom of Solomon 2:19 in Metzger, *The Apocrypha of the Old Testament*; Bagster, *The Apocrypha: Greek and English in Parallel Columns*, 57.

196. Green's Literal Translation. Comparative translations: "Correcting opponents with gentleness. God may perhaps grant that they will repent and come to know the truth" (New Revised Standard Version); "He must speak in a gentle tone when correcting the errors of opponents, in the hope that God will at last give them repentance, for them to come to a full knowledge of the truth" (New Testament in Modern Speech).

197. Calvin, 234.

198. Humphreys, 180.

199. Compare with the following translation, "will come to their senses" (New International Version).

200. Strong, #366.

201. Ellicott, 132.

202. MacKnight, 252.

203. Strong, #3803.

204. Die Schlachter Bibel.

205. Betteridge, 526, s.v. "Schlinge."

206. MacKnight, 251–52.

207. Hillard, 91.

208. Strong, #5467.

209. Humphreys, 180–81.

210. Nouvelle Édition de Genève.

211. Bible in Basic English.

212. "Profane" (Darby Bible Translation); "profanes" (La Sainte

Bible—l'Ancien et le Nouveau Testament). Compare also 1 Timothy 1:9.

213. Barnes, 262.

214. Aristotle, *Ethics*, Nicmachean Ethics 9:8; Bart, *The Etics of Aristotle*, 284.

215. Brown, 75.

216. Nouvelle Édition de Genève.

217. *Webster's Dictionary*, 404, s.v. "egotism."

218. Strong, #5366.

219. Biblia Reina-Valera.

220. Bíblia Sagrada.

221. Die Schlachter Bibel.

222. Statenvertaling, De ganse Heilige Schrift—het Oude en Nieuwe Testament.

223. Hillard, 93.

224. Strong, #213.

225. Ibid., #5244.

226. Hillard, 94.

227. Strong, #546.

228. Young's Literal Translation. Alternatively translated "implacable" (Revised Version—Standard American Edition; Darby Bible Translation); French, "implacables" (La Bible); Spanish, "implacables" (La Biblia de las Américas); German "unversöhnlich" (Die Eberfelder Bibel).

229. Young's Literal Translation; Darby Bible Translation; New International Version.

230. French, "cruels" (Nouvelle Édition de Genève); Spanish, "crueles" (Biblia Reina-Valera); Portuguese "cruéis" (Bíblia Sagrada); German, "grausam" (Die Eberfelder Bibel); Dutch, "wreed" (De ganse Heilige Schrift—het Oude en Nieuwe Testament).

231. Strong, #794.

232. Ellicott, 135.

233. Ibid., 134.

234. Strong, #786.

235. Biblia Sacra Versio Vulgata.

236. Strong, #4689.

237. Hillard 94.

238. Liddell & Scott, 390, s.v. "διάβολ – ή – ος."

239. *Webster's Dictionary*, s.v. "savage."

240. *Webster's Dictionary*, 311, s.v. "cruel."

241. Strong, #865.

242. Die Schlachter Bibel.

243. Young's Literal Translation.

244. English, "reckless;" Dutch, "roekeloos."

245. Dutch *opgeblazen*; Danish *opblæste*; and German *aufgeblasen*—all meaning puffed up, self-important and arrogant.

246. The Interlinear Hebrew-Greek-English Bible; Darby Bible Translation.

247. Also translated traitor in Luke 6:16, and betrayers in Acts 7:52.

248. Barnes, 263.

249. Liddell & Scott, s.v. "προ – δοσία – δότης."

250. Bible in Basic English.

251. New Revised Standard Version.; New International Version; New Testament in Modern Speech.

252. Wordsworth, 462.

253. Strong, #4312.

254. Wordsworth, 463.

255. Strong, #5187.

256. Barnes, 264.

257. "Having denied" (The Interlinear Hebrew-Greek-English Bible; Revised Standard American Version); "have denied" (New American Standard Bible).

258. The Interlinear Hebrew-Greek-English Bible; Darby Bible Translation.

259. Darby Bible Translation.

260. The Interlinear Hebrew-Greek-English Bible; Darby Bible Translation.

261. Ibid.

262. New Revised Standard Version.

263. Hillard, 95.

264. New International Version.

265. Compare a French translation, *des femmes d'un esprit faible*—"women with a feeble spirit" (Nouvelle Édition de Genève).

266. Strong, #4987.

267. Hillard, 95.

268. MacKnight, 257.

269. The Interlinear Hebrew-Greek-English Bible; Darby Bible Translation.

270. Considered to be an oxymoron generated by Paul (Lock, *The Pastoral Epistles*, 107).

271. Young's Literal Translation.

272. God's Word Translation.

273. Eusebius, *Evangelicæ Præparationis*, 3313–314, quoting the philosopher Numenius the Pythagorean from *On the Good*—no longer independently extant.

274. Parry, *The Book of Jasher*, 224; Jasher 79:27–30.

275. Hillard, 96.

276. Barnes, 266.

277. Ellicott, 139. Compare an alternative, "But they shall not advance farther" (Darby Bible Translation).

278. "Their foolishness, like that of the other two [Jannes and Jambres], must become obvious to everyone" (The Jerusalem Bible).

279. The words "as theirs also was" are in reference to Jannes and Jambres in the previous verse.

280. Darby Bible Translation.

281. The Greek reads *te* (τῇ), meaning "the" in front of each attribute in this verse; however, *my* is needed in the first instance to introduce the list as referring to Paul.

282. Darby Bible Translation.

283. The words "in Pisidia" are not in the original text, but are included here to distinguish from the major city of Antioch in Syria.

284. Young's Literal Translation.

285. The Interlinear Hebrew-Greek-English Bible; Darby Bible Translation.

286. Faulring, 533.

287. Barnes, 270; New Revised Standard Version; New International Version.

288. Douay-Rheims Version.

289. Alternatively rendered, "will go from bad to worse" (New International Version); or, "will go on from bad to worse" (New Testament in Modern Speech).

290. Young's Literal Translation.

291. Strong, #1114.

292. Hillard, 97.

293. *Webster's Dictionary*, s.v. "traduce."

294. Hillard, 97.

295. New Revised Standard Version; New International Version; New Revised Standard Version

296. New International Version; New Testament in Modern Speech. Latin "infantia" (Biblia Sacra Versio Vulgata); French "infance" (Nouvelle Édition de Genève).

297. MacKnight, 260.

298. Strong, #1124.

299. Ellicott, 144.

300. Wordsworth, 464.

301. Ibid.

302. Lock, 109.

303. Wordsworth, 464.

304. Faulring, 533.

305. Ibid.

306. Brown, 79.

307. Strong, #1882.

308. Brown, 79.

309. King James Version.

310. Wordsworth, 466; The Interlinear Hebrew-Greek-English Bible; Darby Bible Translation; Young's Literal Translation.

311. Darby Bible Translation.

312. Faulring, 533.

313. Ibid.

314. Brown, 81.

315. Strong, #171.

316. Barnes, 276.

317. "Argument drawn from the future to urge diligence in the present" (Ellicott, 151).

318. Compare with these translations: "For the time is coming when people will not put up with sound doctrine, but having itching ears, they will accumulate for themselves teachers to suit their own desires" (New Revised Standard Version); "For the time will come when they will not endure sound doctrine; but having itching ears, they shall heap to themselves teachers in accordance with their own lusts" (King James Version).

319. Strong, #2002.

320. Calvin, 255–56.

321. Ellicott, 151.

322. The Interlinear Hebrew-Greek-English Bible; Darby Bible Translation; New Revised Standard Version; New International Version.

323. Though not quoting, this passage is possibly inspired from Ezekiel, "And, lo, thou art unto them as a very lovely song of one that hath a pleasant voice, and can play well on an instrument:

for they hear thy words, but they do them not" (Ezekiel 33:32).

324. New International Version.

325. Darby Bible Translation.

326. Wordsworth, 466.

327. Strong, #89.

328. *Spendo* (σπένδω) appears in the Greek Septuagint of the Old Testament: *sponden* (σπονδὴν) Numbers 15:5; 28:7; *sponde* (σπονδὴ) Numbers 28:14. From Brenton, 195, 215.

329. Brown, 82. "Paul as he faces martyrdom is about to pour out his blood as an offering to God" (Falconer, *The Pastoral Epistles*, 96).

330. Huther, 317.

331. Barnes, 279.

332. Strong, #359.

333. Barnes, 279.

334. Huther, 318.

335. "Fight the good fight of faith, lay hold on eternal life, whereunto thou are also called" (1 Timothy 6:12).

336. Strong, #73. "The struggle itself was now all but over, little more than the effects were remaining" (Ellicott, 154).

337. Harvey, 115.

338. The translation "there remains" is not literally, but specifically correct. Compare the alternatives: "for the rest" (The Interlinear Hebrew-Greek-English Bible; Darby Bible Translation); "from now on" (New Revised Standard Version; Bible in Basic English).

339. The translation "who have longed for" is not literally, but specifically correct (New Revised Standard Version; New International Version).

340. Barnes, 281.

341. Sadler, 302.

342. The Interlinear Hebrew-Greek-English Bible; Darby Bible Translation.

343. Darby Bible Translation; New International Version.

344. "We say with some confidence that Titus was the elder brother of Luke and a convert of Saint Paul [Titus 1:4] in the early days at Antioch. . . . The Roman names Titus and Lucanus are quite natural for a pair of brothers, though it is more likely that they were Greeks than Romans, and all the notices of them are satisfied by the hypothesis that they were Antiochene free-men" (Brown, xix).

345. Strong, #80.

346. Bernard, 138.

347. Lock, 117.

348. Ellicott, 157; Humphreys, 196.

349. "Marcus was the Latin surname for John (Johanan)" (Humphreys, 197).

350. Strong, #5190. See also Ephesians 6:21; Colossians 4:7.

351. "Of the subsequent career of Tychicus nothing certain is known. Several cities claim him as their bishop. The Menology of Basil Porphyrogenitus, which commemorates him on April 9, makes him Bishop of Colophon and successor to Sosthenes. He is

also said to have been appointed Bishop of Chalcedon by St. Andrew the Apostle (Lipsius, Apokryphe Apostelgeschichte, 579). He is also called Bishop of Neapolis in Cyprus (Le Quien, Oriens Christ., I, 125 & II, 1061). Some martyrologies make him a deacon, while the Roman Martyrology places his commemoration at Paphos in Cyprus" (Herberman, 106).

352. Wordsworth, 467.

353. "The word [*failonen*] φαιλενην, signifies either a cloak or a bag—if the apostle meant a cloak, he is sending for it at so great a distance" (MacKnight, 267); "We cannot see what use Paul would have for the mantle when he was expecting death so soon" (Huther, 325); Why should "Paul give orders to have either a garment or a chest brought to him from a place so distant, as if there were no workmen, or as if there were not abundance both of cloak and timber? If it be said, that there was a chest filled with books, or manuscripts, or epistles, the difficulty will be solved; for such materials could not have been procured at any price" (Calvin, 265).

354. "'Others translate the rare Greek word as book-holder, and think of a case or bag in which Paul kept his precious rolls. That he had left such a piece of baggage behind him would be more easily understood that than he should after so long a time ask for his cloak.' The books and parchments

would then be the contents of the portfolio" (Köhler, as quoted in Strachan, 255).

355. Calvin, Commentaries on the Epistles to Timothy, Titus, and Philemon, 265. "A bag in which the books were contained" (Brown, 86).

356. Bernard, 146. In other instances, this word may also refer to "a woollen wrap for carrying books safely," as opposed to a box, chest, folder, or vellum wrap (Lock, 118). The type of portfolio depends upon the importance of the documents, and the inclination of the owner.

357. The New Testament: Translated from the Syriac Peshito Version, 390.

358. "There is some foundation for the interpretation 'a book-case' or 'portfolio,' which the Syriac versions support" (Humphreys, 199).

359. Brockelmann, *Lexicon Syriacum*, 37, s.v. ܒܝܬ ܟܬܒܐ

360. Ellicott, 159.

361. Aramaic Peshitta New Testament, 138.

362. Harvey, 118.

363. Bernard, 147.

364. Calvin, 265–66.

365. "The book-carrier {footnote: A bag made of leather or woolen cloth} which I left at Troas with Carpus, bring it with you when you come, and the books, especially the parchment scroll" (Holy Bible: From the Ancient Eastern Text, 1192).

366. Etheridge, *The Apostolic Acts and Epistles from the Peschoto, or Ancient Syriac*, 369.

367. Livius, *Livy—Rome and The Mediterranean*, 223.

368. Hackett, 3324, s.v. "Troas."

369. Strong, #975.

370. Ibid., #3200.

371. "The vellum rolls, what were these? Perhaps among them was the diploma of his Roman franchise" (Livermore, *The Epistles of Paul*, 290).

372. Compare with an earlier incidence of Paul wrongly imprisoned in Acts 16:35–38.

373. In the case of Paul of Tarsus, he told us he was free-born—he inherited Roman citizenship by birth (see Acts 22:25–29).

374. The Old Testament records the earliest mention of identification of diplomatic documents as a passport. These documents were issued to Nehemiah in 445/444 B.C. by King Artaxerxes I (Artaxerxes Longimanus) at Shushan in Persia: "Moreover I [Nehemiah] said unto the King [Artaxerxes], If it please the king, let letters be given me to the governors beyond the River [Euphrates], that they may convey me over till I come into Judah" (Nehemiah 2:7). Nehemiah needed documents of safe passage to all the pashas or provincial governors all the way through to Judea. This verse is expressed with greater clarity in a paraphrased version: "If it please the king, give me letters to the governors west of the Euphrates River instructing them to let me travel through their countries on my way to Judah" (The Living Bible).

375. *Cives Romani* (Roman Citizenship): Children born in legal marriage to Roman man became *de facto* citizens. Freed slaves could obtain a limited form of citizenship via their former owner/patron—their sons became full citizens. Retiring legionary Auxiliaries were sometimes granted citizenship. Occasionally others received citizenship in gratitude for particular service to the state. Citizenship could be purchased at a high price (see an example in Acts 22:27 28). Citizenship rights were hierarchical and varied over the centuries.

The law *Jus suffragiorum* defined citizen voting rights; capital punishment; and military conscription; *Jus honorum*—civil and public office; *Jus commercii*—the right to make legal contracts and own property; *Jus gentium*—citizen relationship with provincials and foreigners; *Jus connubii*—regulated matrimony and the powers of a husband as *pater familias* over his wife and children; *Jus migrationis*—defines citizenship in respect of migration within Italy (also *Jus Latii*), inferior Roman colonies, and foreign lands. Further laws included immunity, to sue and be sued, right to legal trial in court, the right of appeal from lower courts, and indemnity from torture (condensed from Smith,

Dictionary of Greek & Roman Antiquities, 681–702).

376. Paul was born free and inherited the Roman citizenship. There are four primary candidates who were associated with the city of Tarsus and the province of Cilicia, who could have granted citizenship to either his father or grandfather. They are: (1) General Marcus Antonius (Mark Anthony, consul/general); (2) General Pompeius Magnus (Pompey the Great); (3) General Octivanus Augustus (consul/general, and later the Emperor Augustus); (4) General Publius Sulpicius Quirinius (governor/general of Crete and Cyrene in 14 B.C.; legionary general in Galatia and Cilicia 5–3 B.C. fighting the Homonadenses Tribe north-west of Tarsus; and later governor of Syria and Palestine at the birth of Jesus—as mentioned in Luke 2:2). An ancestor of Paul at Tarsus must have accomplished some great service to the Roman state, or directly to one of the above military commanders. Each of these generals was stationed at Tarsus in previous decades during the Roman Republic. With the demise of the Republic, only the Imperial Court at Rome could issue Roman citizenship.

377. Stemma: "A pedigree, genealogical table, genealogical tree" (White, 581, s.v. "stemma").

378. In the case of Paul, military means service to or in one of the Roman legions stationed at or near Tarsus.

379. In the case of Paul this was probably as an elected or appointed official at Tarsus or later during his residency at Antioch-on-the-Orontes-River.

380. Dignitas: "The state or condition of the dingus. . . . Worthiness, merit, desert, . . . dignity, greatness, grandeur, authority, rank, . . . official dignity, honorable employment, office" (White, 184, s.v. "dignitas").

381. Revised Standard American Version.

382. Compare Proverbs 24:12; Psalm 62:12; Romans 2:6.

383. New International Version.

384. The words "I pray God" are not in most Greek texts.

385. Strong, #627.

386. This Greek word also appears in Luke 23:48 (The Interlinear Hebrew-Greek-English Bible; Darby Bible Translation).

387. "Of course St. Paul could have a *patronus* to speak for him if he wished, but in addition to the *patronus*, whom we should call 'counsel for the defense,' it had always been customary to allow a prisoner to produce *advocati*, persons of weight likely to impress the court, who stood by him in the court, giving him the countenance of their public support and their testimony as to his character, and on occasion helping the conduct of his case by their suggestions. The fact that the word *advocatus* was coming to be used as synonymous with *patronus* probably shows

that the position of the *advocati* was becoming a more legal one" (Hillard, 108–9; italics added).

388. Bernard, 148. No one "stood forward with me to plead in my defense, or more probably as an *advocatus* to support by his counsel" (Ellicott, 161; italics added).

389. Harvey, 119.

390. "While in Greece he tried to have a canal cut through the Isthmus, and addressed a gathering of Praetorian Guards, urging them to undertake the task. Nero took a mattlock himself and, at a trumpet blast, broke the ground and carried off the first basket of earth on his back" (Suetonius: "Nero"; Graves, *Suetonius: The Twelve Caesars*, 222).

391. Conybeare, *The Life and Epistles of Saint Paul*, 767.

392. Nero "ruled that, instead of a case being presented as a whole, every relevant charge should be presented separately by one side and then by the other" (Graves, 222).

393. Alternatively "rescued" (New Revised Standard Version).

394. Alternatively "rescue" (New Revised Standard Version).

395. When Paul first arrived in Corinth he "found a certain Jew named Aquila, born in Pontus lately come from Italy, with his wife Priscilla; (because that Claudius had commanded all Jews to depart from Rome:) and came unto them. And because he was of the same craft, he abode with them, and wrought: for by their occupation they were tent makers" (Acts 18:2–3).

396. "A certain Jew named Aquila, born in Pontus, lately come from Italy, with his wife Priscilla" (Acts 18:2).

397. Alternatively expressed as "stayed at his post" (Humphreys, 202).

398. The word *erastos* (ἐραστος) also means "amiable" (Pervanoglu, 305, s.v. "ἐραστος").

399. Liddell & Scott, 1828, s.v. "Τρόφιμος."

400. Hackett, 3325, s.v. "Trophimus"; Ellicott, 164.

401. "Before winter"—compare with 2 Timothy 4:9.

402. Strong, #3044 & 3043.

403. The Roman Catholic Church claims that Linus and then Clement were successors to St. Peter as the second and third Bishops of Rome, and successor in the early legendary papal hierarchy. Linus or Clement could not have been successors to Peter in the Apostleship over the Church in A.D. 66 or 69. We have the undisputed fact that the Lord Jesus Christ appeared to St. John—one of the original Twelve Apostles—then living on Patmos Island, and revealed the Book of Revelation to him in A.D. 97. The successor to St. Peter in the Holy Apostleship was at Patmos and not at Rome!

404. Roberts & Donaldson, *The Ante-Nicene Fathers*, 478. Book 7

"Constitutions of the Holy Apostles," Section 4 "Enumeration ordained by Apostles," chapter 46 "Who were they that the holy Apostles sent and ordained?" Translation of a codex dated A.D. 1056 and discovered by Philotheos Bryennios at the library of the Jerusalem Monastery of the Most Holy Sepulcher at Constantinople in 1873.

The above record indicates that the Apostle Paul ordained Linus as bishop of the first organized congregation. The Apostle Peter ordained Clemens as the second bishop sometime thereafter. This is reiterated in another volume, " . . . as also the church of Rome, which makes Clement to have been ordained in like manner by Peter" (Roberts, 258. *The Writings of Tertullian*, second part, book 1 "The prescription against heretics," chapter 32 "None of the heretics claim succession from the Apostles"). There is reasonable credibility to conjecture that as Linus was bishop of the first organized congregation, and due to an inflow of new converts, Clement was bishop of the second organized congregation. Two bishops (local ecclesiastical leaders) ordained by two different apostles, serving in Rome concurrently. We are not conclusively informed how many congregations were organized by the apostles at Rome. As the early Church enlarged, it is obvious that eventually there were several bishops concurrently serving in different congregations.

The following is included for the sake of complete documentation—even though it is seemingly contradictory to the above: "The blessed apostles, then having founded and built up the Church, committed unto the hands of Linus the office of the episcopate. Of this Linus, Paul makes mention in his Epistles to Timothy. To him succeeded Anacletus; and after him, in the third place from the apostles, Clement was allotted the bishopric" (Roberts, 416; *Irenaeus Against Heresies*, book 3, chapter 3, paragraph 3).

405. Eusebius, *History of the Church*, 3:2 in Williamson, *Eusebius: The History of the Church*, 65.

406. "The theory has been advanced that the Pudens of the same text might have been Linus' father, and that this Pudens and Claudia were the couple mentioned by the Roman author Martial (Epigrams, 4:13, see quote below)" (*The International Standard Bible Encyclopedia*, 141, s.v. "Linus."

"Claudia Peregrina weds, Rufus, with my own Prudens" (Kerr, *Martial: Epigrams*, 239).

407. Faulring, 533.

408. Ibid.

409. The compilation of the epistles of Paul is in descending size from Romans through to Philemon. The placement of the Epistle to the Hebrews after Philemon, instead of before Romans, is because the compilers disputed whether Paul was the actual author of Hebrews.

410. "Make haste to come unto me quickly" (2 Timothy 4:9); and again, "Do thy diligence to come before winter" (2 Timothy 4:21).

411. "Only Luke is with me. Take [John] Mark, and bring him with thee: for he is serviceable to me for the ministry" (2 Timothy 4:11).

412. When Paul first came to Alexandria Troas in A.D. 52, he received the vision in the nighttime to bring the gospel over to Macedonia (Acts 16:8–10).

413. *Via Egnatia* (Greek *Egnatia Odos*, Εγνατία Οδός).

414. *Dyrrachium* (Latin; and Greek *Dyrrhachion*, Δυρράχιον) is today the port city of Durrës, Albania.

415. The Roman censor Appius Claudius Caecus completed the first section of this highway for military purposes from Rome to the south in 312 B.C. during the Samnite Wars; thereafter, the highway became known as the Appian Way in his honor.

416. Tranquillus [Graves translator], Suetonius: *The Twelve Caesars*, "Nero," 24, 226.

417. Ibid., 19, 222.

418. The Senate had passed a law to the effect that a period of ten days must elapse between sentence and execution, to allow the emperor to consider an appeal of clemency.

419. Conybeare, 767.

420. "Stained in his youth with the worst impurities, he retained in his advanced years all his early habits, and closed with disgrace a life begun in infamy. By his vices, the surest road to preferment, he obtained the command, first of the city cohorts, and afterwards of the Pretorian Guards. The rewards which were due to virtue only he obtained by his crimes. To his effeminate qualities he united some of those rougher evils which may be called manly passions, such as avarice and cruelty. Having gained an entire ascent over the affections of Nero, he was in some instances the advisor of the horrors committed by that prince, and in others the chief actor, without the knowledge of his master. He corrupted Nero at first, and in the end deserted him" (Tacitus, *History* 1:72 in Murphy, *Tacitus*, 3:363–64).

421. The Tullianum prison was constructed 640–16 B.C. The prison remained in operation until the 4th century A.D. and thereafter discontinued. No longer functioning as a prison, the facility became a place of pilgrimage to see where Saint Paul and Saint Peter were imprisoned. The name Tullianum was dropped centuries later and it became known as Carcere Mamertino (Mamertine Prison). Eventually the dungeon became the church of San Petrus in Carcere (Saint Peter in Prison). In 1597, construction commenced on a church over the old Tullianum dungeon, and the church of San Giuseppe dei Falegnami (Saint

Joseph the Carpenter) was completed in 1726. Today the church is on the Via di Marforio, Rome.

422. Holzner, Paul of Tarsus, 485. The Pyramid of Cestius—i.e. *Piramide di Caio Cestio* or *Piramide Cestia*.

423. Ibid.

424. Livius 2:6; de Sélincourt, *Livy—The Early History of Ancient Rome*, 110.

425. This church is over 3 km from the original internment location.

426. The Basilica of St Paul's outside the Walls (*San Paolo fuori le Mura*) is located at 186 Via Ostiense, Rome.

427. Lateran Treaty, February 11, 1929 Article 13; On September 20, 1870, the last Papal State was annexed by the then Kingdom of Italy. After a standoff lasting fifty-nine years, the Kingdom of Italy signed the Lateran Treaty (Concordat) with the Holy See on February 11, 1929. The concordat reconstituted the Holy See with political power and diplomatic status as a sovereign state. The Holy See is composed of not only the Vatican enclave, but also several other enclaves as a single sovereign state. In addition to the sovereign enclaves, there are several other enclaved buildings accorded extraterritorial sovereignty in perpetuity. The 1947 Constitution of the new Italian Republic incorporated the Lateran Concord.

428. The Three Fountains Abbey (Abbazia delle Tre Fontane) is located at Via de Acquae Salvie, Rome.

429. Catholic News Agency, 6 December 2006; *Holy See Communiqué*, 11 December 2006.

430. Winfield, 29 June, Guardian News & Media Ltd.; Owen, 29 June *Times-Online*; Messia, 29 June Cable Network News.

431. "Though he [Paul] once, according to his own word, persecuted the Church of God and wasted it, yet after embracing the faith, his labors were unceasing to spread the glorious news: and like a faithful soldier, when called to give his life in the cause which he had espoused, he laid it down, as he says, with an assurance of an eternal crown. Follow the labors of this Apostle from the time of his conversion to the time of his death, and you will have a fair sample of industry and patience in promulgating the Gospel of Christ. . . . None will say that he did not keep the faith, that he did not fight the good fight, which he did not preach and persuade to the last. And what was he to receive? a crown of righteousness. And what shall others receive who do not labor faithfully, and continue to the end?" (Smith, Teachings of the Prophet Joseph Smith, 63–64).

Part Three

TITUS

Titus

PROLOGUE

The Epistle of Paul to Titus is one of the Pastoral Epistles together with First and Second Timothy. This is the last epistle that Paul wrote as a free man. His arrest and transportation to Rome for trial at the imperial court followed shortly thereafter. While in Macedonia—possibly at Philippi—Paul composed this letter to Titus, whom he had recently left on Crete Island to set the Church in order by appointing[1] bishops to the new congregations (Titus 1:5–7). Composition of this letter possibly occurred in September or October of AD 67. When we consider Paul as the primary authority respecting the current Church organization on Crete, then Titus was his empowered agent or authorized representative. The document is, therefore, a *mandatum principiis* in the form of "a letter from a ruler or high official to one of his agents, delegates, ambassadors, or governors helping him set up shop in his new post and gets things in good order and under control."[2]

The letter deals more with specifics and less with generalities. Paul provides instruction and direction for all age and social groups. Some of the comments made are specific to cultural conditions among the Cretan populace and not applicable in other cultures. This letter is one of those rare occasions when Paul specifically quotes local literature in his letter, utilizing lines to highlight a paradigm shift to

Christian doctrinal beliefs. The content of the letter includes clear witness and expression of Christian theology often overlooked in many translations—not only in English but also in several other languages. "Paul's letters are not haphazard collections of isolated bits and pieces; they are carefully composed documents that involve both foresight and rhetorical sensibilities"[3]

WHO WAS TITUS?

We know little about the background and origins of Titus. One observant author considers Titus to be the elder brother of Luke. "We say with some confidence that Titus was the elder brother of Luke and a convert of Saint Paul (Titus 1:4) in the early days at Antioch."[4] This author highlights two particular references in the Second Corinthian Epistle that indicate the brother of Titus is a well-known figure in the leadership of the Christian Church.[5]

"And we have sent with him [Titus] the brother [by implication of Luke], whose praise is in the gospel throughout all the churches" (2 Corinthians 8:18)

"I desired Titus, and with him I sent a brother [by implication of Luke]. . ." (2 Corinthians 12:18)

In both incidences, the word *brother* (Greek *adelphos* ἀδελφόσ) in the literal sense means a brother of the womb, as in "male children of the same parents."[6]

Titus

❧

COMMENTARY

The New Testament contains only one epistle to Titus—no doubt there were many more that did not survive. Most epistles written by Paul were to congregations; however, four personal epistles survived that were written to individuals—Timothy, Titus, and Philemon. This now is the third of those four epistles.

INTRODUCTION (TITUS 1:1–4)

This opening sentence is so rich in its content, but it may present difficulties concerning its meaning to some. Paul is writing to Titus, a Church leader well versed in the doctrines of salvation, not just theology. Titus knows Paul and his complex writing style. He understands the meaning of "the faith of God's elect," and that "hope of eternal life, which God . . . promised before the world began" in the premortal realm of his spirit children. This epistle is for a saint—not a Jew or a Gentile, but a Christian. The familiarity of the term "mine own son," is reminiscent of Paul's affection for Timothy (1 Timothy 1:2) and Onesimus (Philemon 10).

❧

[1:1] Paul, a [slave] ~~servant~~ of God, and an apostle of Jesus Christ, according to the faith of [the elect of God][7]

~~God's elect~~, and [full knowledge] ~~the acknowledging~~ of [what is] the truth [that leads to][8] ~~which is after~~ godliness;

A servant (Greek *doulos* δοῦλος) is a slave in the regular use of the designation. In this verse, Paul calls himself a "slave of God" (*doulos theoy*, δοῦλος Θεοῦ; see appendix C). The meaning of *slave* is lost to our cultural paradigm. First century Christians understood the message of this form of address. From other statements by Paul, we understand that "Christ hath redeemed us" (Galatians 3:13), in that "he hath purchased with his own blood" (Acts 20:28). If we then are redeemed from the sinful condition we were found in, then we are purchased from Satan, that he has no more claim of ownership upon us; therefore we are truly 'bought and paid for.' Paul portrayed this perception in 1 Corinthians: "Know ye not that your body is the temple of the Holy Ghost which is in you, which ye have of God, and ye are not your own? For ye are bought with a price: therefore glorify God in your body, and in your spirit, which are God's" (1 Corinthians 6:19–20). We are all slaves in that we sold ourselves into slavery to the devil, and Jesus bought—or redeemed—us through the Atonement. Therefore, our slave status with God is actually our freedom—our liberation from sin and damnation. Complex though this expression is to us, slaves composed a considerable portion of the membership of the Church under

Roman law. The message had meaning to the target audience, and the Apostle Paul knew how to communicate as "Paul, a [slave] ~~servant~~ of God, and an apostle of Jesus Christ." A considerable portion of the Church membership were slaves—human merchandise. The usual interpretation of *servant* is paid service. However, Paul meant *slave*, in the literal sense.

Elect (Greek *eklektos* ἐκλεκτός) means "select, chosen out; by implication favorite."[9] This word also appears in a well-known verse: "many are called, but few are chosen."[10] Those accepting baptism and confirmation as members of the Church are the chosen of God—the elect.

Godliness (Greek *eysebia* εὐσέβεια) is "the doctrine which is according to godliness [and] signifies that which is consistent with godliness, in contrast to false teachings."[11] This word is translated *holiness* in Acts 3:12. Godliness is among the desirable Christian virtues tabulated by the prophet Peter: (1) knowledge, (2) temperance, (3) patience, (4) godliness,[12] (5) brotherly kindness, and (6) charity. "For if these things be in you, and abound, they make you that ye shall neither be barren nor unfruitful in the knowledge of our Lord Jesus Christ" (2 Peter 1:6–8). The virtue of godliness refers "to both belief and behavior. . . . it is not an either-or matter."[13]

[1:2] In hope of [life] eternal ~~life~~,[14] which [the never-lying] God ~~that cannot~~

lie, promised before [in times eternal] the world began;

Eternal life (Greek *zoes aionioy*, ζωῆς αἰωνίου) should read "life eternal" and is "the blessing of living in the presence of God and His Beloved Son forever."[15] Paul draws a parallel in the second part of the verse with *the world began* (Greek *chronon aionion*, χρόνων αἰωνίων), correctly translated as "time eternal."[16] This play on words carries forward into the next verse.

[1:3] But [at his appointed] hath in due times [revealed][17] manifested his [own] Word [in a proclamation][18] through preaching, [with] which [I am entrusted] is committed unto me [by] according to the [command] commandment of [our Savior] God our Saviour;

Due times (Greek *kairois idiois*, καιροῖς ἰδίοις) should be "times in its own," or, more meaningfully, "his own times" in English. The Greek word *time* (*kairos*, καιρός) in this verse conveys the sense of an occasion or event-time.[19] Specifically, the use of this word is in the plural. Perhaps he is alluding to the various dispensations of the gospel—Adam, Enoch, Noah, Abraham, Moses, and others. In the previous verse, the Greek word *time* (*chronon*, χρόνων) meant "a space of time," implying duration.[20] At a particular occasion (or event) in the eternities—prior to the here-and-now of mortality—this promise of life eternal was made. Long

before Adam and Eve entered the Garden eastward in Eden, a council was convened in the eternal realms. All the children of God attended this eternal council in the presence of "the never-lying God" (v. 2) where "our Savior" (v. 3) was "revealed" (v. 3) "in a proclamation" (v. 3) "promised [by God] before time eternal" (v. 2).

In the great pre-mortal council in heaven, God the Father presided and presented his plan for the mortality and eventual immortality of his children. In this his two principal associates were the pre-mortal Jesus (then known as Jehovah) and the pre-mortal Adam (then known as Michael). The roles of these two were related from the beginning, each having a crucial part to play in providing life to all other children of God—temporal life through Adam and eternal life through Christ.[21]

Manifested (Greek *phaneroo* φανερόω) means "to render apparent (literally or figuratively),"[22] in the context of manifesting by divine revelation, therefore implying something revealed through revelation.

Committed unto me is better translated as "I was entrusted." Paul is a senior member of the Quorum of the Twelve Apostles and has no inhibition referring to his entrusted apostolic calling.[23] He states that he has a divine mandate to proclaim the gospel of salvation and the knowledge of the reality of our Savior God ("Savior of us God"—*soteros emon theoy*, σωτῆρος ἡμῶν Θεοῦ).

[1:4] To Titus, [a loyal] ~~mine own~~ son[24] [in] ~~after the~~ ~~common~~ faith [we share]: Grace, mercy, and peace, from God the Father and [Master], ~~the Lord~~ Jesus Christ, [the] ~~our~~ Savior [of us].

The complex form of writing used by Paul renders the message of this sentence nebulous, not only in most translations, but also in the original Greek. Fortunately, one translation managed to capture the intent without taking too much liberty in the choice of words, "To Titus, my loyal child in the faith we share."[25]

Mine own son, even retranslated to "a loyal son," is still a peculiar statement. However, the following explanation is simple. "If a person taught Torah to someone else's child, it was as if the teacher had begotten that child. The language used refers to the disciple being born into the life to come through this act of discipling. Paul has simply substituted the gospel for Torah as the agent of regeneration."[26]

Appointment of Bishops (Titus 1:5–9)

In this passage, we read a similarity to 1 Timothy 3:1–13. The characteristics and qualities defined in both instances describe individuals who will assume authoritative leadership positions in the everyday affairs of local Church government. Paul well realized the influential position held by a bishop; no other Church leader works so closely with the problems that beset the membership.

Titus was himself an ecclesiastical leader. Through the course of the centuries, the office of bishop distanced itself from its intended position close to the congregation. A bishop who does not know each one of his flock cannot fulfill his calling effectively.

[1:5] For this [purpose] ~~cause~~ [I] left ~~I~~ thee in Crete, that thou shouldest [organize what remains to be done] ~~set in order the things that are wanting,~~ and ordain elders in [each] ~~every~~ city, as I had appointed thee:

Titus is not functioning in the capacity of a congregational bishop, but he *is* to ordain elders and bishops and is, therefore, the presiding priesthood leader over all the congregations on Crete Island.

Thou shouldest set in order (Greek *epidiorthoo* ἐπιδιορθόω) means "to straighten further, (figuratively) arrange additionally."[27] This does not imply that Titus was to rectify a defect. The instruction is to organize the Church in the usual manner: ordain elders and a bishop in each congregation. Titus previously received authorization to do this by apostolic authority. Jerome translated this word to Latin as *constituas*, meaning constitute or appoint[28] leadership in the congregations.

[1:6] If any be [without accusation] ~~blameless,~~ the husband of one wife, having [believing] ~~faithful~~ children

not accused of [debauchery] ~~riot~~ **or [undisciplined]** unruly.

In this verse, Paul specifically directs that one of the qualifications for ordination to the office of bishop is marriage to "one wife." The Hebrew patriarchs were not alone in the practice of polygamy. This has been part of human history and is yet culturally acceptable among many ethnic groups today—particularly Islam and even in Christian Africa. The message of this passage to Titus indicates that among the inhabitants of Crete, polygamy was culturally acceptable. Church membership was available to these polygamists; yet, ordination to the office of bishop was limited to the monogamist. In 1860, Presbyterian minister William Graham addressed the conversion to Christianity of modern polygamist families: "Many believers had several wives, as is often the case in heathenism at the present time, and one of the most difficult questions of modern missions is how to treat such cases. When a man and his two wives, for example, all at the same time become Christians and demand baptism and the Lord's Supper, what am I to do? There is no passage that I know of in the Word of God to guide me in the matter. . . . No text indeed has been more opposed and perverted in the history of the Church than this one."[29]

[1:7] For a bishop must be [irreproachable] ~~blameless~~, **as [a]** ~~the~~ **steward [of the household] of God; not [arrogant]** ~~selfwilled~~, **not [violent]** ~~soon angry~~, **not given to [drunkenness]** ~~wine~~,

[not quarrelsome] ~~no striker~~, **not [profiteering]** ~~given to filthy lucre;~~

Bishop (Greek *episkopos* ἐπίσκοπος) is a superintendent or overseer. The office of bishop is qualified in this chapter and in 1 Timothy 3. Fortunately, we have the definitions given by Paul, and unfortunately, no other apostolic records of the first century elucidate further. A distinct observation here is that "a person who cannot manage his own household certainly should not be entrusted with the task to manage the household of God."[30] This teaching receives endorsement in another comment made by Paul to Timothy. "For if a man know not how to rule his own house, how shall he take care of the Church of God?" (1 Timothy 3:5)

Blameless (Greek *anegkletos* ἀνέγκλητος) simply means irreproachable in the context of "that which cannot be called to account" for something through being innocent.[31]

Steward (Greek *oikonomos* οἰκονόμος) is lacking in meaning for our day. An *oikonomos* was "a house-distributor (i.e. manager), or overseer, (i.e. an employee in that capacity); by extension a fiscal agent (treasurer)."[32] Jesus used this position in reference to those called to positions of executive leadership in His Church. "The Lord said, 'Who then is that faithful and wise steward, whom his lord shall make ruler over his household?' "[33] Later Paul also uses *oikonomos* in reference to himself and the other apostles: "Let a man so account of us, as of the ministers of

Christ, and stewards of the [ordinances]³⁴ ~~mysteries~~ of God. Moreover it is required in stewards, that a man be found faithful" (1 Corinthians 4:1–2).

Self-willed (Greek *aythades* αὐθάδης) directly means self-pleasing or arrogant. This describes a person who, "dominated by self-interest, and inconsiderate of others, arrogantly asserts his own will. He asserts his own rights, regardless of the rights of others. With no motive at all, he is quick to act contrary to the feelings of others."³⁵

[1:8] But [hospitable] ~~a lover of hospitality~~, [benevolent] ~~a lover of good men~~, [self-controlled] ~~sober~~, [equitable] ~~just~~, holy, [self-disciplined,] temperate;

Sober (Greek *sophron* σώφρων) means "safe (sound) in mind, i.e. self-controlled (moderate as to opinion or passion)."³⁶ Luther translated this word to German as *besonnen*, meaning "prudent, circumspect, [or] discreet."³⁷

[1:9] [Clinging]³⁸ ~~Holding fast~~ [to] the faithful [Word] ~~word~~ [according to the teaching]³⁹ ~~as he hath been taught~~, that he may be able [both to exhort the] ~~by sound doctrine both to exhort~~ and to [expose those contradicting] ~~convince the gainsayers~~.

Word (Greek *logos* λόγος) simply means thought. However, in several instances—including this verse—Logos is a designation for Jesus the Christ and

is therefore capitalized as Word.⁴⁰ Jesus, as the Messiah, is the living form of the Word of God.

Convince (Greek *elegcho* ἐλέγχω) "means to rebuke another with the truth so that the person confesses, or at least is convicted of his sin. Although convicted, he may not be convinced" he is, however, exposed.⁴¹ This is the irrefutable evidence in a court of law that convicts the accused.

[1:10] For there are many [undisciplined with a mischievous word] ~~unruly and vain talkers~~ and [mind deluders] ~~deceivers~~, [especially] ~~specially~~ they of the circumcision:

Vain talkers (Greek *mataiologos* ματαιολόγος) means, "an idle (i.e. senseless or mischievous) talker."⁴² This is the only occurrence of this word in the New Testament, selected for the play on words that it provides. Notice that this word contains the ending *logos*, and therefore, *mataio logos* is the *mischievous* word and not the *incarnate* Word (*Logos* Λόγος), or *God* as explained in the previous verse.

Deceivers (Greek *phrenapates* φρεναπάτης) means a mind deluder. The message of this phrase is that mind deluders deliver the deluded word or counterfeit word, therefore offering a counterfeit salvation.

[1:11] [Whom you must muzzle] ~~Whose mouths must be stopped~~, who subvert whole [households] ~~houses~~,

teaching things ~~which~~ **they [have no right to teach]** ~~ought not,~~ **for [sordid gain][43]** ~~filthy lucre's sake.~~

Mouths must be stopped (Greek *episto-mizo* ἐπιστομίζω) in the English Authorized King James Version translates the same Greek word twice (*mouths* and *be stopped*) joined by the word *must*. The Greek word *epistomizo* means "to put something over the mouth"[44] in the sense of muzzling the mouth of a horse or mule. Luther captured this in German with *das Maul stopfen*,[45] meaning stop the mouth of an animal. English applies the same word for mouth to both human and animal. German has *Mund* for the human mouth and *Maul* for the animal mouth.[46] The direct English translation would be "muzzle the snout of the dissidents."

Who subvert whole houses (Greek οἵτινες [*oitines* **who**] ὅλους [*oloys* **whole**] οἴκους [*oikoys* **houses/families**] ἀνατρέπουσι [*anatrepoysi* **overturn/subvert**]).[47] Jerome translated this word to *subvertunt* in Latin. *Subverto* in Latin means to turn upside down, overthrow, ruin, and destroy.[48] In both Greek and Latin, the word describes the "sacking of a city" by a conquering army.[49] *Houses* literally refers to dwellings but also implies families; therefore, the translation of *households* preserves the double application. Knowing Paul and his methods of communication, we can also infer he meant more than just the individual households. The metaphor extends to the congregations of the

Church, referring to those who subvert whole congregations "of the household of Faith" (Galatians 6:10).

[1:12] One of themselves, even a prophet of their own said, The Cretians are [always] ~~alway~~ **liars, evil beasts, slow bellies.**

The Cretian appendage of perpetual lying was infamously preserved in the Greek language with the word *kretizein* (κρητίζειν), "to act like a Cretian."[50] Alternatively *kretizo* (κρητίζω), "speak like a Cretian," or *pros kretas* (πρὸς κρῆτας) "play the Cretian"—inferring that a person is lying.

The quote is from the philosopher Epimenides of Cnossus.[51] Paul surprisingly, though respectfully, designates Epimenides "a prophet of their own." The quote in this verse comes from lines in the poem "Cretica"; however, this work did not survive, and we only know of its existence through quotation and reference by others of a later period. The slander against the Cretians is because they lie when asked the whereabouts of the tomb of Zeus. If Zeus is an immortal god, then he is not dead and therefore has no tomb—so the Cretians must be liars![52]

> They fashioned a tomb for thee, O holy and high—
> The Cretians, always liars, evil beasts, slow bellies!
> But thou art not dead; thou art risen and alive forever,
> For in thee we live and move and have our being."[53]

Paul is not implying that all Cretians are liars, on the contrary, he instructed Titus to ordain elders in every congregation—therefore, many were good and circumspect. Generalities are a dangerous application.

[1:13] This witness is true. Wherefore [refute] ~~rebuke~~ them [rigorously] ~~sharply~~, that they may be [doctrinally[54] healthy] ~~sound~~ in the faith;

Sharply (Greek *apotomos* ἀποτόμως) means abruptly, "in a manner that cuts,"[55] and implies that the action is to be preemptive response—therefore, rigorous and uncompromising.

[1:14] Not giving heed to Jewish [myths] ~~fables~~, and commandments of men, [having turned away] ~~that turn~~ from the truth.

Jewish fables, in this verse, does not have reference to Mosaic Law or practices. The emphasis is on the Jewish interpolation of the law as practiced at the time. Pharisaic and other interpretations and expectations actually burdened the Law and, in many instances, were considered more important than the actual law. These myths were the commandments of men added to the law and never part of the expectations that God had for man upon the earth. The word *fables* (Greek *mythos* μῦθος) is providing an explanation for or of a truth "yet is unreal and fabricated."[56] This deception may be intentional or unintentional; either way, the explanation presented is not the

truth. One who recognizes the deception because they know the facts is in a position to expose the muthos—the myth.

[1:15] [Verily,[57] all things are] ~~Unto the~~ pure [to the] ~~all things are pure:~~[58] but [to those having been] ~~unto them that are~~ defiled and unbelieving[59] ~~is~~ nothing [is][60] pure; but [both][61] ~~even~~ their mind and conscience [have been] ~~is~~ defiled.[62]

That are defiled (Greek *miaino* μιαίνω) means both morally and ceremoniously contaminated. In respect of *mind* see the appendix A; for *conscience* see the appendix D.

[1:16] They profess [to] ~~that they~~ know God; but [by their] ~~in~~ works ~~they~~ deny him, being abominable, and [intractable] ~~disobedient~~, and [incapable of all] ~~unto every~~ good [works] ~~work reprobate~~.

COUNSEL TO MEMBERS (TITUS 2:1–8)

Members of the Church receive are entreated not to compromise the expectation of dignity and reverence. Paul iterates the primary concern for each portion of the congregation: elderly men to be temperate; elderly women refrain from gossip; younger women be good homemakers; younger men be sensible; and slaves be obedient and honest.

[2:1] But speak thou the things [consistent[63] with] which become sound doctrine:

[2:2] That the aged men be [temperate][64] sober, [solemn] grave, [prudent][65] temperate, sound in [the] faith, in charity, in [perseverance] patience.

Sober (Greek *nephaleos/-ios* νηφάλεος/-ιος) means "to abstain from wine or any substance that could cloud one's judgment"[66]—to be temperate. The usual interpretation of these verses about being "sober" and "not given to much wine" is to declare that alcoholism was a specific problem in Crete. This is true, but stopping at that conclusion would understate the fact that "alcoholism was a serious problem in the Greco-Roman world, especially amongst the elderly."[67] The issue is raised by Paul to emphasize "that drunkenness is incompatible with the Christian witness and lifestyle."[68]

Grave (Greek *semnos* σεμνός) means that a person "is well ordered in his earthly life and has a grace and dignity derived from his heavenly citizenship. There is something majestic and awe-inspiring about one who is *semnos*; he does not repel but invites and attracts."[69] This word conveys a sense of solemn respectability,[70] or "as becometh a sacred office."[71]

[2:3] [Likewise] the aged women likewise, that they be in behavior as becometh [venerable] holiness, not [devilish] false accusers, not [enslaved] given

to much wine,[72] [an upright instructor] teachers of good things;

Holiness (Greek *hieroprepes* ιεροπρεπής) is a unique word in the New Testament, and means reverent. The word derives from *hieros* (ιερός), meaning "sacred, consecrated to deity, pertaining to God;"[73] and devolves from *hireopoios* (ιεροποιός) a "performer of sacred rites."[74] Therefore, *hieroprepes* conveys the understanding of being "suited to a sacred character . . . consecrated to God,"[75] or "as becometh a sacred office."[76] The word expresses priestess qualities, formerly in relationship to pagan temples, now adapted to the priestess expectations of a Christian temple-endowed woman.

Given (Greek *douloo* δουλόω), in this instance, means "being enslaved to wine"[77]—by implication, more than addicted (*ekdotos* ἔκδοτος).[78] Paul compares the state of alcohol abuse to that of being deprived of liberty'[79] in mind and body.

[2:4] That they may [admonish] teach the [younger] young women to be sober,[80] to love their husbands, to love their children,

They may teach (Greek *sophronizo* σωφρονίζω) "denotes to be of sound mind."[81] *Teach* does not convey the full extent of the coaching and admonition the elderly women were to undertake for this assignment. More conveniently translated, *admonish* means "to advise of a fault, administer mild reproof."[82]

[2:5] To be discreet, chaste, [good house-keepers] ~~keepers at home, good,~~ [submissive][83] ~~obedient~~ to their own husbands, that the Word of God be not [exposed to reproach][84] ~~blasphemed.~~

Blasphemed (Greek *blasphemeo* βλασφημέω) means to speak impiously.[85] The aim of the concept here is at the Gentile observing the actions of Christians. Seeing bad examples, they may mock Christian morals in the sense of "blasphemy." However, the mocker would not be mocking Christianity directly but indirectly through the bad example of these young wives. The bad example, therefore, exposes the Christian Church to external reproach.

Read verses 3 to 5 as a single sentence. The exhortation for young wives to love their husband may refer to the circumstances of arranged marriages. In the culture of Crete, the marriage of a young wife possibly did not initiate through love but through parental appointment. Therefore, this exhortation may have more impact than our modern cultural interpretation would anticipate. "In many cases the most that was hoped for or exhorted in Greco-Roman ethics was respect and obedience, not love."[86]

[2:6] [Younger] ~~Young~~ men, likewise, [encourage] ~~exhort~~ to be [sensible][87] ~~sober minded.~~

Exhort (Greek *parakaleo* παρακαλέω) implies "to call to one's side" and "encourage with the intent to produce a particular effect."[88]

[2:7] In all things [showing] ~~shewing~~ thyself [an example] ~~a pattern~~ of good works: [with integrity] ~~in shewing uncorruptness,~~ [respectability][89] ~~gravity,~~ sincerity,

Shewing uncorruptness (Greek *adiaphthoria* ἀδιαφθορία) conveys the sense of integrity and honesty.[90]

[2:8] [Speaking] sound [incontestable words] ~~speech, that cannot be condemned;~~ that he that [opposes] ~~is of the contrary part~~ may be ashamed, having [nothing bad] ~~no evil thing~~ to say [about us] ~~of you.~~

That cannot be condemned (Greek *akatagnostos* ἀκατάγνωστος) means unblamable in the sense "that cannot be condemned."[91] This is the only incidence of this word in the New Testament. "The term *akatagnostos* comes from the courts" and means "incontestable."[92]

You (*ymon* ὑμῶν) appears in the Greek Textus Receptus version.[93] However, the Novum Testamentum Graece version has *us* (*hmon* ἡμῶν) instead of *you*.[94] *Us* is consistent with the exhortation in verse five above, "that the Word of God be not exposed to reproach."

COUNSEL TO SLAVES (TITUS 2:9–10)

We must preface the next two verses

with an observation. Verse nine commences with "exhort slaves" and not "exhort the masters of slaves." This is important as "this advice is to be given directly to the slaves . . . so the slave is treated as a person with a conscience capable of making moral, indeed Christian, decisions and responding accordingly."[95] The introduction of Christian belief into the Greco-Roman world raised human dignity to a level unknown to the culture of the time. Paul not only expects masters to consider their slaves as fellow-Christians, but the slaves were to divest themselves of a slavish mentality as well. They were to "submit unto their own masters in everything" (v.9). "Paul is calling for voluntary submission to something that these slaves by their individual willing could in no wise change."[96]

——————— ❧ ———————

[2:9] Exhort [slaves] ~~servants~~ to be [submissive] ~~obedient~~ unto their own masters [in everything], and to [be obliging,] ~~please them well in all things;~~ not [objecting] ~~answering again;~~

Regarding slaves and servants, see appendix C.

To be obedient (Greek *ypotasso* ὑποτάσσω) "was originally a Greek military term meaning to arrange (troop divisions) in a military fashion under the command of a leader. In nonmilitary use, it was a voluntary attitude of giving in, cooperating, assuming responsibility, and carrying a burden."[97] In this sense, Paul is exhorting the members who are slaves to be disciplined Christian soldiers. Take the slavery out of your work by changing your attitude towards your condition. See yourself as a free son or daughter of God, owing only allegiance to Him, and you are free.

Answering again (Greek *antilego* ἀντίλεγω) means speaking against, disputing, contradicting,[98] or objecting.[99] This is objecting or refuting to obey a command in the sense of military insubordination—noncompliance or disobedience. We should like to comprehend how the slaves on Crete Island implemented this apostolic counsel, and throughout Christendom across the following centuries until the eventual eradication of institutional slavery from Europe.

[2:10] Not [embezzling] ~~purloining~~, but [showing] ~~shewing~~ [perfect loyalty] ~~all good fidelity~~; that [in all things] they [make] ~~may adorn~~ the doctrine of God our Savior [more attractive] ~~in all things~~.[100]

Purloining (Greek *nosphizomai* νοσφίζομαι) means to sequestrate for oneself, or embezzle.[101] Apparently, slavery had resulted in the degradation of character, and the lack of motivation to improve one's ethics and morals. In such circumstances, "the comportment of a slave who was utterly devoted and scrupulously honest could not fail to provoke wonder"[102] from the external observer. The observation of a slave with commendable Christian ethical and moral character would generate missionary enquiry.

[2:11] For the grace of God [which][103] ~~that~~ **[hath appeared bringing]** ~~bringeth~~ **salvation [to all men]**[104] ~~hath appeared to all men,~~**[105]**

[2:12] Teaching us that, denying ungodliness and worldly lusts, we should live [prudently] ~~soberly~~**, righteously, and godly, in [the]** ~~this~~ **present [age]** ~~world;~~**[106]**

Soberly (Greek *sophronos* σωφρόνως) means with sound mind, prudent,[107] "and suggests the exercise of that self-restraint that governs all passions and desires, enabling the believer to become conformed to the mind of Christ."[108]

Godly (Greek *eysebos* εὐσεβῶς) means piously; however, *godly* must be retained because of the play on words in the verse—*ungodly* and *godly*. This emphasis continues into the next verse awaiting "the great God."

[2:13] [In expectation of] ~~Looking for~~ **that blessed hope, and the [manifestation of the glory]** ~~glorious appearing~~ **of [our]** ~~the~~ **great God and** ~~our~~ **Savior Jesus Christ;**

Savior (Greek *soter* σωτήρ) means deliverer. "The term *soter* was a common description in the Hellenistic world for a God who rescues, helps, heals, or in some way intervenes on behalf of someone or some group. Indeed, the most powerful deity in the Greek pantheon was called Zeus [Ζεύς or Ζωτὴρ] Soter, and his daughter Artemis was called Artemis Soteira [Ἀρτεμᾶς Σώτειρα]."[109] It is of particular note that Paul omits the use of Lord in this epistle and specifically uses other titles for the Divinity. We may conclude that the purpose of Paul was to displace Zeus and the Greek pantheon of gods with the Great God Jesus Savior (Soter)—the Christ/Messiah. The message of this dialog seems to indicate there must have been a significant issue with non-Jewish converts on Crete who did not disengage their former devotions to Zeus as their *Soter* (Savior). In many respects, many people are no different today. The only difference is that the modern Zeus is materialism.

[2:14] Who gave himself [on our behalf] ~~for us~~**, that he might redeem us from all iniquity, and purify unto himself a peculiar people,**[110] **zealous of good works.**

Iniquity (Greek *anomia* ἀνομία) "refers not to one living without law, but to one who acts contrary to law; where there is no law given there can be *hamarita* [ἁμαρτία—error] but not [iniquity] *anomia*."[111]

Peculiar (Greek *perioysios* περιούσιος) conveys the concept of being beyond or special.[112] "Peculiar in its old sense from *peculium*, the property which a son or slave was allowed to possess as his own."[113] This unusual word is used in the Greek Septuagint translation of the Old Testament[114] for the Hebrew word *segulla* (סְגֻלָּה). The English translation to peculiar people distorts the Hebrew meaning. A close preservation of the Hebrew concept is captured in another verse, "If ye will obey . . . and keep my covenant, then ye shall be a peculiar treasure unto me above all people" (Exodus 19:5). When God termed His chosen people *peculiar*, he intimates that they are a "carefully preserved and privately possessed people."[115]

[2:15] These things speak, and exhort, and rebuke with all authority. Let no man despise thee.[116]

SALVATION FOR ALL (TITUS 3:1–7)

The opening verses of this chapter are an injunction to all members of the Church to be subject to civil authority in worldly matters. There is also an exhortation to conduct themselves without contention toward one another—both in and out of the Church.

[3:1] Put them in mind to [willingly] be subject to [Imperial Rome] ~~principalities~~ and [authorities] ~~powers~~, to obey magistrates, [and] to be ready to [do any honorable kind of][117] ~~every good~~ work,

Principalities and powers (Greek *archais kai exoysiais*, ἀρχαῖς καὶ[118] ἐξουσίαις) is literally rulers and authorities. And since rulers *are* authorities, this translation can cause confusion. An alternative translation renders this as "the rulers who are in authority."[119] Paul teaches that the Cretians should be willing to obey civil authority—indicating opposition existed among the populace. Metellus Creticus subjugated Crete to Roman rule in 67 BC. Thereafter, "Crete was annexed to Cyrene [Libya] as a Roman Province, under a Proprætor, with the title of Proconsul. . . . Paul charges Titus to inculcate loyalty to the authority of Rome," and the Emperor Nero.[120]

[3:2] [Not to slander[121] any] ~~To speak evil of no~~ man, [not] to be [contentious][122] ~~no brawlers~~, but gentle, [demonstrating] ~~shewing all~~ meekness unto all men.

No brawlers (Greek *amachos* ἄμαχος) means not contentious,[123] not quarrelsome,[124] or without active participation in a fight.[125] Jerome curiously translated this word to *litigiosos* in Latin, appearing as litigious in a comparative English translation.[126] This interpretation would imply that Cretan contention consequently resulted in court litigation.

[3:3] For we ~~ourselves~~ also were [one-time senseless][127] ~~sometimes foolish~~, disobedient, deceived, [in slavery to] ~~serving~~ divers lusts and pleasures,

living in malice[128] and envy, hateful, and [persecuting] one another.

Serving (Greek *doyleia* δουλεία) refers to slavery, either in ceremony or figuratively in servitude.[129] See Appendix C. The English word *serving* no longer conveys the understanding of *servitude* as implied in this verse by Paul. An alternative modern translation to *servitude* in this instance could be addiction. Paul specifically says "addicted to diverse lusts and pleasures." The status and consequences of slavery extends beyond physical slavery. Many elect to subject themselves to the slavery of alcoholism, drug addiction, and sexual promiscuity.

THE CONDESCENSION OF GOD (TITUS 3:4–8)

The following verses speak of the hope that we have of the promise of eternal life—heirs of an eternal glory. Through the gospel saving ordinances of the baptism of regeneration and the confirmation of the Holy Ghost, a sanctifying process commenced. The works of righteousness qualify us, but it is the mercy of God through the epiphany of Jesus as the Christ and Savior that salvation comes.

[3:4] But [when] ~~after that~~ the [goodness][130] ~~kindness~~ and [condescension] ~~love~~ of God [appeared in the Epiphany of] our Savior ~~toward man appeared,~~

Love (Greek *philanthrophia* φιλανθρωπία), from which is derived the English word *philanthropy*,[131] this word is here expressing the benevolence of God for His children. Jerome translated this word to *humanitas* in Latin—from which we obtain the English word *humanitarian*. In the Greek text, the next word is "appeared" (Greek *epiphaino* ἐπιφαίνω)—unfortunately the two words are *decoupled* in most English translations.[132] This is the source of the English word *epiphany*, meaning "a bodily manifestation, as of a deity."[133]

The kindness that we extend to our fellowmen is termed *philanthropy*. This philanthropy is an expression of our condescending to mitigate the wretched circumstances of our fellow beings. When God mitigates our wretchedness with his philanthropy, this is termed "the condescension of God."[134]

This **epiphany of condescension** is in contrast to the claims to divinity of the Roman emperors. Satan knew that the time of the coming of Christ was at hand and probably inspired divining men to introduce the worship of human leaders. This started with the Julius Caesar cult and extended on through the Julio-Claudian emperors—Augustus (Divine), Caligula, and Claudius. Satan knew that the Living God would come upon the Earth; therefore, he sought to counter that epiphany with a cultic deception. In the cult of emperor worship, the populace considered the emperor as a savior and god of humanity. "The Living Christ was the only God in that era that made a real epiphany."[135] *God* and *he* in verses 4–6 refer to Heavenly Father who condescended to send his Son Jesus the Christ. Paul formulates his words to contrast the difference between "contemporary ruler-cults in order to assert more impressively the claims of Christianity."[136]

[3:5] [It was] not by works of righteousness which we have done, but according to his mercy[137] he [gave] ~~saved~~ us [salvation],[138] [through] ~~by~~ the washing of regeneration, and renewing of the Holy Ghost;

Not by works of righteousness is a direct reference to the Jewish focus on works of the Mosaic Law. This becomes clear when he adds **which we have done**—reminiscent of his Pharisaic background prior to conversion. No amount of personal pedantic righteousness on our part can produce salvation. Divine intervention and priesthood authority is necessary to make saving ordinances efficacious.

The washing of regeneration (Greek *loytroy paliggenesias*, λουτροῦ παλιγγενεσίας) is a term meaning the ordinance of baptism by immersion. This is a beautiful expression, and very descriptive. The word *washing* (*loytron* λουτρόν) means a bath or a wash basin. The word *regeneration* (*paliggenesia* παλιγγενεσία) appears only twice in the New Testament (Matthew 19:28; Titus 3:5). This word literally means a rebirth. Classical writers use this word in reference to the changes produced by

the return of spring.

Renewing (Greek *anakainosis* ἀνακαίνωσις) in this instance refers to a revival or restoration of what previously existed. This conveys the concept of a restoration to the fellowship we once enjoyed. On three other occasions, Paul referred to the gift of the Holy Ghost as "the earnest of our inheritance" back in the kingdom of God.[139]

[3:6] Which he [poured] ~~shed~~ on us abundantly through Jesus Christ our Savior;

[3:7] That [having been][140] ~~being~~ justified by [the] ~~his~~ grace [of that Holy[141] One[142]], we should be made heirs according to the hope of eternal life.

The doctrine of this verse was previously elucidated by Paul in his Epistle to the Romans, "The Spirit itself beareth witness with our spirit, that we are the children of God: And if children, then heirs; heirs of God, and joint-heirs with Christ; if so be that we suffer with him, that we may be also glorified together" (Romans 8:16–17).

[3:8] ~~This is a~~ Faithful [is the] saying, and [concerning] these things I [desire] ~~will~~ that thou affirm [confidently][143] ~~constantly,~~ that [those believing] ~~they which have believed~~ in God [should] ~~might~~ be [thoughtful] ~~careful~~ to maintain good works. These things are good and [advantageous] ~~profitable~~ unto men.

[3:9] But [turn away from] ~~avoid~~ foolish questions, and genealogies, and contentions, and [wrangling] ~~strivings~~ about the Law, for they are unprofitable and vain.[144]

Genealogies (Greek *genealogia* γενεαλογία) has reference to the claim to noble descent. Jesus encountered certain Jews asserting a purported hereditary superiority. He issued a stern rebuke at the time: "Think not to say within yourselves, we have Abraham to our father: for I say unto you, that God is able of these stones to raise up children unto Abraham" (Matthew 3:9; Luke 3:8). Even in Crete, certain Jews claimed Abrahamic, priestly, or rabbinical pedigree.[145]

The Bible is replete with genealogical tables, not only of royal lineage of Abraham, Moses, and Solomon, but also of Jesus. However, purported superiority, not genealogical records, is the issue in this remark by Paul. This is evidenced by his use of the word *vain* (Greek *mataios* μάταιος) to emphasize the vanity of their claims. Among certain Christian denominations, this can occur when a member of the congregation implies superiority or special status over a recent convert—also for vanity. Ancestral origins do not enhance our salvation options; rather, they increase the expectations placed upon the individual to excel even more.

[3:10] A [heretical] man, ~~that is an heretick~~ after the first and second admonition reject;[146]

Heretick (Greek *hairetikos* αἱρετικός) actually means a person "who chooses or adopts some particular course or opinion."[147] During the time of Paul, the word *heretic* (modern spelling) had a slightly more refined definition as a "freely chosen opinion."[148] In a theological sense, a heretic is someone "who is doctrinally aberrant,"[149] or "who entertains erroneous opinions in religion."[150] The more common choice of this theological word today is *apostate*.

Reject (Greek *paraiteomai* παραιτέομαι) means to depreciate or avoid. Luther translated this word in German as *meide* meaning "to avoid or keep clear of"; the French translated it to *éloigne*,[151] meaning "to distance." "There is nothing in this or the associated words which favors any definite reference to formal excommunication [Greek *ekballe* ἔκβαλλε]."[152]

[3:11] Knowing that he [who] ~~that~~ is such [has been] ~~is~~ subverted, and sinneth, being condemned of himself.

Subverted (Greek *ekstrepho* ἐκστρέφω) means "to turn inside out or upside down, invert."[153] In this verse, the Greek word is written as *exestraptai* (ἐξέστραπται), translating as "has been subverted," implying a process of change instigated from external influences.

[3:12] When I shall send Artemas unto thee, or Tychicus, be diligent to come unto me to Nicopolis: for I have determined there to winter.

Even now at the conclusion of this epistle, Paul is unsure who will actually deliver this letter. He indicates that he will send either Artemas (*Arteman* Ἀρτεμᾶν) or Tychicus (*Tychikon* Τυχικόν). The conclusion is that he selected Artemas over Tychicus, which we infer this from the words of 2 Timothy 4:12, "Tychicus have I sent to Ephesus."

[3:13] Bring Zenas,[154] the lawyer and Apollos[155] on their journey diligently, that nothing be [lacking to] ~~wanting unto~~ them.

[3:14] And let [our own] ~~ours~~ also learn to [take the lead in] ~~maintain~~ good works for necessary [wants] ~~uses~~, that they be not unfruitful.

[3:15] All ~~that are~~ with me salute thee. [Salute those who] ~~Greet them that~~ love us in the faith. Grace be with you all. Amen.[156]

[postscript] ~~It was~~ Written to Titus, [who was ordaining] ~~ordained~~ the first [bishops] ~~bishop~~ of the church [among] ~~of~~ the Cretians, from [somewhere in] ~~Nicopolis of~~ Macedonia [en route to Nicopolis].

This epistle postscript was not part of the original document but has since become a traditional part of the biblical legacy. The postscript suggests the composition of this epistle occurred at Nicopolis in Epirus—on the west coast of Greece. However, Paul indicated in 3:12 that he "will go" there for the winter, not that he was already there!

Titus

---❦---

EPILOGUE

There is no indication where Paul was in the Province of Macedonia when he dispatched this epistle to Titus. We also do not know who the courier was that delivered the epistle to Crete. The likelihood is that the courier traveled south through Greece and took ship from Athens or Corinth south to the Island of Crete. There is also no indication as to where Titus was on Crete Island. Traditions place him in several locations—depending upon local claims.

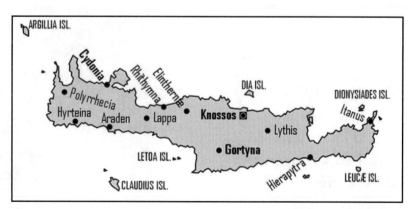

GRECO-ROMAN CRETE[157]

TITUS AND CRETE

Tradition records that Titus was born to Greek parents (Galatians 2:3) at Gortyna (Γορτυνα), Crete.[158] This would explain why Paul entrusted Titus with the assignment of organizing the Church in Crete. In the epistle from the Apostle Paul, we conclude that Titus received authorization to select, call, and ordain bishops (Titus 1:5–7) of the various Cretian congregations. We must therefore assume that Titus was already ordained to a more senior office than that of a bishop. Titus apparently only remained on Crete to conclude his assignment there, for we next hear of him at Rome a few months later.

CRETE IN RELATION TO MACEDONIA[159]

THE CIRCUMSTANCES OF PAUL

Paul's arrest occurred sometime after dispatching his letter to Titus. Classified as an imperial prisoner, Paul was transferred to the Mamertine Prison in Rome. During the final winter of despair, Paul awaited judgment from Emperor Nero. Working backward from comments in the Second Timothy letter, we know that Titus and

several others gathered to Paul at Rome. Once again, Paul could reecho his words to the Corinthians, "I had no rest in my spirit, because I found not Titus my brother" (2 Corinthians 2:13). Eventually "the coming of Titus" provided comfort to the apostles "that are cast down" (2 Corinthians 7:6). Finally, conditions became dangerous at Rome, and many left the city for safer locations. Paul wrote, "For Demas hath forsaken me, having loved this present world, and is departed unto Thessalonica; Crescens to Galatia, Titus unto Dalmatia" (2 Timothy 4:10). Respecting the departure of Titus for Dalmatia and the faltering faith of Demas, one author expressed the following consideration: "There is warrant for supposing that his visit to Dalmatia subsequent to the present epistle had anything in common with the state of Damas. The frequent and most honorable mention of his service in the epistles of Paul ought to leave no doubt of his fidelity and devotedness from first to last."[160]

WHAT HAPPENED TO TITUS?

The departure of Titus for Dalmatia is the last recorded event in the life of Titus. Crete tradition ascribes the office of the first bishop of Crete to him, both in the Catholic and Orthodox traditions of the office of bishop.[161] Titus is purported to have died the death of martyrdom and was "buried [at Gortyn] in Crete in his ninety-fourth year"[162]—AD 96 or 107. During the sixth century, the imposing Basilica of St. Titus (Agios Titos, Ἅγιος Τίτος) was erected to house the legendary mortal remains of Titus. However, the historical turbulence of the following centuries played a significant role in the transportation of the skull of St. Titus. A Saracen invasion in AD 524 severely damaged Gortyna and the basilica. Once again, the basilica suffered further damage in an earthquake in AD 670. Each time the basilica incurred damage, a restoration occurred, until the Saracen invasions in AD 824/832 necessitated the hiding of the St. Titus skull. In consequence of this invasion, the basilica was never reconstructed and has remained an archeological ruin ever since. The Saracens remained in control of Crete until repulsed by a counter invasion under the Byzantine general Nicephoros Phokas in AD 961. The St. Titus skull was eventually enshrined in a new church at Heraklion. Over the next seven centuries, the St. Titus skull remained housed at Heraklion, until the Ottoman invasion in 1699 necessitated the evacuation of the relic from Crete. The skull was enshrined in the Cathedral of St. Mark at Venice, Italy.[163]

The Cathedral of St. Mark at Venice is Roman Catholic, and Crete is under the jurisdiction of the Greek Orthodox Church. A protracted negotiation between the two churches over the return of the St. Titus skull to the Orthodox Church lasted from 1957 until 1966. On May 15, 1966, the legendary St. Titus skull returned to the Greek Orthodox Church. The skull is now enshrined at Heraklion, Crete.[164]

NOTES FOR TITUS

1. "Authoritative nomination" (Kelly, *The Pastoral Epistles of Paul*, 3:8).

2. Witherington, *Letters and Homilies for Hellenized Christians*, 90.

3. Ibid, 99.

4. Brown, *The Pastoral Epistles*, xix.

5. "The Roman names Titus and Lucanus are quite natural for a pair of brothers, though it is more likely that they were Greeks than Romans, and all the notices of them are satisfied by the hypothesis that they were Antiochene freemen" (Ibid.).

6. Strong, #80.

7. See Romans 8:17; 9:11; 11:5; Colossians 3:12; 1 Thessalonians 1:4; 1 Peter 1:2; and 2 Peter 1:10.

8. Today's New International Version. The literal words are "according to" (*tes kat*, τῆς κατ), but do not convey the message of the expression.

9. Strong, #1588.

10. See Matthew 22:14. Compare also "the chosen of God" (Luke 23:35).

11. Strong, #2150.

12. "Godliness . . . is seen as a combination of internal reverence or piety combined with right behavior" (Witherington, 99).

13. Ibid, 102.

14. "They who keep their second estate shall have glory added upon their heads for ever and ever" (Abraham 3:26).

15. M. Russel Ballard, "The Atonement and the Value of One Soul," *Ensign*, May 2004, 84; "If you keep my commandments and endure to the end you shall have eternal life, which gift is the greatest of all the gifts of God" (D&C 14:7); compare also, "Blessed are they who are faithful and endure, whether in life or in death, for they shall inherit eternal life" (D&C 50:5; cf. 51:19).

16. "Time eternal" softly translated to "ages ago" in The Revised Standard Version

17. New Revised Standard Version German translations correctly translate to *offenbart*, (i.e. *offenbarung*), meaning "revealed" as in revelation (Luther's Heilige Schrift des Alten und Neuen Testaments).

18. The Greek word *kerygma* (κήρυγμα) appears eight times in the New Testament and is consistently translated as "preaching." However, in this instance it relates to God and not the activity of Paul. The word was *proclaimed* by God and *preached* by Paul.

19. Strong, #2540.

20. Strong, #5550. Compare with 2 Timothy 1:9.

21. Jeffrey R. Holland, *Christ and the New Covenant*, 198; "God also revealed to Abraham the great doctrine of the eternal nature of time, of space, and of matter, and of the eternal existence of intelligences. He was shown a vision of the great

council in heaven, where the plan of salvation was presented and the Son of Man was selected to become the Savior of the world. At that council the Heavenly Father made a covenant with his children to give them eternal life on condition of their obedience to the Gospel" (Howard W. Hunter, *The Gospel Through the Ages*, 75).

22. Strong, #5319.

23. Witherington, 103.

24. The Greek word *teknon* (τέκνον) appears ninety-nine times in the New Testament and means "genuine, literal, or true child"; it is translated as "child" seventy-seven times, "daughter" once, and "son" twenty-one times (Strong, #5043). "Son" is retained in this verse since Titus is clearly intended, not just implied.

25. New Revised Standard Version.

26. Witherington, 105.

27. Strong, #1930.

28. Cassell's Latin Dictionary, 142, s.v. "constituo, constitus, constitutum."

29. Graham, *A Practical and Exegetical Commentary on the Epistle to Titus*, 31.

30. Witherington, 111; "A man that has a disobedient, disorderly, unruly, or riotous family, is not a proper man to be a bishop" (Graham, 32–33).

31. Strong, #410.

32. Strong, #3623.

33. See Luke 12:42. Compare also the parable of the unwise steward in Luke 16:1–8. *Oikonomos* is translated "chamberlain" in Romans 16:23, and "governors" in Galatians 4:2.

34. *Mysteries* (Greek *musterion* μυστήριον) relates to a secret "through the idea of silence imposed by initiation into religious rites" (Strong, #3466).

35. Strong, #829.

36. Strong, #4998.

37. Cassell's German–English/English–German Dictionary, 106, s.v. "besonnen."

38. Green's Literal Translation

39. Interlinear Hebrew-Greek-English Bible

40. 21st Century King James Version.

41. Strong, #1651.

42. Strong, #3151.

43. New Revised Standard Version; "For the love of money is the root of all evil: which while some coveted after, they have erred from the faith, and pierced themselves through with many sorrows" (1 Timothy 6:10).

44. Strong, #1993.

45. Luther's Heilige Schrift des Alten und Neuen Testaments.

46. A derogatory expression in German is to say to someone, *"Maul* halten" instead of *Mund* halten"—"Shut your mouth!"

47. Interlinear Hebrew-Greek-English Bible

48. Cassell's Latin Dictionary, 580, s.v. "subverto (subvorto)."

49. "The metaphor is taken from the military practice of besieging cities, and is here beautifully applied to houses, taken in the sense of families" (Graham, 52).

50. Horne, *Critical Study and Knowledge of the Holy Scriptures*, 4:558.

51. "The poet in question here is, according to Clement of Alexandria (Strom i.59.2), Epimenides of Cnossus, in Crete, a religious teacher and wonder-worker of the sixth century BC The line has at times been attributed to Callimachus (circa 305–circa 240 BC) because the first half occurs in his Hymn to Zeus, but it is probable that he was citing a phrase, which was already in proverbial use by his time. Paul calls Epimenides a prophet, thus emphasizing the authority of his judgment; but it is interesting to note that Plato, Aristotle, Cicero, and others speak of him as an inspired, prophetic man" (Kelly, *The Pastoral Epistles of Paul*, 3:235).

52. "The Cretians got a bad name by fabricating a tomb, which they pretended to be Jupiter [in Latin, Zeus in Greek], and it stuck to them for ages" (Graham, 59); "Diodorus Siculus, writing in the first century BC, tells us that Cretians believed that they were the original Greeks, having emerged from the earth itself (5.64.1). Cretians even claimed that the Olympian gods were in fact men and women of Crete elevated to the status of deities because of their benefactions that they did for humankind (5.64.2). It is not surprising, that they also believed that their island was the birthplace of most of the gods, particularly Zeus, who was thought to be buried there (5.77.3). This allowed Cretians even to claim that worship of the gods began on Crete" (Witherington, 87).

53. Barrs, *Apologetics & Understanding*, lesson 20; Callimachus of Cyrene in his Hymn I. to Zeus also makes a similar statement. The first two paragraphs of this work is quoted here: "At libations to Zeus what else should rather be sung than the god himself, mighty for ever, king for evermore, router of the Pelagonians, dealer of justice to the sons of Heaven? How shall we sing of him—as lord of Dicte or of Lycaeum? My soul is all in doubt, since debated is his birth. O Zeus, some say that thou wert born on the hills of Ida; others, O Zeus, say in Arcadia; did these or those, O Father lie? 'Cretians are ever liars.' Yea, a tomb, O Lord, for thee the Cretians builded; but thou didst not die, for thou art for ever" (Callimachus of Cyrene [300–240 BC], Hymn to Zeus, 1:1–9. Mair & Leob [translators], "Hymn 1 to Zeus," lines 1–9, Callimachus:

Hymns and Epigrams; Lycophron; Aratus).

54. Excuse the liberty taken here with an additional word to convey the intent.

55. Strong, #664.

56. Strong, #3454.

57. The Greek word *men* (μέν) was omitted in the Authorized King James Version. This word appears 194 times in the New Testament, and it translated "verily" fourteen times—predominantly in Hebrews and Romans. The Gospels consistently record Jesus uttering the word *amen* (ἀμήν)—correctly translated to English as "verily." Jesus spoke in Aramaic and Hebrew, and, therefore, actually said *ak* (אַךְ). Understanding that Paul is also from the same cultural background, we conclude that he intended the same meaning (Strong, #3303 s.v. "men"; #281 "amen"; Hebrew/Aramaic Dictionary, #389. s.v. "verily").

58. "Unto the pure, let all things be pure" (Faulring, 535).

59. This word means actively disbelieving the faith with repugnance that the individual formerly embraced.

60. Faulring, 535.

61. *Sowohl* in German means "both" or "as well" (Luther's Heilige Schrift des Alten und Neuen Testaments).

62. "To the pure—Those whose hearts are purified by faith this we allow. All things are pure—All kinds of meat; the Mosaic distinction between clean and unclean meats being now taken away. But to the defiled and unbelieving nothing is pure—The apostle joins defiled and unbelieving, to intimate that nothing can be clean without a true faith: for both the understanding and conscience, those leading powers of the soul, are polluted; consequently, so is the man and all he does" (Wesley, *Notes on the Bible*, Titus 1:15.

63. International Standard Version.

64. Temperate: "Observing moderation or self-control; specifically, by extension, not indulging in intoxicating liquors" (*Webster's Dictionary*, 1291, s.v. "temperate").

65. Prudent: "Habitually careful to avoid errors and in following the most politic and profitable course . . . exercising sound judgment" (Ibid., 1017, s.v. "prudent").

66. Strong, #3524.

67. Witherington, 134.

68. Ibid., 135.

69. Strong, #4586.

70. Pervanoglu, 700, s.v. "σεμνός."

71. Humphreys , 218.

72. Compare Romans 6:16; 2 Peter 2:19.

73. Strong, #2413. An intimation of this meaning appears in the following translation: "The aged women, in like manner, in holy attire" (Douay-Rheims Version).

74. Pervanoglu, 362, s.v. "ἱεροποιός."

75. Strong, #2412.

76. Humphreys, 218.

77. Strong, #1402.

78. Jannaris, *A Concise Dictionary of the English and Modern Greek Languages*, 6, s.v. "addicted ἔκδοτος."

79. Groves, Greek and English Dictionary, 159, s.v. "Δουλόω."

80. These words are not in the Greek text or in other translations.

81. Strong, #4994.

82. *Webster's Dictionary*, 20, s.v. "admonish."

83. Weymouth, New Testament in Modern Speech, 3rd edition.

84. Ibid.

85. Strong, #987.

86. Witherington, 133.

87. New American Standard Bible.

88. Strong, #3870.

89. Luther's Heilige Schrift des Alten und Neuen Testaments, *mit Ehrbarkeit*, meaning, "respectability."

90. Groves, 10, s.v. "ἀδικαφθορία."

91. Strong, #176.

92. Witherington, 140.

93. Interlinear Hebrew-Greek-English Bible

94. Aland, *The Greek New Testament.*

95. Witherington, 141.

96. Ibid.

97. Strong, #5293.

98. Strong, #483.

99. Pervanoglu, 72, s.v. "ἀντιλέω."

100. Compare the following version: "Or steal from them. Instead, they are to show complete and perfect loyalty, so that in every way they may make the teaching about God our Savior more attractive" (International Standard Version, v.1.4.8.).

101. Groves, 408, s.v. "Νοσφίζω."

102. Murphy-O'Connor, "Community and Apostolate: Reflections on 1 Timothy 2:1–7," *The Bible Today*, October 1973, 1263.

103. Faulring, 535.

104. Ibid.

105. New American Standard Bible.

106. One author made the simple equation respecting the message of these verses, "Let doctrine inspire duty" (Humphreys, 223).

107. Pervanoglu, 772, s.v. "σωφρόνως."

108. Strong, #4996.

109. Witherington, 103.

110. Compare Exodus 19:5; Deuteronomy 14:12; 26:18; 1 Peter 2:9; D&C 60:4.

111. Strong, #458.

112. Strong, #4041.

113. Humphreys, 226. Compare a similar expression in the Old Testament: "If ye will obey my voice indeed, and keep my covenant, then ye shall be a peculiar treasure unto me above all people: for all the earth is mine" (Exodus 19:5).

114. Brenton, *The Septuagint with Apocrypha: Greek and English*, 250, Deuteronomy 14:2 (περιούσιον).

115. Strong, #5459.

116. Alternatively translated, "Let no one look down on you" (New Revised Standard Version).

117. International Standard Version 1.4.8.

118. Several authorities "omit καὶ [kai] here: perhaps ἀρχαῖς [archais] may be a gloss" (Wordsworth, 3:1).

119. New Testament in Modern Speech, 3rd edition; "The difference between the two words is that the former expresses a governing *de facto*, whether also *de jure* or not, the latter a governing *de jure*, a duly constituted authority" (Humphreys, 229).

120. Wordsworth, 3:1; "If the Apostle had been merely a secular teacher of human knowledge, or a champion of a human sect, and had not been endued with divine wisdom, he would not have ventured to inculcate these lessons of subordination to a foreign authority, now wielded by Nero; but he would either have been silent on the subject, or, perhaps, have flattered the vanity and inflamed the passions of the Cretians, and have courted their favor, by following the example of those teachers, who excited them to throw off the yoke of Roman rule, and to recover their ancient Liberty" (Wordsworth, 3:1).

121. Translated *lastern* in German (Luther's Heilige Schrift des Alten und Neuen Testaments), and other German and Dutch translations.

122. Darby Bible Translation.

123. Strong, #269.

124. Groves, 30, s.v. "ἄμαχος."

125. Benseler, *Griechisch-Deutsches Schul-Wörterbuch*, 39, "ἄμαχος."

126. Douay-Rheims Version.

127. Green's Literal Translation; Groves, 51, s.v. "ανόητος."

128. "Malice is the evil habit of mind which manifests itself in . . . evil and harm-doing. . . . It comes between a state of envy and the actual working of ill to a neighbor" (Humphreys, 231).

129. Groves, 159, s.v. "δουλεία."

130. Pervanoglu, 899, s.v. "χρηστότης."

131. Groves, 588, s.v. "φιλανδρωπία"; Philanthropy is the "disposition or effort to promote the happiness or social elevation of mankind" (*Webster's Dictionary*, 948, s.v. "philanthropy").

132. Preserved in the Latin translation, "cum autem benignitas et humanitas apparuit salvatoris nostri Dei" (Jerome, Biblia Sacra Versio Vulgata).

133. *Webster's Dictionary*, 427, s.v. "epiphany."

134. "Condescension" see 1 Nephi 11:16, 26; 2 Nephi 4:26; 9:53; Jacob 4:7; "The condescension of God (meaning the Father) consists in the fact that though he is an exalted, perfected, glorified Personage, he became the personal

and literal Father of a mortal Off-spring born of mortal woman. And the condescension of God (mean-ing the Son) consists in the fact that though he himself is the Lord Omnipotent, the very Being who created the earth and all things that in it are, yet being born of mortal woman, he submitted to all the trials of mortality, suffer-ing 'temptations, and pain of body, hunger, thirst, and fatigue, even more than man can suffer, except it be unto death' (Mosiah 3:5–8), finally being put to death in a most ignominious manner" (McConkie, *Mormon Doctrine*, 155).

135. Witherington, 157.

136. Kelly, *The Pastoral Epistles of Paul*, 3:251.

137. Eleos (ἔλεος) is consistently trans-lated "mercy" all twenty-eight times in our New Testament. However, the word can also be translated "compassion" and retain its mean-ing.

138. "His kindness contemplates all, while it is valid only for those who believe" (Kelly, 3:98).

139. (I) "After that ye believed, ye were sealed with that Holy Spirit of promise, which is the earnest of our inheritance until the redemp-tion" (Ephesians 1:13–14). (II) "Now he which stablisheth us with you in Christ, and hath anointed us, is God; who hath also sealed us, and given the earnest of the Spirit in our hearts" (2 Corinthi-ans 1:21–22). (III) "God, who also hath given unto us the earnest of the Spirit" (2 Corinthians 5:5).

140. Young's Literal Translation Past tense in a future sense—as though the eternal judgment had already taken place.

141. The word "holy" is not in the Greek text, but is added here to qualify the use of "One" as a spe-cific reference or title for God.

142. Green's Literal Translation.

143. New American Standard Bible.

144. "Vain is added to intensify unprof-itable; from its use here then it should mean vain in its results and be opposed to good, which is seen to be good" (Humphreys, 236–237). Interpret the word "vain" as something "from which nothing of true value results" (Ellicott, *Com-mentary on the Pastoral Epistles*, 197).

145. "Judaism got itself entangled in a new Platonism. Those endless gene-alogies, which had always charmed the Israelite as he traced his own pedigree from Seth, and Abra-ham, and David, were now begin-ning to soar into higher heights of speculation, till at length they dealt with angelic relationships and lost themselves in interminable mazes of celestial emanations" (Vaughan, *The Wholesome Words of Jesus Christ*, 7).

146. Liberally translated into modern

English as "Warn divisive people once, and then warn them a second time. After that, have nothing to do with them" (Today's New International Version).

147. Groves, 17, s.v. "Αἱρετικός."

148. Cheyne, *Encyclopædia Biblica*, *2:2019*, s.v. "heresy, heretic, sect."

149. Witherington, 163.

150. Reid, *A Dictionary of the English Language*, 197.

151. Nouvelle Édition de Genève.

152. Ellicott, *Commentary on the Pastoral Epistles*, 198.

153. Groves, 187, s.v. "ἐκστρέφω."

154. Zenas (Greek *Zenas* Ζηνᾶς) means "Zeus given" and is the Greek form for the Latin name *Zenodorus* derived from "of Zeus" (Greek *Zeus* Ζεύς).

155. Apollos (Ἀπολλώς), the name of the primary Greek god.

156. Not all Greek manuscripts include the "Amen" at the end of this verse.

157. Map by the author William V. Blacoe, 2009.

158. Ibid.

159. "Apostle Titus," *Orthodox Messenger* 8, July/August 1997.

160. Kelly, 3:4.

161. "Timothy [is] stated to have been the first bishop appointed to the See of Ephesus, as was Titus to the churches of Crete" (Eusebius, *Historæ Ecclesiastæ—The History of the Church*, 3:4, 67).

162. Huther, *Critical and Exegetical Handbook to the Epistles to Timothy and Titus*, 5.

163. "St. Titus," Saints & Angels. *Catholic Online*. http://www.catholic.org/saints/saint.php?saint_id=2352

164. "Apostle Titus," *Orthodox Messenger*.

Part Four

PHILEMON

Philemon

❧

PROLOGUE

Following a very adventurous and life-threatening maritime journey from Caesarea to Rome, Luke recorded that "Paul dwelt two whole years in his own hired house [at Rome], and received all [visitors] that came in unto him, preaching the Kingdom of God, and teaching those things which concern the Lord Jesus Christ, with all confidence, no man forbidding him" (The Acts 28:30–31).

During this time Paul encountered a man named Onesimus (Greek *Onesimos* Ὀνήσιμος)—which is interpreted to mean useful. With the passing of several months, a great bond of friendship developed between Paul and Onesimus. Paul even goes so far as to refer to Onesimus as "my son . . . whom I have begotten in my bonds" (Philemon 10). However, this friendship is not without extraneous complications: Onesimus is a runaway slave (Latin *fugitivus*) from the household of his

dear friends, Philemon and Apphia, who live at Colossae in the province of Asia Minor.[1]

In the summer of AD 62, Paul is now about fifty-six years of age. This is the second year of his house arrest at Rome while waiting for the conclusion of his case before the imperial court. Paul will continue under these circumstances until acquitted in a few months. Being a man of uncompromising integrity, Paul elects to surrender his compassionate endorsement of retaining Onesimus with him at Rome and returns the runaway slave to his rightful and lawful master. It must be understood that before Paul could write this letter, Onesimus must have already accepted his return to his masters, Philemon and Apphia—"the unheard-of act of voluntary returning to servitude."[2] This young man became a Christian not only in name, but also in nature. He must already "have experienced a change of heart" (Alma 5:26). Therefore, Paul elects to equip Onesimus with a letter of introduction to Philemon and Apphia. In effect, Paul composes a mercy plea respecting the misdemeanors of Onesimus.

We must understand that irrespective of what Paul should write, it is Onesimus who has to make the personal commitment to undertake the journey back to Colossae and surrender to the will and judgments of Philemon. A *fugitivus* slave is not an easy life to live. A Latin maxim of the time stated: "*Servile caput nullum jus habet*"[3]—meaning, the slave has no right! In reality, Philemon could do whatever he liked

ONESIMUS MOSAIC[5]

with his disobedient fugitivus Onesimus—kill, torture, or emancipate him at will. Not only the purpose, but also the emotional content of this letter will greatly affect the physical wellbeing and future of Onesimus. Just as Paul had been a *fugitivus* from the Law, his Lord, and the gospel; so

too was Onesimus a *fugitivus* from the law and his masters, Philemon and Apphia. The Lord forgave Paul; would Philemon forgive Onesimus?

"It is sometimes an awkward thing to become a Christian. For you feel impelled to do the right thing, which is so often a very unpleasant thing. The religion, which Paul taught, was very practical. Onesimus must not merely tell God that he is sorry, he must go back to his master and confess and take his punishment and make what restitution he can."[4]

ONESIMUS

Onesimus is not an uneducated peasant slave of agrarian labor. On the contrary, he is apparently well educated and therefore belonged to the household staff. Onesimus was an educated slave as ascertained from the postscript of the epistle, which indicates that Onesimus was scribe to Paul in the actual writing of this letter to Philemon: "Written from Rome to Philemon, by Onesimus, a servant" (Philemon epistle postscript). In respect of the Colossian epistle, the postscript indicates that Onesimus was co-scribe with Tychus in penning the epistle: "Written from Rome to the Colossians by Tychius and Onesimus" (Colossians epistle postscript).

How the epistle to Philemon survived

to be included within the canon of the Holy Bible is somewhat of a mystery.[6] We may presume that the teaching value of this letter enabled its preservation as an example and as strength to those who found themselves in the institution of bondage and slavery to others. Since the Empire of Rome was wholly given over to the enslavement of so many men, women, and children, we can believe that this—the shortest epistle of Paul—meant more to that portion of the membership of the Church who were in the same circumstances as Onesimus than any other of Paul's works. This letter must have offered consolation to those who endured the feudal system and later the enslavement of a transported Negro population in the Americas. In such circumstances, this letter may well have served as a standard of faith in the Gospel of Jesus Christ for that oppressed portion of the human family. By this reasoning, we may say that divine intervention dictated, guided, preserved, and ensured the inclusion of this morsel of hope within the canon of the Holy Bible.

Paul had a close friendship with Philemon and his family; he refers to him as his "brother" in a more personal tone than merely the Christian usage of brotherhood (Philemon 1:1–2, 20). Apparently, the family consisted of Philemon, his wife Apphia and their son, Archippus (Philemon 2). This son, Archippus, was currently serving as bishop to the Colossian congregation (Colossians 4:16–17). We say "bishop" since Paul refers to Archippus as a "fellow-soldier" (Philemon 1:2)—though it might also mean full-time missionary service. One tradition holds that Philemon, his wife Apphia,[7] their son Archippus,[8] and Onesimus,[9] all suffered death under the later Roman persecutions.[10]

Timothy, Tychius, and Onesimus depart from Rome south on the Via Appia, crossing the Adriatic Sea and traversing Greece, possibly calling at Thessalonica and Philippi en route to Asia Minor. The whole journey from Rome to Colossae is a distance of about 1,600 km. Eventually they arrive at Ephesus and deliver the epistle to the Bishop of the Ephesian congregation. A short time later, Onesimus departs in company with Tychius and proceeds inland up the Lycus Valley: a very lonely journey, not without fear and trepidation. All the while, Paul is back in Rome, doubtless in prayerful concern for the welfare of the young man he so dearly loves.

Perhaps they first delivered the epistle to the Loadiceans, where

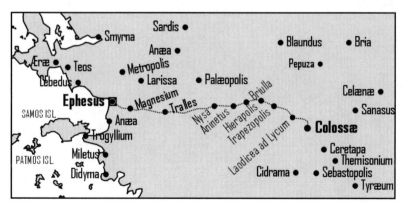

COLOSSAE IN RELATION TO EPHESUS[12]

Onesimus would be known by name and by condition. He continued the final phase of the journey across the valley and up the hill to Colossae. He would pass through the village to the villa of Philemon and deliver the epistle to the bishop of the Colossian congregation, and the private letter to Philemon. This one single sheet of papyrus was filled with love and hope for freedom. "The keynote of all is love. Love beseeches when it might command."[11] In the Colossian letter we read the tender words: "For I bear him record, that he [Onesimus] hath a great zeal for you, and them that are in Laodicea, and them in Hierapolis" (Colossians 4:13).

Philemon

COMMENTARY

Each of the letters of the New Testament are designated an epistle. In the first century, a letter in Latin was an *epistula* or *epistola*, and an *epistole* (ἐπιστολή) in Greek. In this instance, the letter to Philemon is so short that it is only a "note" or a "little letter," and therefore, an *epistolium* in Latin or an *epistolion* (ἐπιστόλιον) in Greek.[13]

[1:1] Paul, a prisoner [for] of Jesus Christ, and Timothy [thy] our brother, unto Philemon our dearly [the] beloved, and [fellow-worker] fellowlabourer,

In the majority of letters from Paul, he introduces himself in verse one as an apostle. Considering the purpose and tone of this letter, we soon discover that Paul somewhat endeavors to communicate on the level of private citizen and not with apostolic authority. "Apostolic authority

will not go half so far as personal influence in this case. So he drops all reference to it, and, instead, lets Philemon hear the fetters jangling on his limbs—a more powerful plea."[14] The intention of the declaration "a prisoner" is to draw sympathy from Philemon for Paul prior to introducing the primary purpose of writing this letter. Paul was "a prisoner" at Rome for preaching the gospel—or Word (*Logos* Λόγος)—of Jesus Christ.

Fellowlaborer (Greek *sunergos* συνεργός)

is more familiar to us as fellow-worker. This is the Greek word from which we derived the English word *synergy*—meaning "combined and correlated force; united action."[15] Paul indicates that they worked so well together that they created a synergy. This means that collectively they achieved more than the sum of their individual efforts. The same is applicable to a missionary companionship today.

[1:2] **And to ~~our beloved~~ Apphia [our beloved sister][16], and [to] Archippus[17] our fellow-soldier, and to the [congregation *meeting*][18] ~~church~~ in thy house:**

It is of particular consequence that Paul in his introduction to Philemon (Φιλήμων) includes Apphia (Ἀπφία) in the address of this letter. "In the house at Colossae there was a Christian wife by the side of a Christian husband."[19] Since the subject of this letter is the fugitivus slave Onesimus, it is understandable. As wife of Philemon, Apphia would have exercised household stewardship over the slaves. Paul therefore includes an indirect mercy plea for Onesimus to Apphia for her consideration. According to protocol, Paul must direct the specific plea to Philemon and only indirectly to his wife Apphia.

From the Colossian epistle, we learn that Archippus (*Archippo* Ἀρχίππῳ) is the bishop of the congregation at Colossae; wherein Paul wrote, "And say to Archippus, Take heed to the ministry which thou hast received in the Lord, that thou fulfill it" (Colossians 4:17). As bishop of the congregation, Archippus is minister to his father Philemon. Paul may have been seeking to invite Archippus to add his ecclesiastical voice in counsel to his father respecting the mercy plea.

Fellow-soldier (Greek *sustratiotes* συστρατιώτης) is a military term meaning "co-campaigner." This means that like Paul, Archippus is serving in the army of God. See appendix B, "The Imperial Roman Army."

We are to understand by this statement that the congregation of the church (Greek *ekklesia* ἐκκλησία) of the saints at Colossae met for worship services in the home of Philemon. The Jews had their synagogue and the worshippers of the pantheon of gods had their temples; however, the Christians had not yet established a chapel. It is therefore postulated that the house was a villa, spacious enough to accommodate the family in comfort and include slave quarters—as implied later in respect to the returning household slave Onesimus.

[1:3] **Grace to you, and peace, from God [the] ~~our~~ Father[20] [of us] and ~~the Lord~~ Jesus Christ [our Lord].**

The greeting extended by Paul refers to two members of the Godhead by name and by title: from God, who is our Heavenly Father, and Jesus, who is Lord and the Christ (Greek *Christos* Χριστός, Hebrew Mashiach מָשִׁיחַ).

[1:4] I thank my God, [always] making mention of thee ~~always~~ in my prayers,

Paul indicates that he prays for the welfare of his friend Philemon.[21] Considering that he is awaiting trial before the Imperial court at Rome, he is the one in need of the prayers of the saints; yet his thoughts are for the welfare of his friend.

[1:5] Hearing[22] of [the faith that thou hast in the Lord Jesus, and] thy love ~~and faith, which thou hast toward the Lord Jesus, and~~ [for] ~~toward~~ all saints;[23]

The two words here translated **toward** are not the same in Greek. **Toward the Lord** is *pros* (πρός) indicating "forward to" as in direction or pertaining to something.[24] **Toward all saints** is *eis* (εἰς) "indicating the point reached or entered, of place, time, or figuratively purpose."[25]

Saints (Greek *agios* ἅγιος) means "sacred (physically pure, morally blameless or religious, ceremoniously consecrated) . . . separated from sin and therefore consecrated to God."[26] The Greek word *agios* may have become the Christian expression of the Old Testament Hebrew designation *qadowsh* (קָדוֹשׁ), likewise meaning sacred. There is an equation of *sacredness* with *sanctity* in another verse: "For I am [Jehovah] ~~the Lord~~ your God: ye shall therefore sanctify yourselves, and ye shall be holy; for I am holy" (Leviticus 11:44; cf. Leviticus 20:26; Numbers 6:8; Deuteronomy 6:8; 14:2, 21).

[1:6] [So] that the [sharing] ~~communication~~ of thy faith may [be effective, when you recognize all that is] ~~become effectual by the acknowledging of every~~ good [which ye have] ~~thing which is in you~~ in Christ Jesus.[27]

The replacement of *communication* with a more appropriate translation of *sharing* raises the question of whether Paul meant not only "the sharing of Philemon's faith" but also his "sharing of temporal necessities because of his faith." In addressing the values of faith and love in the character of Philemon and Apphia in this and previous verses, Paul is highlighting the premise by which they will be making judgment on the Onesimus mercy plea.

[1:7] For we have [much grace] ~~great joy~~ and [encouragement] ~~consolation~~ in thy love, because [brother,] the [inward affection] ~~bowels~~ of the saints [have been] ~~are~~ refreshed by thee, ~~brother.~~

Joy (Greek *charis* χάρις) means graciousness. "Grace indicates favor on the part of the giver, and thanks on the part of the receiver. . . . Grace removes guilt; mercy removes misery."[28]

Bowels (Greek *splagchnon* σπλάγχνον) was a Jewish idiom symbolizing pity or sympathy, "as the seat of human tender affections."[29] The word is comparatively translated "inward affection" in 2 Corinthians 7:15.

THE CASE FOR ONESIMUS (PHILEMON 1:8–21)

With the prologue and felicitations concluded, Paul now turns to the primary reason for writing to Philemon.

AN APPEAL RATHER THAN A COMMAND

Verses 8 and 9 must be read together to comprehend that Paul elects to forego the option of an apostolic order and instead makes an appeal to Philemon on the basis of love as he entreats for the welfare of Onesimus. Paul seeks a tactful approach to introduce the object of this letter. "So much persuading and sanctified ingenuity does it sometimes take to induce good men to do plain duties which may be unwelcome."[30]

The hard approach, "I could order you" (v.8), is followed immediately by the soft approach, "instead I entreat you" (v.9). Compare the following translation, "And so, though I might in the name of Christ give you orders to do what is right, still, because of love, in place of an order, I make a request to you."[31]

—————— ❧ ——————

[1:8] [And so] ~~Wherefore,~~ [although in Christ] ~~though~~ I might be [direct] ~~much bold in Christ~~ to [command] ~~enjoin~~ thee [to do] that which [ought to be done] ~~is convenient,~~

Wherefore (Greek *dio* διό) means *consequently* and implies "and so to the point,"

"for this reason," or "for that reason." "The careful limits put to apostolic authority here deserve notice. . . . He had no authority in himself, but he has 'in Christ.' "[32] Paul is now turning attention to the object of this letter to Philemon. He lays it clear that he does not intend to use his apostolic authority to decree, but to plea for Onesimus.

That which is convenient (Greek *aneko* ἀνήκω) "means primarily 'to have arrived at, reached to, pertained to,' came to denote 'what is due to a person, one's duty, what is befitting.' "[33]

[1:9] [Rather because of love] ~~Yet for love's sake~~ I rather [entreat] ~~beseech~~ thee, being such an one as Paul the [ambassador][34] ~~aged,~~ and now also [constrained] ~~a prisoner~~ of Jesus Christ.[35]

Aged (Greek *presbytes* πρεσβύτης) refers to an old man, though in this instance it is possibly an erroneous transcription of *presbeytes* (πρεσβευτής) which is an ambassador, minister, or envoy.[36] Considering the content of the letter, the translation of *ambassador* is more meaningful, restoring the letter »ε« into the Greek word above.

Prisoner of Jesus Christ is an unusual statement in the light of gospel liberty. Paul is currently living under house arrest at Rome pending the judicial decision of the Imperial court. If he were a prisoner, in the true meaning of the word, he would be incarcerated (*prison* in Latin is *carcer*) in the

Mamertine Prison (Latin *Tullianum*). It is therefore concluded that Paul had a specific intent when he used the Greek word *desmios* (δέσμιος), which means "a binding"—though it "denotes 'a prisoner in bonds.' "[37] In many respects, the house arrest at Rome was an enforced sabbatical upon the unyielding ministerial commitment of Paul. He was constrained in his movements but not in his capacity.[38] Paul is making a stirring sympathetic appeal for the sake of love rather than duty and compulsion—"Love naturally beseeches, and does not order."[39]

THE ONESIMUS MANUMISSION PLEA (PHILEMON 1:10–14)

These verses are the core concern of the letter. Paul provided ample introduction and now comes to the main point—the manumission of the slave. The previous verses highlighted the relationship between Paul and Philemon. The following verses highlight the relationships between Paul and Onesimus, then between Onesimus and Philemon.

[1:10] I [entreat] ~~beseech~~ thee [concerning] ~~for~~ my son Onesimus, whom I have [become the father of] ~~begotten~~ in my [imprisonment] ~~bonds~~:

Take note that Paul does not introduce Onesimus into the letter in the role of a runaway slave, but as a son. Paul is presenting the change of perspective that for him the status of Onesimus has already changed from bond to free, from servant to brother. He invites Philemon and Apphia to endorse a proposal that is already a fact from his perspective. Several years earlier Paul had composed the following words to the Corinthians, "For he that is called in the Lord being a [slave] ~~servant~~, is the Lord's freeman: likewise also he that is called, being free, is Christ's [slave] ~~servant~~" (1 Corinthians 7:22).

Bonds (Greek *desmos* δεσμός) refers to a band or shackle by which a prisoner is constrained. As mentioned in the previous verse, Paul was not in prison rather but under house arrest. However, while under house arrest, he was not at liberty to leave the premises. The authorities would have assigned a soldier to guard him—day and night. The general interpretation is that Paul had a chain at the ankle or the wrist extending to the soldier or mounted to the wall. This, however, is not consistent with the condition of house arrest practiced by the Romans. Once again, Paul is apparently abusing a figure of speech for his own purpose. Only one reputable translation apparently recognized this context and translated this verse accordingly, "I am appealing to you for my child, Onesimus, whose father I have become during my imprisonment."[40]

[1:11] [Formerly he] ~~Which in time past~~ was [useless] to thee ~~unprofitable~~, but now [is useful] ~~profitable~~ to thee and to me:

Unprofitable (Greek *achrestos* ἄχρηστος) means unprofitable in the sense of being useless. If Onesimus had been unprofitable in the sense of being hurtful or aggressive, then he would have used the word *achreios* (ἀχρεῖος) used in reference to the parable of the unprofitable servant in Matthew 25:30.

Profitable (Greek *euchrestos* εὔχρηστος) means useful or easy to make use of.[41] Paul used this word in a comparative context elsewhere, "Only Luke is with me. Take Mark, and bring him with thee: for he is [useful] profitable [*euchrestos* εὔχρηστος] to me for the ministry" (2 Timothy 4:11).

There is a play on words in Greek that is not evident in English in this verse. The name Onesimus (*Onesimos* Ὀνήσιμος) also means "profitable" or "useful." Therefore, when we read again verses 10–11 we understand his pun: "I [Paul] entreat thee [Philemon] for my son, Onesimus [*Useful*], whom I have begotten in my bonds: which in time past was to thee *useless*, but now *useful*, to thee and to me." By implication, we could read the following: "Previously *Useful* was *useless* to you, but now *Useful* has become *useful* both to you, Philemon, and to me, Paul." Onesimus is a changed man in his rebirth as a faithful Christian (*Christianos* Χριστιανός). There is an obvious similarity in Greek between Useless, Useful, and Christian—compare above. This may have been intended by Paul as a subtle additive.

[1:12] Whom I have [returned to you][42] sent again: [that is mine own inward affection,] thou therefore receive him, that is, mine own bowels:

Sent again (Greek *anapempo* ἀναπέμπω) is a legal term denoting "send up to a higher authority."[43] There is a specific intention in the use of this word by Paul. At the time of writing this letter, Paul was in Rome pending the judicial decision of the Imperial court. He had appeared before a lower provincial court in Caesarea and had exercised his right of citizenship by declaring, "I appeal unto Caesar" (Acts 25:11). As the charge against Paul was deferred to the higher judicial authority, so too is the charge against Onesimus deferred to the higher judgment of Philemon.

Mine own (Greek *emos* ἐμός) is a term generally equated with children in relation to their parents.[44] Paul is pleading with Philemon to receive Onesimus hospitably. He expresses his own anxiety concerning the reception Philemon will extend to Onesimus. "The message of Christianity is primarily to individuals, and only secondarily to society. It leaves the unit, which it has influenced to influence the mass. . . . It acts on spiritual and moral sentiment, and only afterwards and consequently on deeds or institutions."[45]

[1:13] Whom I [was desirous to retain] would have retained with me, [so] that in thy stead he might have [minister to] ministered unto me [during my imprisonment for] ~~in the bonds of the gospel~~:

Paul indicates that Onesimus was useful to him and that he was "desirous to retain Onesimus"—he had need of him.

Bonds of the gospel (Greek *desmois tou euaggeliou*, δεσμοῖς τοῦ εὐαγγελίου) is complicated to translate. It might well be translated "the bonds for the gospel."[46] Once again, the gospel is a gospel of freedom, not of bondage. Idiomatic forms of expression are cumbersome when translated to some languages. The first rule of translation is to preserve the concept and message and not the literal meaning of words.

[1:14] **But without thy [consent, I would not take the liberty]** ~~mind would I do nothing~~; **that thy [good deed might not be imposed]** ~~benefit should not be~~ **as it were** ~~of necessity~~, **but [voluntary]** ~~willingly~~.

It is as though Paul were indicating to Philemon that he has his best interests at heart respecting the request to change the status of Onesimus. Though the translation above provides better clarity, the concept is still vague to the modern English reader. The message of this verse is, "I wanted to give you the opportunity to do me a favor."

A NEW TRIPARTITE RELATIONSHIP (PHILEMON 1:15–21)

It is obvious from the contents of this letter that Paul and Philemon had an established relationship reaching back many years. The contents also echo the

relationship that has recently developed between Paul and Onesimus. However, the letter now invites Philemon to discover a new relationship with Onesimus—no longer as a slave, but now as a friend in a three-way relationship which includes Paul.

[1:15] ~~For~~ **Perhaps [for this purpose he was separated]** ~~he therefore departed~~ **for a season, that [everlastingly] thou [may]** ~~shouldest~~ **receive him** ~~for ever~~;

Thou shouldest receive (Greek *apecho* ἀπέχω) means to receive in full. By implication, though the departure of Onesimus was as a runaway slave, his return and everlasting salvation more than compensate in the eternal perspective. Paul plays down the reality of the runaway and charges Onesimus with departing or separating "for a season"—temporarily, as though he were on assignment instead of being a fugitive.

[1:16] **Not now as a [slave]** ~~servant~~, **but above a [slave]** ~~servant~~, **a brother beloved, [especially]** ~~specially~~ **to me, but how much more [now] unto thee, [as a man]** ~~both in the flesh~~, **and [as a brother] in the Lord?**

Servant (Greek *doulos* δοῦλος) is a slave in the regular use of the designation. See appendix C.

Verses 15–16 must be read together to preserve the message: "[15] Perhaps the reason he was separated from you for a little while was that you might have him back forever—[16] no longer as a slave, but better than a slave, as a dear brother. He is very dear to me but even dearer to you, both as a fellow man and as a brother in the Lord."[47]

The previous verse redesignated the runaway to a separation. This verse now purports that Onesimus has undergone a transformation in attitude and value. He departed as a slave, and now returns "as a man" and "as a brother" in Christian brotherhood. "Quietly caring for 'the life of the soul' is still what matters most."[48]

[1:17] If thou [consider] ~~count~~ me therefore a partner, receive him as myself.

Partner (Greek *koinonos* κοινωνός) means one who has a share or is an associate in any respect. It is difficult to discern if Paul means a "business partner" or "missionary companion" in the gospel. Being aware of his style of writing, he may actually have meant both. The message of this verse that Paul wishes to convey to Philemon is to receive Onesimus as he would Paul. We have here Paul taking a stand beside Onesimus in defense of him not only in words but also in deed.

[1:18] If he hath wronged thee, or oweth thee [a debt] ~~ought~~, [charge that to me] ~~put that on mine account~~;

This verse commences with an "if," as though Paul was not sure, when in fact he knew very well that Onesimus had stolen;

"for no doubt Onesimus had told him all his faults, and the whole context shows that there was no uncertainty in Paul's mind."[49] Paul says wronged instead of stolen with intent to play down the crime.

In verse 10, Paul indicated that he had assumed a position of father to Onesimus. Now in this verse he takes upon himself the financial debt of his adopted son in regular Greco-Roman fashion. The theft may have been cash (silver or gold coin), jewelry (belonging to Apphia), or other valuable objects. This verse is alternatively translated, "But if he has wronged you in any way or owes you anything, let me pay for it."[50] Verse 18 is the declaration by Paul that he assumes responsibility for the outstanding financial commitments of Onesimus to Philemon. Verse 19 follows with the written witness of the debt transfer. One other observation is necessary in respect of any debt owed by Onesimus to Philemon. Verse 13 observed that the ministration of Onesimus to Paul at Rome was in proxy for Philemon. Therefore, any debt owed has already been cleared in that Philemon owed ministration to Paul, whom Onesimus delivered. Philemon now owes a debt to Onesimus that should cancel any debt owed by Onesimus to Philemon.

[1:19] I Paul [am writing this] ~~have written~~ it with mine own hand, I will repay it: [However,] ~~albeit~~ I ~~do not~~ say [nothing] to thee [about] ~~how~~ thou [owing] ~~owest unto~~ me even thine own self ~~besides~~.

We know that Onesimus was the scribe of this letter, but the wording here indicates that Paul took the pen for a moment to write these words, as though he were writing to verify the offer to redeem that which Onesimus stole at his departure.

With pen in hand, Paul wrote—

ΕΓΩ	ΠΑΥΛΟΣ	ΕΓΡΑΨΑ	ΤΗ
Ego	*Paulos*	*egrapsa*	*te*
I	Paul	wrote	with

ΕΜΗ	ΧΕΙΡΙ	ΕΓΩ	ΑΠΟΣΤΙΣΩ[51]
eme	*cheiri*	*ego*	*apostiso.*
my	hand	I	will repay.

Paul turned this letter into a penned personal bond, transferring debt and other consequences from Onesimus to Paul in an act of noble sincerity. "The formal tone of the promise [is] rendered more formal by the insertion of the name."[52] The thought-provoking question that we must consider is, "Would I be willing to do the same for someone in a similar situation, either then or now?" Some years later, Paul performed a similar action in writing to Timothy. "The salutation of Paul with mine own hand, which is the token in every epistle: so I write" (2 Timothy 3:17).

By implication: "Since I saved your soul by bringing the gospel to you, I reckon that you owe me for spiritually redeeming your life." Philemon receives the invitation to extend temporal saving to Onesimus. This is a personal letter between friends. The form of writing is overbearing to our twenty-first century social acceptability. Paul alludes to the indebtedness of Philemon to him through the phraseology of mentioning the unmentionable.

[1:20] **Yea, brother, let me have [profit]** ~~joy~~ **of thee in the Lord: [unburden]** ~~refresh~~ **my [anxieties]** ~~bowels~~ **in [Christ][53]** ~~the Lord.~~

Joy (Greek *oninemi* ὀνίνημι) means benefit or profit. Paul "is doubtless continuing his credit and debit metaphors and using the verb in the sense of 'profit.' "[54] The previous verse is the debit—taking on the debt—and this verse is the credit—alluding to a metaphorical cancellation of the transferred debt. There may also be another intention in the selection of this particular word. Just as oninemi means profit, Onesimus not only means useful, it also means profitable. In a definite selection of words, Paul is subtly asking, "Yea, Philemon, let me have Onesimus repaid by thee in the Lord."

From the content of this letter, we conclude that Paul had every expectation that Philemon and Apphia would expedite the mercy plea of Paul in behalf of Onesimus. In our own personal relationships with dear friends and colleagues, we also manifest expectations of predictability based upon our experiences from the legacy of the association.

[1:21] **[Trusting]** ~~Having confidence~~ **in thy obedience I [write]** ~~wrote~~ **unto thee, knowing that thou wilt** ~~also~~ **do more than I [ask!]** ~~say.~~

The tone of this letter is a goodwill gesture, not out of a need to obey an order given. Throughout the letter, Paul avoided mentioning the word obedience until now. He now used "the word 'obedience' and that in such a way as to present it as the child of love, and the privilege of his friend."[55] How far does Paul expect Philemon to take this mercy plea? In the verse above he also says, "I know that you will do more than I ask"—"when love enjoins there should be trust in its tones."[56] The friendship between Paul and Philemon must have been considerable to qualify such a bold assertion in this and other passages of this letter.

[1:22] [In addition,] ~~But withal~~ prepare [for me a hospitable reception] ~~me also a lodging~~: for I [hope] ~~trust~~ that [in answer to] ~~through~~ your prayers I shall be [freed to come] ~~given~~ unto you.

But withal . . . also (Greek *ama de kai*, ἅμα δὲ καὶ—literally "withal but also") is an expression that is simply translated by Luther in German as *daneben*,[57] meaning "in addition" or "as well."[58] Other German translations use another single word, *zugleich*,[59] meaning "at the same time."[60]

A lodging (Greek *xenia* ξενία) means hospitality or a place of entertainment;[61] specifically applicable for this verse as a hospitable reception. We might liberally interpret this verse to mean that Paul is asking Philemon to prepare a homecoming reception for him following his anticipated release from imperial custody. Paul will expect to find Onesimus at the homecoming reception. The emperor will free Paul; will Philemon free Onesimus?

CONCLUDING GREETINGS (PHILEMON 1:23–24)

These concluding greetings are in the form of a postscript, since the greetings are from other friends and associates. A greeting addendum is actually outside of the formal letter content. It permits others to append their greetings to the recipient, even though they do not initiate the correspondence. In modern terms, it is like saying, "Since you are writing to him, say hello from me."

[1:23] [Greetings from] ~~There salute thee~~ Epaphras, my fellow-prisoner [for] ~~in~~ Christ Jesus;

Fellow-prisoner (Greek *sunaichmalotos* συναιχμάλωτος) actually means a prisoner of war. Therefore, Paul is metaphorically applying this to the imperial confinement of Epaphras[62] and himself for preaching the gospel of Jesus Christ.

[1:24] Marcus, Aristarchus, Demas, Lucas, my [fellow-workers] ~~fellow-labourers~~.

Marcus is John Mark, author of the gospel. There is further mention of Aristarchus in Acts 19:20, 20:4, 27:2 and

Colossians 4:10; Demas is mentioned in Colossians 4:14 and 2 Timothy 4:10; and Lucas is the author of the Gospel according to Luke and the Acts of the Apostles.

[1:25] The [mercy] ~~grace~~ of our Lord Jesus Christ be with [you][63] ~~your spirit. Amen.~~[64]

By implication: "God be with you until we meet again."

[postscript] Written from Rome to Philemon, by Onesimus, a [slave] ~~servant~~.

The postscript never was a component part of the actual letter composed by Paul; it dates from the compilation of the Authorized King James Version. In respect of slave/servant see appendix C, "Slavers (Servus)."

Philemon

EPILOGUE

This letter is more than a mercy plea for a runaway slave; it challenges the very concept of slavery as being incompatible with the gospel of Jesus Christ. The institution of slavery is repugnant to Christian values. Respect for our fellowmen as coequal "children of God" means that no one can be born a slave; they can only be enslaved after birth. Paul directs the thesis of this letter to Philemon and his wife Apphia to evaluate where they stand with respect to gospel values and accepted social practices. Though they have the legal right to impose suffering in the name of justice upon Onesimus, such action would be repugnant to Christian values. How can anyone retain his fellowmen in the condition of slavery and at the same time implore God for liberation from the slavery of sin through His atoning sacrifice? Through conversion and repentance, God has pronounced Onesimus free. It would be a paradox if Philemon and Apphia could not also accept the changed status of their relationship to Onesimus. If the acts of faith and the charitable disposition of this family (v.5–6) exclude the enslaved portion of society, is there real Christian virtue, or only the appearance of it? We are all slaves to sin seeking divine intervention to buy freedom for our soul.

Perhaps, Philemon and Apphia had a private council with their son Archippus, the bishop of the Colossian congregation. There would have been deliberation, evaluation, and observation of Onesimus to see for themselves that a transformation was evident. No doubt, Archippus would relate a statement he observed in the Colossian epistle specifically relevant to this deliberation: "Where there is neither Greek nor Jew, circumcision nor un-circumcision, Barbarian, Scythian, bond nor free: but Christ is all, and in all" (Colossians 3:11). Tradition preserves for us the belief that eventually they reached the conclusion to endorse the plea of Paul.

Consider the following words of Isaiah: "Thus saith God [Jehovah] ~~the Lord~~, he that created the heavens, and stretched them out; he that spread forth the earth, and that which cometh out of it; he that giveth breath unto the people upon it, and spirit to them that walk therein: I [Jehovah] ~~the Lord~~ have called thee in righteousness, and will hold thine hand, and will keep thee, and give thee for a covenant of the people, for a light of the Gentiles; To open the blind eyes, to bring out the prisoners from the prison, and them that sit in darkness out of the prison house" (Isaiah 42:5–7).

The Epistle of Paul to Philemon was a private letter written by a member of the Quorum of the Twelve Apostles. Though a private letter, it significantly added value to the cannon of scripture. The doctrine of the letter did not abolish slavery, but it did illuminate the gospel standard concerning the judgment of slave owners with respect to the temporal enslavement of a significant portion of the children of God.

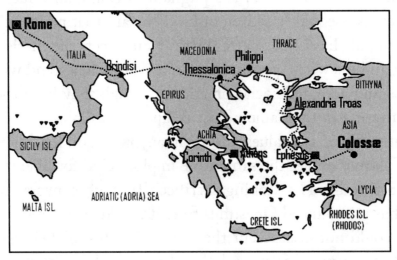

FROM COLOSSAE TO ROME[65]

NOTES FOR PHILEMON

1. Today Colossae is, for the most part, an unexcavated ruin near the present-day village of Honaz just south of the hot springs of Pamukale in west-central Turkey.

2. MacLaren, *The Expositors Bible—Colossians and Philemon*, 417.

3. Lightfoot, *St. Paul's Epistles to the Colossians and to Philemon*, 377, note 5.

4. Smyth, *The Story of Saint Paul's Life and Letters*, 221.

5. Steven Enich, "St. Onesimus" (St. Onisim), St. Petka Serbian Orthodox Church, Kalemegdan, Belgrade, Serbia. ©Hilandar Research Library, 14 October 2009. http://hdl.handle.net/1811/39610.

6. "If the New Testament were simply a book of doctrinal teaching, this epistle would certainly be out of place in it; and if the great purpose of revelation were to supply material for creeds, it would be hard to see what value could be attached to a simple, short letter, from which no contribution to theological doctrine or ecclesiastical order can be extracted. But if we do not turn to it for discoveries of truth, we can find in it very beautiful illustrations of Christianity at work" (MacLaren, 417).

7. Stoned to death by a mob at Colossae late in the first century (*Patron Saint Index*. http://saints.sqpn.com/sainta.htm).

8. In the Greek Orthodox Church and the Roman Catholic Church, Saints Philemon, Apphia, and Archippus share a "Feast Day" on November 22 each year. Archippus has a separate Feast Day on March 20 in the Roman Catholic calendar (http://saints.sqpn.com/saintadd.htm).

9. In the Greek Orthodox Church, Saint Onesimus is the patron of the imprisoned. His Feast Day is on February 15 each year.

10. "According to tradition, Philemon and his wife Apphia were stoned to death at Colossae by an anti-Christian mob" (Catholic Online, http://www.Catholic.org/saints);

"Kontakion in the Second Tone: We praise Christ's Apostles as bright stars illumining the ends of the world, glorious Philemon, Onesimus, Archippus, and with them, wise Apphia, crying: Pray unceasingly in behalf of us all" (Courtesy of Holy Transfiguration Monastery, Greek Orthodox Archdiocese of America).

11. Map by the author, William V. Blacoe, 2009.

12. MacLaren, 490.

13. Cassell's Latin Dictionary, 216, s.v. "epistolium."

14. MacLaren, 420.

15. Strong, #4904; *Webster's Dictionary*, 1273, s.v. "synergy."

16. The word "sister" appears in most

translations, such as The Revised Standard Version; The Jerusalem Bible; New International Version; and so forth.

17. See Colossians 4:17.

18. The word "meeting" is not in the Greek text, and is only included for clarity.

19. MacLaren, , 423.

20. Compare with use of "Father" in Colossians 1:2–3.

21. "Paul's was one of those regal natures to which things are possible that other men dare not do. No suspicion of weakness attached to him when he pours out his heart in love, nor any of insincerity when he speaks of his continual prayers for his friends, or when he runs over in praise of his converts. Few men have been able to talk so much of their love without betraying its shallowness and self-consciousness, or of their prayers without exciting a doubt of their manly sincerity. But the Apostle could venture to do these things without being thought either feeble or false, and could unveil his deepest affections and his most secret devotions without provoking either a smile or a shrug" (MacLaren, 432).

22. Several versions translate as "Because I hear" instead of "hearing."

23. "Paul conducts his siege of Philemon's heart skillfully" (MacLaren, 439).

24. Strong, #4314.

25. Strong, #1519.

26. Strong, #40.

27. "Jesus" is not found in most translations.

28. Strong, #5485.

29. Strong, #4698.

30. MacLaren, 447.

31. Hooke, *Bible in Basic English,* Philemon 8–9.

32. MacLaren, 448.

33. Strong, #433; compare, "Neither filthiness, nor foolish talking, nor jesting, which are not convenient [*aneko* ἀνήκω]: but rather giving of thanks" (Ephesians 5:4); "Wives, submit yourselves unto your own husbands, as it is fit [*aneko* ἀνήκω] in the Lord" (Colossians 3:18).

34. Revised Standard Version—Catholic Edition.

35. Consider the following evaluation of the expression in this verse: "If you hesitate to take him back because you ought, will you do it because I ask you? And, before you answer that question, will you remember my age, and what I am bearing for the Master?" (MacLaren, 454).

36. Pervanoglu, 658, s.v. "πρεσβευτής."

37. Strong, #1198.

38. The prophet Joseph Smith experienced a similar circumstance (D&C 122:7–9).

39. MacLaren, 449; "Love is the weapon of a strong man who can

cast aside the trappings of superiority, and is never loftier than when he descends, nor more absolute than when he abjures authority, and appeals with love to love" (Ibid., 450).

40. New Revised Standard Version.

41. Strong, #2173.

42. The words "to you" appear in most translations.

43. Strong, #375.

44. Conybeare, *The Life and Epistles of St. Paul*, 690, note 1.

45. MacLaren, 461.

46. The word "for" is found in The New Revised Standard Version and The New International Version.

47. Today's New International Version.

48. Neal A. Maxwell, "Care for the Life of the Soul," *Liahona*, May 2003, 68.

49. MacLaren, 478.

50. The Jerusalem Bible.

51. Interlinear Hebrew-Greek-English Bible

52. MacLaren, 479.

53. "Christ" not "Lord" is the reading of most translations (The Revised Standard Version; Jerusalem Bible; New International Version).

54. Strong, #3685.

55. MacLaren, 486.

56. Ibid., 487.

57. Luther's Heilige Schrift des Alten und Neuen Testaments.

58. Cassell's German–English/English–German Dictionary, 141, s.v. "daneben."

59. Die Schlachter Bibel; Die Eberfelder Bibel.

60. Cassell's German–English/English–German Dictionary, 751, s.v. "zugleich."

61. Strong, #3578.

62. *Epaphras* appears also in Colossians 1:7 and 4:12.

63. Faulring, 535.

64. The word "Amen" is not in all Greek texts.

65. Map by the author, William V. Blacoe, 2009.

Appendixes

A. THE SOUL: MIND, SPIRIT, AND BODY

B. THE IMPERIAL ROMAN ARMY

C. SLAVERY (*SERVUS*) WHAT IS
SLAVERY?

D. CONSCIENCE, ETHICS, AND
MORALITY

Appendix A

✣

THE SOUL:

MIND, SPIRIT, AND BODY

Sectarian Christianity diversely understands the theological concept of the human soul. The doctrine of the soul is understood in The Church of Jesus Christ of Latter-day Saints; however, there is inconsistency with respect to the application of the terminology. In respect to the New Testament, there is considerable misapplication of the Greek words. Hebrew words of the Old Testament are not consistently matched to the Greek word of the same meaning. Jesus preached in Aramaic, and the gospel and epistle authors wrote in Greek. Almost two millennia after the authors of the New Testament documents, our modern languages and translators have preserved the inconsistencies. Avoidance of change perpetuated inconsistencies and frustrated the clarity in understanding.

In particular, the word *body* is generally used when the soul is actually the intent.

There is further theological confusion with respect to the application of the term *soul*.

In some instances, the word is used interchangeably with *spirit*. Here we review the various words of the New Testament and the applicability. "The term soul is used in two ways in the scriptures. First, a spirit that is united with a physical body, whether in mortality or after resurrection, is called a soul (see D&C 88:15–16). Second, our spirits are sometimes called souls (see Alma 40:15–18; Abraham 3:23)."[1]

The individual is composed of a *mind* (intellect), *spirit* (spirit body), and *body* (*physical* body). Together the mind, spirit, and body constitute the soul of the individual.[2] Depending upon the nature and nurture of the individual, this union may be in internal harmony or opposition. "We need so much for body, mind, and spirit to unite in one healthy, stable soul."[3]

BODY (GREEK *SOMA* ΣΩΜΑ)

Defined as the physical body and the relative component limbs and organs. Limbs: "let not thy left hand know what thy right hand doeth" (Matthew 6:3). Organs: "all his bowels gushed out" (Acts 1:18). In the poignant words of Paul, "The body is not one member, but many" (1 Corinthians 12:14). One particular scriptural verse mentions the body relative to its composition of the soul and the thoughtful mind. "A perishable body weighs down the soul, and this earthy tent burdens the thoughtful mind" (Apocrypha, Wisdom 9:15).

FLESH (GREEK *SARX* ΣΑΡΞ)

Defined as "the body as opposed to the soul (or spirit), or as the symbol of what is external . . . by implication human nature with its frailties."[4] Used in context as, "the spirit indeed is [eager] ~~willing~~, but the flesh is weak" (Matthew 26:41, cf. Mark 14:38). Succinctly used by Jesus, "Behold my hands and my feet, that it is I myself: handle me, and see; for a spirit hath not flesh and bones, as ye see me have" (Luke 24:39).

MIND (GREEK *NOYS* NOYΣ)

Defined as "intellect, mind, or understanding. Paul uses this word several times in the epistle to the Romans, "But I see another law in my members, warring against the law of my mind, and bringing me into captivity to the law of sin which is in my members. . . . So then with the mind I myself serve the law of God; but with the flesh the law of sin" (Romans 7:23, 25). Another example, "And even as they did not like to retain God in their knowledge, God gave them over to a reprobate mind, to do those things which are not convenient" (Romans 1:28). Paul also uses the word in respect to the mind of God in several instances, "For who hath known the mind of the Lord? or who hath been his counselor?" (Romans 11:34, cf. Romans 12:2; 1 Corinthians 1:10; 2:16)

This word *mind* (*noys* νοῦς) corresponds in most instances of the same word in the Doctrine and Covenants. "See that ye serve him with all your heart, might, mind, and strength, that ye may stand blameless before God at the last day" (D&C 4:2).

MIND (GREEK DIANOIA ΔΙΑΝΟΙΑ)

The Greek word *mind* is defined as

deep thought, mind, imagination, understanding. This word is used in the following well-known scriptural context, "Thou shalt love the Lord thy God with all thy heart, and with all thy soul, and with all thy mind" (Matthew 22:27). The mind of man was ensconced in a spirit body in the pre-mortal realm. This mind existed prior to the premortal experience—"the mind of man is as immortal as God himself."[5]

This word *mind* (*dianoia*) corresponds, in most instances, to the word *intelligence* in the Doctrine and Covenants, "Intelligence, or the light of truth, was not created or made, neither indeed can be" (D&C 93:29). This is the mind infused with intelligence through divine quickening that enhances the capacity of the soul. The mortal condition provides for certain experiences that induce learning and development of the mind. "Whatever principle of intelligence we attain unto in this life, it will rise with us in the resurrection" (D&C 130:18).

MIND (GREEK *PHRONHMA* ΦΡΟΝΗΜΑ)

The Greek word refers to the mental inclination. This word appears in the following context, "And he that searcheth the hearts knoweth what is the mind of the Spirit, because he maketh intercession for the saints according to the will of God" (Romans 8:27).

MIND (GREEK *PHRONEO* ΦΡΟΝΕΩ)

The Greek word refers to "exercise the mind, have an opinion, or be mentally engaged." This word is used in the following context by Paul, "Be of the same mind one toward another. Mind not high things, but condescend to men of low estate. Be not wise in your own conceits" (Romans 12:16).

SPIRIT (GREEK *PNEYMA* ΠΝΕΥΜΑ)

The Greek word is defined as the rational soul. In Hebrew, *spirit* (*ruwach* רוּחַ) similarly means wind, breath, or a rational being. This concept is used in context by Paul when he said, "as absent in body, but present in spirit" (1 Corinthians 5:3). Another example in similar context, "the spirit indeed is [eager] ~~willing~~, but the flesh is weak" (Matthew 26:41).

A definition of the spirit of man is given by the Prophet Joseph Smith: "The spirit is a substance; that it is material, but that it is more pure, elastic and refined matter than the body; that it existed before the body, can exist in the body; and will exist separate from the body, when the body will be moldering in the dust; and will in the resurrection, be again united with it."[6]

SOUL (GREEK *PSYCHE* ΨΥΧΗ)

Soul may be defined as the breath of life. This is the word used by James: "He which converteth the sinner from the error of his way shall save a soul from death" (James 5:20). The Hebrew equivalent appears in Genesis 35:18 also as *soul* (Hebrew *nefesh* נֶפֶשׁ) defined as in the essence of life. One Christian theologian correctly defined: "Far from being a 'part' which joins with the body to form the human being, the soul denotes the entire man, insofar as he is animated by the spirit of life."[7] The three main words appear in a single verse from Paul: "Your whole spirit and soul and body be preserved blameless" (1 Thessalonians 5:19).

Satan endeavors to capture our soul—all of it: mind, spirit, and body. To that end, "he goeth up and down, to and fro in the earth, seeking to destroy the souls of men" (D&C 10:27). The celestial salvation that we seek is to draw near unto God to "treasure up for his soul everlasting salvation in the kingdom of God" (D&C 11:3). Salvation is only attainable for the whole person—all component parts, both spiritual and physical. The mind and spirit of man must rule over the physical body and subdue its tempting passions. Jesus Christ became our example. "Christ grew grace by grace and lived the perfect life. The divine spirit within him—not the flesh—gained control of his soul."[8]

CONCLUSION

The components of the soul are the intellectual reasoning mind, the spirit body, and the physical body. In the premortal condition, the mind and the spirit body became eternal and inseparably united. In the process of mortal conception, the human spirit (composing the mind and the spirit body) entered into a physical body.

We are currently experiencing mortality as a living soul. When the time comes, physical death will induce a condition in which the collective spirit entity of mind and spirit disembody or disengage from the physical body. Eventually, the spirit being will be resurrected—a process by which the physical body will be restored to its proper frame and be fused with the spirit entity. "And shall come forth; they who have done good in the resurrection of the just; and they who have done evil, in the resurrection of the unjust" (D&C 76:17).

With the fulfillment of the resurrection process, the individual becomes an inseparable composition of mind, spirit, and body as an eternally fused soul. "The spirit and the body are the soul of man. And the resurrection from the dead is the redemption of the soul" (D&C 88:15–16). The "why" of this process is captured in the following words: "There was a purpose in the union of the spirit with the body. . . . The union of the spirit with the body constitutes the soul of man; and the resurrection from the dead, the reunion of that spirit with an immortal, indestructible body, constitutes the redemption of that soul. . . . That [is] the outstanding purpose of human existence is to give the spirit union with the body."[9]

ENDNOTES

1. The Church of Jesus Christ of Latter-day Saints, *True to the Faith*, 164.

2. "The nurturing in body, mind, and spirit" (Heber J. Grant, "Message from the First Presidency," *Conference Report*, October 1942, 12–13);

"We are to train our bodies, our minds, and our spirits" (Spencer W. Kimball, "Beloved Youth, Study and Learn," in David O. McKay, *Life's Directions*, 177–78.

3. Holland, *On Earth as it Is in Heaven*, 88.

4. Strong, #4561.

5. Dyer, *Who Am I?*, 174.

6. Smith, *Teachings of the Prophet Joseph Smith*, 207.

7. Léon-Dufour, *Dictionary of Biblical Theology*, 565–566.

8. Carlos E. Asay, *In the Lord's Service*, 53.

9. Gordon B. Hinckley, *Sermons and Missionary Services of Melvin Joseph Ballard*, 178–179.

Appendix B

❧

The Imperial Roman Army

Legion

Each *legion* (Greek *legion* λεγιών, Latin *legio*) comprised of ten cohorts (Latin *cohors*, equal to a modern battalion or regiment) equivalent to sixty centuries (Latin *centuriae*) of infantry (Latin *Milites Gregarius*), and a further six centuries (Latin *sex suffragia*) of cavalry. In the time of Augustus, numerically a full-strength legion consisted of 6,826 men—6,100 foot soldiers (Latin *legionaries*), and 726 horsemen. After the Battle of Actium in 31 BC there were sixty Roman legions, and Augustus systematically reduced the army and stabilized it at twenty-eight legions.[1] "It has been calculated that at the end of Augustus's reign, the Roman army numbered from 250,000 to 300,000 men, of whom half served in the legions and half in the auxiliaries."[2]

The word *legion* appears unmodified in the English New Testament translations. There are four[3] references in the three synoptic gospels. Three of the four are in relation to the exorcism of the man possessed with demons in "the country of the Gergesenes" (Matthew 8:28). The fourth is in respect to celestial legions of angels.

- "Presently give me more than twelve legions of angels?" (Matthew 26:53).[4]
- "My name is Legion: for we are many" (Mark 5:9).
- "What is thy name? And he said, Legion" (Luke 8:30).

LEGATE

A *legate* (Latin *legatus legionis*) commanded the legion. In modern military organization, the legate is equivalent to a colonel. "Legati may be divided into three classes: 1. Legati as ambassadors sent to Rome by foreign nations;[5] 2. Legati or ambassadors sent from Rome to foreign nations and into the provinces;[6] 3. Legati who accompanied the Roman generals into the field, or the proconsuls and praetors in the provinces."[7] This third class is the legate of the Roman legions, and "they were nominated (*legabantur*) by the consul or the dictator under whom they served, but the sanction of the senate (*senates consultum*) was an essential point without which no one could be legally considered a legatus."[8] A Camp Prefect (Latin *Praefectus Castrorum*) acted as deputy assisting the legate.

TRIBUNE

There were six tribunes (Latin *tribuni*, Greek *chiliarchos* χιλίαρχος)[9] with command over the ten cohorts (equivalent to battalions) of the legion.[10] The Emperor or Senate appointed one tribune who was the son of a senator (Latin *Tribunus Laticlavius*) and second in command to the legate. The other five tribunes (Latin *Tribuni Angusticlavii*) were equestrian knight–class citizens and career officers. There

were sometimes additional tribunes (Latin *Tribuni Cohortium*)[11] over auxiliary cohorts attached to a legion.[12] In modern military organization, the tribune is equivalent to a captain. The career tribunes would have "served for ten years in the infantry or five years in the cavalry."[13]

Cohorts 1 and 2 were termed Millarian Cohorts,[14] commanded by the senior tribunes, Tribuni Militum (Greek *chiliarchoi* χιλίαρχοι)[15] of the legion. "The authority of each tribune was not confined to a particular portion of the legion, but extended equally over the whole."[16] A "pair [of tribunes] undertook the routine functions" on a rotating basis.[17] In addition, the tribunes "nominated the centurions, and assigned to each the company which he was to command."[18]

In the New Testament, the Roman *tribune* is consistently translated captain.

"Then the [cohort] ~~band~~ and the [tribune] ~~captain~~ and [centurions] ~~officers~~" (John 18:12).

"Tidings came unto the [tribune] ~~chief captain~~ of the [cohort] ~~band~~ . . . immediately took [legionnaires] ~~soldiers~~ and centurions, and ran down unto them: and when they saw the [tribune] ~~chief captain~~ and the [legionnaires] ~~soldiers~~, they left beating of Paul. Then the [tribune] ~~chief captain~~ came near . . . he said unto the [tribune][19] ~~chief captain~~" (Acts 21:31–33, 37).

CENTURION

A *centurion* (Latin *centurio*, Greek *hekatontarchos* ἑκατόνταρχος) commanded a century (Latin *centum*) of soldiers—the century actually ranged between 60–160 soldiers. In modern military organization, the centurion was the captain of an infantry company, and a senior centurion was equivalent to a major. The senior centurion named "Centurio Primus, and afterwards Centurio Primipili, or simply Primipilus," had responsibility for "the eagle [standard] of the legion."[20] This was carried by the legion *Aquilifer*—a soldier comparable to the highest-ranking non-commissioned officer. The centurion appointed assistants as his second-in-command, a legionnaire called the *optio* as his assistant, and another legionnaire called the *tesserarius*—guard commander.

The Millarian Cohorts 1 and 2 had five centurions each, who were termed *primi ordines*. The senior centurion of the first cohort became the *primus pilus*—literally "first spear." In the second cohort, the senior centurion was the *princes secundus*. Cohorts 3 through 10 had six centurions each; the senior centurion of each was the *pilius prior*.

The centurion rank was sufficient to qualify to ride a horse when his century of soldiers was on the march. He was a middle ranking officer of considerable experience and rigorous discipline. "The moral qualities desirable in a centurion . . . were persons not so much remarkable for daring valor as for calmness and sagacity; men not eager to begin a battle at all hazards, but who would keep their ground although overwhelmed by a superior force, and die rather than quit their post."[21] In battle, they led their legionnaires from the front to inspire and motivate their soldiers. Consequently,

centurion casualties were disproportionately high in battle.

Centurions appear in the three synoptic gospels, but interestingly not in the divinity gospel of John. However, the word *centurion* appears more times in Acts, written by Luke, than in the sum of all the gospel accounts.

- "There came unto him a centurion. . . . The centurion answered" (Matthew 8:5, 13; cf. Luke 7:1–10).
- "Now when the centurion" (Matthew 27:54).
- "The centurion, [that] which stood over against him. . . . When he knew it of the centurion" (Mark 15:39, 44–45).
- "When the centurion saw" (Luke 23:46–47).
- "There was a certain man in Caesarea called Cornelius,[22] a centurion of the [cohort] band called the Italian [cohort] band. . . . Cornelius the centurion, a just man" (Acts 10:1, 8).
- "Paul said unto the centurion that stood by. . . . When the centurion heard that, he went and told the [tribune] chief captain" (Acts 22:25–26).
- "One of the centurions . . . unto the [tribune] chief captain" (Acts 23:17).
- "And he commanded a centurion to keep Paul" (Acts 24:23).
- "One named Julius[23], a centurion of Augustus' [cohort] band. . . . But the centurion" (Acts 27:1, 43–44).

ENDNOTES

1. Carry, *A History of Rome*, 338.

2. Ibid.

3. The word "Legion" also appears in the Latin translation of Luke 8:36 (Jerome, Biblia Sacra Versio Vulgata)—even though *legion* is not present in the Greek original for that verse.

4. Translated as *legiones angelorum* in Latin.

5. Examples of this type of *legati* is mentioned by Titus Livius in *Livy: The War with Hanibal*, 645–46 (translated by Sélincourt); *Livy: Rome and the Mediterranean*, 519, (translated by Bettenson).

6. "Legati to foreign nations in the name of the Roman republic [and later the empire] were always sent by the senate. . . . A Roman ambassador; according to Dionysius, had the powers (*exioysia kai dynamis*, ἐξουσία καὶ δύναμις) of a magistrate and the venerable character of a priest" (Dictionary of Greek and Roman Antiquities, 678).

7. Ibid., 677.

8. Ibid., 678.

9. Strong, #5506.

10. Dictionary of Greek and Roman Antiquities, 504.

11. Ibid.

12. "Under Augustus and his successors Tribunus was employed with reference to many military officers . . . Tribunus Castrorum . . . Tribunus Praetorianus . . . Tribunus Fabrum Navalium, and many others" (Ibid).

13. Ibid.

14. *Millarian* is equal to 1,000 legionaries of double strength cohorts.

15. Dictionary of Greek and Roman Antiquities, 503.

16. Ibid.

17. Ibid

18. Ibid.

19. The tribune in this passage is later identified as Claudius Lysias (Greek *Klaudios Lusias* Κλαύδιος Λυσίας), the only Roman tribune named in the New Testament (see Acts 23:26; 24:7, 22).

20. Dictionary of Greek and Roman Antiquities, 504.

21. Ibid.

22. Given in Latin as "*Cornelius centurio cohortis quae dicitur Italica*" (Jerome, Biblia Sacra Versio Vulgata).

23. Given in Latin as "*Centurioni nomine Iulio cohortis Augustae*" (Jerome, Biblia Sacra Versio Vulgata).

Appendix C

SLAVERY (SERVUS)

There are several references to slaves in the New Testament gospels and epistles. In particular, the Epistle to Philemon is a short letter in the form of a mercy plea for a fugitive slave. The Philemon epistle alone justifies the necessity of this appendix to comprehend the institutional and cultural acceptability of slavery in the Greco-Roman world. Some readers have considerable understanding of slavery from the legacy of their ancestors in the southern United States, Brazil, Caribbean Islands, and a host of other locations across the globe.

In simplistic terms, slavery is the loss of personal liberty through subjugation and enforced servitude. Respecting the Roman practice of slavery, it is the institution and social practice of human beings owned as property by another. Slavery exists when one human controls the body—and often the mind—of another human for labor with forms of restraint and through fear with the threat of inflicting consequences.

The Greco-Roman world considered a slave "a living working-tool and possession."[1]

GRECO-ROMAN SLAVERY

The English word *slave* corresponds to the Latin word *servus* and the Greek word *doylos* (δοῦλος).[2] The Latin word for a master who owned a slave was a *dominus*. Further status of ownership called *dominum* had reference "to the slave merely as a thing or object of ownership."[3] Slave trading was an enormous commercial enterprise in Roman times and attracted considerable investment opportunities.

Where did the Romans get their slaves? The answer to that question is a shifting answer. Geographically, the ethnic origin of slaves was dependent upon where the Roman legions were fighting. During the period of conquest in the Italian Peninsula in the third century BC, the slaves were gathered from among the respective conquered tribes. Later, in the second century BC, the Iberian Peninsula, North Africa, and the Balkans became the new source for slaves. In the first century BC, conquest shifted to the remainder of the former Greek territories in the east and the enormous conquest of Gaul in the north. The first century AD brought slaves from Britannia, Germania, and additional eastern conquests. There was ongoing import of slaves throughout these centuries from beyond the Roman frontiers with other slave markets.[4]

To comprehend the cultural acceptance of slavery, it is necessary to recognize that slaves were a human currency. In many instances, human currency was the method of payment for other products. As a practical example, Romans sold wine in north and east Gaul and received payment in human currency to the extent of 15,000 slaves each year. The harvesting of these slaves came from among the Germanic and Scandinavian tribes. "From the emergence of the Roman empire to its eventual decline, at least 100 million people . . . [were] sold as slaves throughout the Mediterranean and its hinterlands."[5]

SLAVE TRADING

A slave trader or slave dealer was a *mango/ mangonis*[6] (Greek *magganon* μάγγανον),[7] alternatively called a *venalicius*,[8] and they often operated in *societas/societatis*,[9] or stock-holding companies, "because of the capital requirements of their ventures."[10] A slave-market (*venalicum*)[11] both sold newly acquired slaves and brokered the purchase of unwanted or surplus slaves for resale to a new slave owner. There is even the indication that slave trading was subject to a state tax of 2–3 percent.[12]

Usually the *mangonis* slave trader conducted the *venalicum* slave market in public, with all the advertising and marketing of any other commercial product.[13] These human products were displayed with a purchase warrant (*titulus*)[14] hanging from their neck on the chest.[15] A *titulus* included the legally required information about the origin (*natio*)[16] of the slave,[17] as well as the slave's background, experience, and known physical or mental impediments. It was, however, common for a *mangonis* slave-trader "to conceal personal defects," wounds, or deformities.[18] It was usual for a *dominus* to bring a medical doctor to inspect the slave prior to closing the sale.[19] When presented in the market, the slaves were naked for customer inspection.[20]

The display of young slaves that possessed exceptional physical beauty took place in private auction for sale to the highest bidder. "The increase of luxury and the corruption of morals led purchasers to pay immense sums for beautiful slaves, or such as ministered to the caprice or whim of the purchaser. Eunuchs always fetched a very high price, and . . . beautiful boys [were] sold for as much as 100,000 or 200,000 sesterces each."[21]

THE SCOPE OF THE SLAVE POPULATION

Estimating the extent of slavery in the Greco-Roman world is not an exact science. There are various estimates for the city of Rome and the Roman Empire in the late Republic and early Imperial times. During the era of Augustus, the estimated population for the city of Rome was 900,000–950,000, composing of 300,000–350,000 slaves. An estimate for the Peninsula of Italy was a population of circa 6,000,000, composing circa 2,000,000 slaves. Projections for the entire Roman empire was circa 8,000,000–10,000,000 slaves, equivalent to 17–20 percent of the inhabitant population.

The productive lifespan of heavy labor slaves was about 20 years. This necessitated the production or commercial acquisition of 250,000–400,000 new slaves each year to sustain the status quo.[22] The empire met the maintenance needs of state-operated mines, utilities, and other services through state-owned slaves called public slaves (*servi publici*).[23] The primary source of new slaves was from war captives—military and civilian—wherein the conquered army and native population were summarily enslaved.[24] "Prisoners taken in war" were termed *captivus*[25] in Latin and *dorialotoi* (δοριάλωτοι) in Greek.[26] As an example, the Jewish revolt of AD 67–73 resulted in the enslavement of 97,000 Jews from Palestine.[27]

Non-domestic slave labor occurred in agriculture; open-cast and subterranean mining; on the docks, loading and unloading ships; and other labor-intensive state and private production and maintenance operations.[28] Purchased domestic slaves were termed *argyronetoi* (ἀργυρώνητοι) or *chrysonetoi* (χρυσώνητοι) in Greek.[29] Considerably fewer slaves were engaged in domestic servitude, maintaining and catering to the lethargy, opulence, or decadence of the free citizens. A Latin maxim of the era was, "*Servi aut nascuntur aut fiunt*"— translated as "slaves are either born or made."[30] In the republic and early empire, most slaves were purchased with comparatively few conceived from among the slave population.[31]

ABANDONED INFANTS

The saddest condition whereby individuals became enslaved was in consequence of the widespread practice of parents abandoning their newborn infants. Abandoned infants were termed "foundlings" (*infans expositicius*).[32] The practice of abandoning newborn infants was not specifically limited to the destitute.

Institutional or charitable orphanages did not exist—nor had the concept ever been entertained. Parents abandoned their children as crude means of birth control or in consequence of economic difficulty. Most foundlings were absorbed into slavery.[33] Raising infants to a marketable age was a business practice of Greco-Roman culture. The only positive result of exposing infants is that childless couples rescued a small portion of the foundling infants and reared them as their own children through legal recognition and adoption.

JUDICIAL CONVICTS

Greco-Roman understanding was that imprisonment served only as a temporary measure until the passing of the sentence. The usual consequence of judicial conviction (*servi poenae*) was penal servitude and enslavement, condemnation to the arena as gladiators, or banishment to the galley oars or mines (*damnatio ad metalla*).[34] "*Servi poenae* were persons whose crimes caused them to be reduced to slave status in a process known as *capitis deminutio*."[35] In addition to criminal prosecution, the consequence of evading military service in the legions resulted in the degrading of citizenship to *dediticii* or even slavery if they came within one hundred miles of Rome.[36]

COMMERCIAL KIDNAPPING

Throughout the years of the New Testament era in the Julio-Claudian dynasty, the occurence of war diminished considerably. This circumstance resulted in a significant reduction in the number of prisoners of war to enslave en mass. Therefore, bandits called *grassatores*[37] took to kidnapping travelers in remote areas—both free and slave—and selling these souls called *ergastula* into slavery. Emperor August and his successor Tiberius enacted measures to curb this practice, but their efforts proved unsuccessful.[38]

SLAVERY THROUGH INSOLVENCY

The use of slave labor on the large estates deprived many small landowners of market share for their produce. They could no longer compete with the labor costs of the larger estates.[39] Those who were not indebted gravitated to the cities, thereby swelling urban populations with free but poor citizens and exacerbating the unemployment problem.[40] The only asset these free peasant citizens possessed was the right to vote and offer political support; their liability was the perpetual struggle for temporal existence.[41] Where mortgages existed, insolvency resulted. The peasant farmer became a bankrupt debtor and was given up (*addictus*) to the creditor.[42] In consequence, the Roman farmer—and possibly his family—was sold into slavery to recoup the debt. The "two cognate social evils" of the time were "slavery and the wholesale paupering of the urban population."[43]

SELLING ONESELF INTO SLAVERY

Roman territorial expansion resulted in an enormous increase of available slave labor. The poor Roman citizens saw their employment opportunities progressively diminish as slaves supplanted them. Small farm holdings could no longer market their produce at the competitive prices of slave-operated estates. Further incursions arose from the substantial import of cheap grain crops from the provinces—particularly Egypt—with cheaper labor.[44] The displaced agrarian Romans eventually gravitated to the cities out of economic necessity, becoming a proletariat of pauper citizens in their own nation. "Genuine self-sales may arguably have occurred for the sake of upward mobility, with an eye to a career and later manumission."[45] Regardless of the justification, self-sale was a "voluntary and legally binding procedure."[46] Slave owners had a vested financial interest in the wellbeing and maintenance of their slaves. This resulted in a condition where slaves were better cared for than poor free Romans.

A consequence of this economic environment was so frustrating to many individuals that they elected to relinquish their rights of Roman citizenship and sell themselves into slavery. The negotiated purchase price for the self-sale passed to family members, thus deferring them from the same consequences. Alternatively, destitute Romans offered themselves into slavery without price in the hope of improving their temporal circumstances. Either way, the intention was the same—to relieve themselves from their pauper condition.[47]

HOME-BORN SLAVES

Marriage—institutional or religious—between slaves did not exist. The cohabitation of male and female slaves was designated *contubernium*,[48] "and no legal relation between him and his children was recognized."[49] A child born to another slave was a *de facto* slave and designated a *verna* in Latin, and an *oikotrips* (οἰκότριψ) in Greek. Alternatively, a new slave that was "purchased" was known as an *oiketes* (οἰκέτης).[50] The offspring of two slaves were also designated *verna* in Latin, but *amphidoylos* (ἀμφίδουλος) in Greek. When the parents were *oikotribes* (οἰκότριβες), their children were *oikotribaios* (οἰκότρίβαιος).[51] During the expansion phase of the republic and empire, "the cohabitation of slaves was discouraged, as it was considered cheaper to purchase than to rear slaves."[52]

Solidification of the empire boundaries resulted in the evaporation of supply through conquest enslavement. Eventually the cohabitation of domestic slaves must have become desirable in reproducing the domestic slave population.[53]

FUGITIVE SLAVES

Runaway slaves were termed *fugitivus/fugitivi*[54]—from which is derived the English word *fugitive*. The harboring and concealing of a fugitive slave was termed *furtum*,[55] which was a criminal offence. Those who pursued runaway slaves were bounty hunters known as *fugitivarii*.[56] Once recaptured, slaves "were branded on the forehead with a mark called a stigma, whence they were thereafter said to be *notati* or *inscripti*."[57] The fugitive business was so lucrative that much earlier, the Greeks had already established insurance companies for slave owners to indemnify against the financial loss incurred by runaway slaves.[58]

SLAVE CATEGORIES AND SKILLS

The portfolio of slaves owned by one master (*dominus*) was termed a *familia*. "Private slaves were divided into urban (*familia urbana*) and rustic (*familia rustica*); but the name of urban was given to those slaves who served in the villa or country residence as well as in the town house so that the words *urban* and *rustic* rather characterized the nature of their occupations than the place where they served."[59] The rustic agrarian slaves were managed by an overseer called a *praefecti* in Latin and an *epitropos* (ἐπιτροπος) in Greek. Male domestic household slaves were managed by a steward *tamias* (ταμίας), and the female slaves by a stewardess *tamia* (ταμία).[60]

The large Roman estates each had their own prison (Latin *ergastula*) "where slaves were forced to work in fetters."[61] A very large villa with a large number of slaves usually divided them into groups of ten (Latin *decuriae*). A further classification of slaves was according to the rank of their skills and occupation. The main ranks were literary/*literati* (*anagnostae*, *librarii*, and *amanuensis*); medical/*mediastini*, ordinary or general/*ordinarii* (which included *actores*, *procuratores*, *dispensatores*, *celarii*, *promi*, *condi*, *procuratores peni*, and others); skilled/*vulgares* (*pistores*, *coqui*, *dulciarii*, *salmentarii*, *ostiarii*, *cubicularii*, *lecticarii*, and others); and menial or generic/*quales-quales* (the lowest class of slave).[62] With the acquisition of education, skills, and qualifications, slaves could obtain promotion through the slave hierarchy. Some slave owners contracted their slaves to work for others in a business designated *apophora* (ἀποφορά) in Greek.[63]

With the expansion of slave ownership, agricultural labor became the domain of slaves, and freemen eventually declined to work the land as laborers. The process continued to expand as the skill base among the slaves increased. Eventually, the domain of slave labor, trades, arts, and academics expanded to such an extent that the free population considered several job opportunities "degrading to a freedman."[64]

MANUMISSION OF SLAVES

In Greek culture, manumitted slaves were called *apeleytheroi* (ἀπελεύθεροι) and "were obliged to honor their former masters as their patron" *prostates* (προστάτης).[65] Some slave owners shared the profits (Latin *peculium*)[66] of their slave-operated business with the slaves. Occasionally, a slave owner would permit a slave to amass funds (Latin *peculium*) to purchase his freedom.[67] During the reign of Augustus, he significantly curtailed the manumission of slaves for fear of diluting the pure Roman race with freed foreigners.[68]

Many eventually accepted the condition and status of being a slave—depending upon the expectations and consequences. For others, the condition of being enslaved was so repugnant and unacceptable that suicide became the only alternative. Slavery was "an institution of society, death was considered to put an end to the distinction between slaves and freemen."[69]

Centuries later, "after the establishment of Christianity" in the later Roman Empire, a slave could become free "by becoming a monk."[70]

SLAVES IN THE NEW TESTAMENT

- **Servant** (Greek *doylos* δοῦλος, Latin *servus*) is a slave in the New Testament.

- **Fellow-servant** (Greek *syndoylos* σύνδουλος, Latin *conserves*) is a co-slave or another slave under the same master.

- **To bring into subjection** (Greek *doylagogeo* δουλαγωγέω) is a slave driver or someone who enslaves.

- **Bondage** or **serving** (Greek *doyleia* δουλεία, Latin *servitutis*), meaning slavery or servitude.

- **Serve** or **bondage** (Greek *doyleyo* δουλεύω) means to be a slave or to serve as a slave.

- **Lord** (Greek *kyrios* κύριος, Latin *domine*) means one with authority.

- "No man can [be in slavery to] ~~serve~~ two masters: for either he will hate the one, and love the other; or else he will hold to the one, and despise the other. Ye cannot [be in slavery to] ~~serve~~ God and mammon" (Matthew 6:24).

- "[Slave] ~~servant~~" (Matthew 8:9); "[teacher] ~~master~~, nor the [slave] servant above his lord. It is enough for the disciple that he [is like] ~~be as~~ his [teacher] ~~master~~, and the [slave like]

~~servant as~~ his lord" (Matthew 10:24–25); "[slaves] ~~servants~~ . . . [Master/Domine] Sir . . . the [slaves] ~~servants~~" (Matthew 13:27-28); "[servitude/*servitutis*] ~~bondage~~" (Romans 8:15); [*servitude*/servitute] "~~bondage~~" (Romans 8:21); "[enslave it] ~~bring it into subjection~~" (1 Corinthians 9:27); "[servitude/*servitutem*] ~~bondage~~" (Galatians 4:24); "[servitude/*servitutis*] ~~bondage~~" (Galatians 5:1); "[servitude/*servituti*] ~~bondage~~" (Hebrews 2:15).

- "Therefore is the kingdom of heaven likened unto a certain king, which would take account [with] ~~of~~ his [slaves/*servis*] ~~servants~~. And when he had begun to reckon, one was brought unto him, which owed him ten thousand talents. But forasmuch as he had not to pay, his [master/*dominus*] ~~lord~~ commanded him to be sold, and his wife, and children, and all that he had, and payment to be made. The [slave/*servus*] ~~servant~~ therefore fell down, and worshipped him, saying, [Master/*Dominus*] ~~Lord~~, have patience with me, and I will pay thee all. Then the [master/*dominus*] ~~lord~~ of that [slaves/*servus*] ~~servants~~ was moved with compassion, and loosed him, and forgave him the debt. But the same [slave/*servus*] ~~servant~~ went out, and found one of his [fellow-slaves/*conservis*] ~~fellowservants~~, which owed him an hundred pence: and he laid hands on him, and took him by the throat, saying, Pay me that thou owest.

And his [fellow-slave/*conservis*] ~~fellowservant~~ fell down at his feet, and besought him, saying, Have patience with me, and I will pay thee all. And he would not: but went and cast him into prison, till he should pay the debt. So when his [fellow-slaves/*conservi*] ~~fellowservants~~ saw what was done, they were very sorry, and came and told unto their [master/*dominus*] ~~lord~~ all that was done. Then his [master/*dominus*] ~~lord~~, after that he had called him, said unto him, O thou wicked [slave/*serve*] ~~servant~~, I forgave thee all that debt, because thou desiredst me" (Matthew 18:23–32).

THE DECLINE OF GRECO-ROMAN SLAVERY

With the advancing influence and acceptability of Christianity within the society and culture of the Roman Empire, the institutional endorsement of slavery began to diminish.[71] Centuries of cultural entrenchment did not evaporate at once; indeed, it took a few more centuries before slavery was no longer culturally or socially acceptable. The process of social reconditioning concerning slavery did not happen within the lifetime of the apostolic New Testament. "The spread of Christianity tended most to ameliorate their condition, though the possession of them was for a long time by no means condemned as contrary to Christian justice."[72] The principles of social justice did not even exist in the Greco-Roman mind. The same paradigm existed later in the Middle Ages with regard to serfs bonded to the estates of aristocratic feudal lords and respecting the social classification of domestic servants through the early twentieth century. "Any attempt to grapple vigorously with these problems must have offended many rooted prejudices and antagonized numerous vested interests."[73]

CONCLUSION

In a later era, John Quincy Adams declared that in slavery, the "distinction between a person and a thing is annihilated."[74] More recently, the United Nations convention on slavery declared, "Freedom is the birthright of every human being."[75] We should point out that even now, in the twenty-first century of the Christian era, there are between 12 and 27 million children of God living in the bonds of physical slavery in the world.[76] That is significantly more than at any known time in history. However, modern slavery is more subtle; it is not institutionally endorsed, though the practice is tolerated and seldom prosecuted. Human kidnapping and trafficking for prostitution is a primary cause of slavery in many—if not most—countries of the world. There is theoretical protection against institutional and criminal enslavement for all inhabitants of United Nations member states. The 1948 "Universal Declaration of Human Rights" and the 1956 "UN Supplementary Convention on the Abolition of Slavery, the Slave Trade, and Institutions and Practices Similar to Slavery" guarantee the protection of personal rights and liberty.

There are, unfortunately, considerably

many more souls living in the slavery of abundant addictions and financial bondage. In consequence, self-slavery is more prevalent in modern society through loss of personal freedom. It far exceeds the conditions of physical self-sale in Roman slavery discussed above. "Fear, futility, discouragement, and sin—[remain] the great enslavers of men's souls."[77]

ENDNOTES

1. Dictionary of Greek and Roman Antiquities, 1034.

2. Ibid; Strong, #1401.

3. Dictionary of Greek and Roman Antiquities, 1036.

4. "Black slaves from as far away as Somalia and the occasional import from India made for comparatively rare but consequently high-prestige retainers" (Scheidel, *The Roman Slave Supply*, 14). Respecting the early Christian era: "There is no evidence either that the cost of slaves spiraled upwards during this period, it seems sensible to infer that the supply of slaves needed annually to replenish the normal depletion of their numbers was more or less available" (Madden, *Slavery in the Roman Empire—Numbers and Origins*, 3:5).

5. Scheidel, *The Roman Slave Supply*, 18.

6. Dictionary of Greek and Roman Antiquities, 1040; "Merchants often followed Roman armies and bought up newly captured slaves"

(Scheidel, 8).

7. Cassell's Latin Dictionary, 360, s.v. "mango – onis."

8. Cassell's Latin Dictionary, 633, s.v. "venalicius – i."

9. The Latin word *societas* means a commercial "partnership, companionship, fellowship, [or] association" (Cassell's Latin Dictionary, 559, s.v. "societas –atis").

10. Scheidel, 12.

11. Cassell's Latin Dictionary, 633, s.v. "venalicius –a – um."

12. "Tariff records from Palmyra from AD 137 stipulate customs dues equivalent to not more than 2 or 3 percent of the value of teenage slaves" (Scheidel, 12).

13. "It is remarkable that when the place of origin of slaves is indicated in Roman literature, this is almost invariably from within rather than from without the Empire" (Madden, 3:26).

14. The Latin word *titulus* also indicates, "a notice on a house that is to let" (Cassell's Latin Dictionary, 606, s.v. "titulus").

15. Dictionary of Greek and Roman Antiquities, 1040.

16. The Latin word natio indicates, "a tribe, race, people, especially uncivilized" (Cassell's Latin Dictionary, 386, natio).

17. Scheidel, 13.

18. Dictionary of Greek and Roman Antiquities, 1040.

19. Ibid.

20. "Accordingly obliged both matrons and ripe virgins to strip, for a complete examination of their persons, in the same manner as if Thoranius, the dealer in slaves, had them under sale" (Suetonius, *The Twelve Caesars*, "Augustus," 69).

21. Dictionary of Greek and Roman Antiquities, 1040.

22. Scheidel, 6.

23. Dictionary of Greek and Roman Antiquities, 1039.

24. "The Roman legal tradition makes it clear that capture in war caused loss of freedom" (Scheidel, 7); "Whole villages with their entire population were often taken and sold into slavery. . . . There were fewer wars through expansion during the Roman imperial time, which significantly reduced the offer of new slaves. At the same time, there was such a significant increase of the manumission of slaves; this caused the numbers of slaves during the imperial time to significantly reduce" (translation of Koester, *Einführung in das Neue Testament*, 58).

25. Cassell's Latin Dictionary, 799, s.v. "prisoner of war."

26. Dictionary of Greek and Roman Antiquities, 1034.

27. "The number of those that were carried captive during this whole war was collected to be ninety-seven thousand" (Josephus, *Wars of the Jews*, 6.9:3).

28. Koester, 59.

29. Dictionary of Greek and Roman Antiquities, 1034.

30. Madden, 3:10.

31. Dictionary of Greek and Roman Antiquities, 1034.

32. "Infántes expósiti et invénti" (Stelten, *Dictionary of Ecclesiastical Latin*, 130).

33. "The enslavement of exposed babies . . . may conceivably have been the leading domestic source of free-born slaves in the mature Empire. . . . Ethnic groups that raised all their children were considered exceptional. . . . The enslavement of foundlings played a major role in the local slave supply" (Scheidel, 10); Foundlings "supplied considerably more slaves . . . than had been usually thought" (Madden, 3:29). "The custom was not made illegal until AD 374" (Ibid, 30).

34. Carry, *A History of Rome*, 381.

35. Scheidel, 10.

36. Ibid.; Dictionary of Greek and Roman Antiquities, 1038.

37. Cassell's Latin Dictionary, 267, s.v. "grassor."

38. Augustus: "Bandit parties infested the roads armed with swords, supposedly worn in self-defense, which they used to overawe travelers—whether free-born or not—and force them into slave-barracks built by the landowners.

Numerous so-called 'workmen's guilds,' in reality organizations for committing every sort of crime, had also been formed. Augustus now stationed armed police in bandit-ridden districts, had the slave-barracks inspected, and dissolved all workmen's guilds except those that had been established for some time and were carrying on legitimate business" (Suetonius, *The Twelve Caesars*, "Augustus," 32); Tiberius: "had undertaken two special commissions: to reorganize the defective grain supply and to inquire into the state of slave-barracks throughout Italy—the owners having made a bad name for themselves by confining lawful travelers in them, and by harboring men who would rather pass as slaves than be drafted for military service" (Suetonius, *The Twelve Caesars*, "Tiberius," 8).

39. "There can be little doubt that despite their potentially vital contribution to agricultural production, slaves were disproportionately concentrated in the cities" (Scheidel, 3).

40. Dictionary of Greek and Roman Antiquities, 1039.

41. Carter, *The Religious Life of Ancient Rome*, 51.

42. Madden, 3:28.

43. Carry, 449.

44. There is an uncanny similarity between ancient Rome and our

modern world. Slavery caused the unemployment of the lower classes two millennia ago. Today, the cheap labor of immigrants is evaporating domestic employment opportunities. The *modus operandi* was different; however, the result is the same—the poor lose.

45. Scheidel, 11.

46. Ibid., 9.

47. "It is unlikely that Roman fathers ever had a formal right to sell their children; in classical law, family members could not be sold into slavery or pawned" (Ibid., 11).

48. "Companionship, intimacy . . . especially the living together of slaves as man and wife" (Cassel's Latin Dictionary, 149, s.v. "contubernium"). This Latin word is the course of the English word "concubine."

49. Dictionary of Greek and Roman Antiquities, 1037.

50. Ibid., 1034.

51. Ibid.

52. Ibid.

53. "Logic dictates that the larger a slave population becomes, the more difficult it is for capture to retain a dominant position as a source of supply, whereas the relative contribution of natural reproduction is bound to increase with overall size" (Scheidel, 6).

54. Cassell's Latin Dictionary, 258, s.v. "fugitives"; Dictionary of Greek

and Roman Antiquities, 1042.

55. Ibid., 1038. *Furtum* means, "a theft, robbery . . . stolen property," involving "underhand methods" (Cassell's Latin Dictionary, 260, s.v. "furtum").

56. Dictionary of Greek and Roman Antiquities, 1038.

57. Ibid., 1042.

58. Ibid., 1035.

59. Ibid., 1041.

60. Ibid., 1035–1036.

61. Madden, 3:15.

62. Dictionary of Greek and Roman Antiquities, 1041.

63. Ibid., 1035.

64. Ibid., 1039.

65. Ibid., 1036.

66. *Peculium* means a "property which members of a familia were allowed to regard as their own; of the savings of slaves" (Cassell's Latin Dictionary, 429, s.v. "peculium").

67. Dictionary of Greek and Roman Antiquities, 1037.

68. "Considering it of extreme importance to preserve the Roman people pure, and untainted with a mixture of foreign or servile blood, he not only bestowed the freedom of the city with a sparing hand, but laid some restriction upon the practice of manumitting slaves" (Suetonius, "Augustus," 40). On another occasion, Augustus vented anger when "he found many slaves had been

emancipated and enrolled amongst the citizens" (Augustus, 42; cf. 44).

69. Dictionary of Greek and Roman Antiquities, 1042.

70. Ibid., 1038.

71. "Does Christianity sanction slavery? Certainly not, its principles cut it up by the roots. A gospel, of which the starting-point is that all men stand on the same level, as loved by one Lord, and redeemed by one cross, can have no place for such an institution. A religion that attaches the highest importance to man's awful prerogative of freedom, because it insists on every man's individual responsibility to God, can keep no terms with a system that turns men into chattels. Therefore, Christianity cannot but regard slavery as a sin against God, and as treason toward man. The principles of the gospel worked into the conscience of a nation destroys slavery" (MacLaren, 460).

72. Dictionary of Greek and Roman Antiquities, 1039; "Jesus Christ, by becoming the Redeemer of the slaves as well as their masters, has lifted them from their degradation, and shown that all souls are equally valuable in the sight of God" (Graham, *A Practical and Exegetical Commentary on the Epistle to Titus*, 87).

73. Carry, 449.

74. Adams, *What is Slavery?* Project

Gutenberg, eText #9595.

75. United Nations High Commission for Human Rights, (1956), Supplementary Convention on the Abolition of Slavery, the Slave Trade, and Institutions and Practices Similar to Slavery, Preamble, §1.

76. "A wide range of estimates exist on the scope and magnitude of modern-day slavery. The International Labor Organization (ILO)—the United Nations agency charged with addressing labor standards, employment, and social protection issues—estimates that there are 12.3 million people in forced labor, bonded labor, forced child labor, and sexual servitude at any given time; other estimates range from 4 million to 27 million" (US Department of State, *Trafficking in Persons Report*, 7).

77. Fosdick, *Twelve Tests of Character*, 87–88.

Appendix D

✤

CONSCIENCE, ETHICS, AND MORALITY

CONSCIENCE

Conscience (Greek *syneidesis* συνείδησις) is that portion of the mental faculty that interprets and establishes ethical values, morals, limitations, and expectations by or from our actions.[1] This does not exclude the driving forces of our mental faculty from rejecting or overwhelming the limitations established in the principles of our conscience. Our conscience is capable of accepting new values and modifying and removing existing ones. The cultural values and traditions that surround us influence our perception and adoption of the ethical values we embrace. Not everyone will embrace and develop the same set of ethical or moral values. In many instances, values are subjective and are interpreted according to the mental faculty and experience of each individual.

211

"Conscience [is] the perception of moral distinctions accompanied by the feeling of personal obligation to do what is morally right."[2]

The conscience can be educated through experience. "Conscience not only may be educated; it is also the product of education. A man ought always to follow conscience, but ought equally to make sure that he does not identify conscience with a mere inherited emotion which his reason criticizes."[3] As a man educates his mind with knowledge, he reevaluates his perception of his own personality and values. Knowledge received creates further knowledge "line upon line, precept upon precept" (D&C 98:12). Through disciplining his thought process to compatibility with the values of his conscience, he attains a greater level of freedom.[4]

The English word *conscience* derives from the Latin word *conscientia*, meaning "consciousness" or "knowledge in oneself," specifically a "consciousness of right or wrong"[5]—good and evil. This Latin expression derives from the Greek word *syneidesis* (συνείδησις), meaning moral consciousness or judgment of the mind. "It is generally supposed that Paul took the word over from Greek philosophy, and baptized it into a newer and deeper connotation."[6]

"The word is stressing that we receive input from our surroundings (temptations, decision-making events, etc.) and we are driven to make a decision. We compare what we know with our conscience (con—'with,' science—'knowledge'), our knowledge base about this input. If we follow our conscience, we act according to what we [accept] ~~know~~ to be true. . . . We can violate our conscience by overriding that knowledge."[7]

Religious perceptions do not necessarily induce the experience of a "guilty conscience." A sense of guilt occurs when an individual contravenes his or her own ethical values in the conscience portion of the human mind. "Blessed is he whose [conscience] ~~heart~~ does not condemn him, and who has not given up his hope" (Sirach [Ecclesiasticus] 14:2).[8]

PERSONAL ETHICAL PRINCIPLES

We now move on to consider ethics and morals. Ethics are philosophical—whether in theory or practice—and classified as right or wrong from the current personal or cultural point of view. Morals are theological—doctrinally established in religious belief—and classified as right or wrong by God through His prophets. Man may redefine his ethics, but only God, through His prophets, may redefine the requirements of our morals.

Ethics (Greek *ethikos* ἠθικός) comprise our personal sense of right and wrong, irrespective of any paradigm influenced by religious affiliation. Each of us develops personal ethical principles by which we live. Among the ancient Greek philosophies, "Stoicism exalted ethics to the supreme position."[9] The adoption of ethical principles comes through social expectations of the community or culture.[10] The community not only adopts shared ethical principles, it also will create a common perception of what those ethical expectations should be. "The existence of a feeling of obligation is undeniable. Such a feeling is indispensable to high-minded living. The great loyalties, which we admire, presuppose it. It is desirable that a man should feel uneasy in the presence of duty unfilled, and that he should feel pleasure at duty performed. This is the fact of conscience."[11]

The English word *ethic* and the French word *ethique* derive from the Latin words *ethica* and *ethice*, meaning "moral philosophy."[12] These Latin words come from the Greek words *ethikos* (ἠθικός) and *ethike* (ἠθική).[13] These two Greek words stem from *ethos* (ἦθος), meaning manner or conduct,[14] describing individual character and social custom.[15]

Consider a man having an ethical sense of duty and fidelity to his wife. Should this man engage in a sexual relationship with another woman, his conscience would rack him with an awakening to his dereliction of ethical duty and a sense of guilt. If the same man is also religious, his conscience will rack him with an awareness of his adultery and transgression—a sense of sin—toward the commandments of God. "The [religious] law of conscience convinces of sin."[16]

CHRISTIAN MORALITY

Morality (Greek *ethike* ἠθική)[17] is the religious sense of ethical values.[18] A person may live by excellent personal ethical principles; yet "morality consists in the submission of our personal life to absolute law."[19] An ethical life does not require religious belief, but a moral life does. This does not exclude the chance that human ethics will coincide with Christian morals on several points in human history. "The sense of moral obligation is indispensable to moral conduct."[20] The contravening of Christian moral principles induces not only guilt, but also a sense of sin in the conscience as a "natural response to the pain of sin."[21]

In respect to sin, there is a distinction between sin committed with intent and sin committed in ignorance. Sin committed with intent necessitates acting contrary to the values we have established in our conscience. The sin committed in ignorance has no sense of remorse or guilt conflicting with any value of conscience. An action may not be contrary to the commandments of God or gospel understanding. However, it may be contrary to our own internalized conscience values and therefore generate a sense of guilt and mental anguish for that individual. He who has so seared his conscience through repeated selective rejection of his own principles of conduct eventually closes down his conscience—bypassing all personal sense of constitutional charter. This person operates by passions and lusts without regard to his own welfare and often without regard to the welfare of others who become victim to his choices. "In many there is often a strong desire to surrender themselves to that spirit of pleasure that deadens the conscience and gives self-justification after wrong doing."[22]

THE LIGHT OF CHRIST

The Light of Christ is the module of divine implant attached to the conscience of all individuals. That Light is the divine spark prompting and infusing the conscience with understanding and comprehension of virtues, morals, and boundaries. "The ability to have an unsettled conscience is a gift of God to help you succeed in this mortal life. It results principally from the influence of the Light of Christ on your mind and heart."[23]

John speaks of this Light of Christ in his gospel account. The first two passages emanate from John as he introduces a theological statement on the divinity of Jesus as the Christ. The final passage is Jesus bearing witness as he extends to us an invitation to embrace that light.

"In the beginning was the Word, and the Word was with God, and the Word was God. The same was in the beginning with God. All things were made by him; and without him was not any thing made that was made. In him was life; and the life was the light of men. And the light shineth in darkness; and the darkness comprehended it not. . . . That was the true Light, which lighteth every man that cometh into the world" (John 1:1–5).

"Then spake Jesus again unto them, saying, I am the light of the world: he that followeth me shall not walk in darkness, but shall have the light of life" (John 8:12).

THE JEWISH PERCEPTION OF CONSCIENCE

The word *conscience* or any derivative form of the word does not appear in Hebrew.[24] The Mosaic law prescribed the ethical standard for the people, which they embraced without recourse to philosophical analysis of the impact upon the conscience. "The chief moral fact in the post-exilic period was the putting into strict practice of the Levitical and Deuteronomic Law, and the consequent triumph of ritual morality."[25] The inability to live a higher law upon leaving exile in Egypt necessitated Jehovah issuing a more simplistic standard of expectation.

The Greek philosophers were seeking ethical principles for the human conscience, whereas the Israelites received the ethical principles in the law from God but did not recognize that this defined their conscience. The internalization of the law was so total that "their ethical point of view did not lead them so to analyze their experience as to create a demand for such terms."[26] The Israelite nation existed in an entrenched cultural isolation. Even when Israelites emmigrated to other lands and became the Jewish Diaspora,[27] they retained their cultural isolation.

Though the Israelite people did not philosophically deliberate on the subject of conscience, they nonetheless expressed it with alternative Hebrew terminology. The concept of *conscience* equates with "the heart." The Proverbs contain many examples: "pureness of heart" (Proverbs 22:11); "create in me a clean heart, O God; and renew a right spirit within me" (Psalm 51:10); "counsel in the heart of man is like deep water; but a man of understanding will draw it out" (Psalm 20:5). The word *integrity* also conveys the same concept: "the integrity of my heart" (Genesis 20:5); "a perfect and an upright man . . . and still he holdeth fast his integrity" (Job 2:3); and lastly, "till I die I will not remove mine integrity [innocence] from me" (Job 27:5).

Jewish thought certainly formed a base for the development of Christianity. However, the Judaism of Alexandria in Egypt had a greater influence on the Jewish legacy in Christianity than the Judaism of Palestine. Alexandria produced the Greek version of the Old Testament and enabled the transition of a record of the dealings of God with man on Earth to a wider audience. The Greek Old Testament empowered the spread of Christianity with additional endorsement and credibility.

THE GRECO-ROMAN PERCEPTION OF CONSCIENCE

Psychology is the study of the mental process of the human soul.[28] The philosophical study of psychology had its origins in ancient Greece.[29] "There is no witness so terrible, no accuser [as] so powerful as conscience which dwells within us,"[30] declared the philosopher Sophocles (495–406 BC). Greek philosophical concepts evolved over several centuries, and with it, the language capability to express these concepts into new words. In these early centuries, conscience was communal or tribal and not individual. Sparta is a classical example imbued with the doctrine of collective conscience. As city-states evaporated and the new concept of Greece emerged, the philosophers sought a new sense of duty to replace the state.[31] Contact with eastern religion and thought awakened an understanding of individualism.[32] Philosophy concluded that man possessed an eternal soul, and this raised new avenues of thought: "We may obtain a soul, but how do we explain its sense of guilt?"[33]

Greek philosophical thought and the language to describe it did not reach Rome until centuries later; the Romans had no understanding of these concepts. At this time, "If one had spoken to a Roman concerning his soul, its sinfulness, and its need of salvation, there would have been no discussion possible, for the person addressed would not have understood what it was all about."[34]

THE SERMON ON THE MOUNT: A TRANSITION

The Mosaic Law taught, "Eye for eye, tooth for tooth, hand for hand, foot for foot, burning for burning, wound for wound, stripe for stripe" (Exodus 21:24–25). Christianity taught, "Love your enemies, [and] bless them that curse you, do good to them that hate you, and pray for them which despitefully use you" (Matthew 5:44). The Mosaic conscience needed a reformation of thought.

"Sacrifices could not relieve men's conscience but served rather to call sin to mind."[35] In seeking for a turning point when we can close the old and introduce the new, the Sermon on the Mount becomes the transition.[36] Generations of rabbis and philosophers yearned for and sought to discover and articulate what the human conscience should become. Rabbis and philosophers withdrew, and "the Son of Man" (Matthew 8:20) supplanted the Mosaic morals and Socratic ethics with a new Christian charter of conscience. Jesus introduced this charter in an extended sermon across Matthew chapters 5, 6, and 7. Jesus "taught them" a new understanding incomparable to anything they had heard previously. He declared with conviction, "Think not that I am come to destroy the Law, or the prophets: I am not come to destroy, but to fulfill" (Matthew 5:17). Earlier we discussed the issue of adultery and its resulting impact upon the conscience of a man. Now Jesus raises the expectation of a new conscience. "Ye have heard that it was said by them of old time, Thou shalt not commit adultery: But I say unto you, that whosoever looketh on a woman to lust after her hath committed adultery with her already in his heart" (Matthew 5:27–28).

Never before had moral expectations been so defined. "Christianity was not only a new religion; it was also a new ethic and moral perception."[37] The Beatitudes not only taught us a new individual expectation, they also taught us a new expectation for society.[38] In summarizing the first phase of the sermon, Jesus gave the mandate, "Be ye therefore perfect, even as your Father which is in heaven is perfect" (Matthew 5:48). One perceptive author in 1913 summed up Matthew 5 with these words: "God is an infinite missionary force. His entire purpose is bound up in the moralization of man. 'Let us make man in our image, after our likeness' (Genesis 1:26) is the motive; 'Be ye holy, for I am holy' (Leviticus 19:2; 1 Peter 1:16) is the goal. . . . The heart of it is that the standard for human perfection is the character of God."[39]

At the conclusion of this three-chapter discourse on new ethics and morals, the enthralled audience pondered these new expectations.[40] "And it came to pass, when Jesus had ended these sayings, the people were astonished at his doctrine: For he taught them as one having authority, and not as the scribes" (Matthew 7:28–29).

CONSCIENCE IN THE NEW TESTAMENT

The Greek word *syneidesis* (συνείδησις) appears thirty-two times in the New Testament and is consistently translated as "conscience":

- "Convicted by their own conscience [*syneideseos* συνειδήσεως]" (John 8:9).

- "I have lived in all good conscience [*syneidesei* συνειδήσει] before God" (Acts 23:1).

- "Have always a conscience [*syneidesin* συνειδήσιν] void of offence" (Acts 24:16).

- "Written in their hearts, their conscience [*suneideseos* συνειδήσεως]" (Romans 2:15).

- "I lie not, my conscience [*syneideseos* συνειδήσεώς] also bearing me witness" (Romans 9:1–2).

- "For conscience [*syneidesin* συνείδησιν] sake" (Romans 13:5).

- "For some with conscience [*syneidesei* συνειδήσει] of the idol . . . and their conscience [*syneidesis* συνείδησις] being weak . . . shall not the conscience [*syneidesis* συνείδησις] of him which is weak . . . wound their weak conscience [*syneidesin* συνείδησιν]" (1 Corinthians 8:5–13).

- "Asking no question for conscience [*syneidesin* συνείδησιν] sake . . . asking no question for conscience [*syneidesin* συνείδησιν] sake . . . and for conscience [*syneidesin* συνείδησιν] sake . . . conscience [*syneidesin* συνείδησιν], I say, not thine own . . . my liberty judged of another man's conscience [*syneideseos* συνειδήσεως]" (1 Corinthians 10:25–33).

• "The testimony of our conscience [*syneideseos* συνειδήσεως]" (2 Corinthians 1:12).

• "Commending ourselves to every man's conscience [*syneidesin* συνείδησιν]" (2 Corinthians 4:2).

• "Charity out of a pure heart, and of a good conscience [*syneideseos* συνειδήσεως]" (1 Timothy 1:5).

• "Holding faith, and a good conscience [*syneidesin* συνείδησιν]" (1 Timothy 1:19).

• "Holding the mystery of the faith in a pure conscience [*syneidesei* συνειδήσει]" (1 Timothy 3:9).

• "Having their conscience [*syneidesin* συνείδησιν] seared with a hot iron" (1 Timothy 4:2).

• "I serve from my forefathers with pure conscience [*syneidesei* συνειδήσει]" (2 Timothy 1:3).

• "Their mind and conscience [*syneidesis* συνείδησις] is defiled." (Titus 1:15).

• "Pertaining to the conscience [*syneidesin* συνείδησιν] . . . purge your conscience [*syneidesin* συνείδησιν] from dead works" (Hebrews 9:8–10, 14).

• "Had no more *conscience* [syneidesin συνείδησιν] of sins" (Hebrews 10:2).

• "Having our hearts sprinkled from an evil conscience [*syneideseos* συνειδήσεως]" (Hebrews 10:22).

• "We trust we have a good conscience [*syneidesin* συνείδησιν]" (Hebrews 13:18).

• "If a man for conscience [*syneidesin* συνείδησιν] toward God endure" (1 Peter 2:19).

• "Sanctify the Lord God in your hearts . . . having a good conscience [*syneidesin* συνείδησιν] . . . the answer of a good conscience [*syneideseos* συνειδήσεως] toward God" (1 Peter 3:15–16, 21).

We also have the unusual circumstance that the Revised Standard Version introduced into the Old Testament the term "pangs of conscience": "My lord shall have no cause of grief, or pangs of conscience, for having shed blood without cause or for my lord taking vengeance himself" (1 Samuel 25:31).

The Authorized King James Version translated this word as "stumbling of heart." In Hebrew, this is composed of two words (*ulmichshol lev*, וּלְמִכְשׁוֹל לֵב). The word *lev* (לֵב) has fifteen different applications: (1) heart as a body organ; (2) "the inner part or middle of a thing;" (3) personality; (4) the "seat of desire;" and on to (10) "it may be the seat of conscience and moral character."[41] An older Hebrew dictionary interpreted this word as "the heart as the seat of life"[42]—representative in the absence of the word *conscience*.

CONCLUSION

Greek "philosophy ... bequeathed a language"[43] that enabled Christianity to articulate new concepts. With the Greek language, the New Testament authors— all from one generation—expressed revolutionary thinking in individual ethics and morals and defined new concepts.[44] We owe much to the emergence of Stoic philosophers and the language of ancient philosophy that was so well suited to articulating the higher Law of God.[45] Articulating the doctrines of Jesus the Christ in Greek enables us to understand that conscience is a divine gift inherent in all of us. "Conscience permits the Lord to be there, whether in early warnings or final warnings."[46]

ENDNOTES

1. "There is a defense mechanism to discern between good and evil. It is called conscience. ... Conscience strengthens through use. Paul told the Hebrews, 'But strong meat belongeth to them that are of full age, even those who by reason of use have their senses exercised to discern both good and evil' (Hebrews 5:14). Those who have not exercised their conscience have their conscience seared with a hot

iron' (1 Timothy 4:2). A sensitive conscience is a sign of a healthy spirit" (James E. Faust, "A Crown of Thorns, a Crown of Glory," *Ensign*, May 1991, 69).

2. Mathews, *A Dictionary of Religion and Ethics*, 111, s.v. "conscience"; "Even with peace of conscience you can have temporary periods when your peace of mind is interrupted by external concerns" (Richard G. Scott, "Peace of Conscience and Peace of Mind," *Ensign*, November 2004, 16).

3. Mathews, 112, s.v. "conscience."

4. "Liberty and conscience thus became a sacred part of human nature. Freedom not only to think, but to speak and act, is a God-given privilege" (Ezra Taft Benson, *So Shall Ye Reap: Selected Addresses of Ezra Taft Benson*, 241).

5. Cassell's Latin Dictionary, 137–138, s.v. "conscientia."

6. Falconer, *The Pastoral Epistles*, 121.

7. Strong, #4893.

8. New Revised Standard Version with Apochrypha.

9. Nash, *Genesis of the Social Conscience*, 50.

10. "Ritual is powerful so long as conscience is dormant, but once rouse the moral sense and it will turn upon ritual and either reject it entirely or modify it so as to destroy its original form. This process of transformation was undoubtedly

going on as early as the first century. Parallel with the spread of these cults was a growing ethical movement represented by certain philosophies, particularly Stoicism. No religion, least of all such cults as these, can withstand the transforming criticism of ethics, and it was a regnant morality that gradually undermined their influence" (Kirk, *The Religion of Power*, 73).

11. Mathews, 111, s.v. "conscience."

12. Stelten, *Dictionary of Ecclesiastical Latin*, 89, s.v. "éthice, éthica."

13. Jannaris, *A Concise Dictionary of the English and Modern Greek Languages*, 136, s.v. "ethic."

14. Pervanoglu, 338, s.v. "ἦθος."

15. "Both ethics and morality can refer to social regulations that are embedded in cultural and historical traditions governing people's character and behavior" (Bunnin, *The Blackwell Dictionary of Western Philosophy*, 228).

16. von Haering, *The Ethics of the Christian Life*, 66; Sin "is the cause of waywardness of conscience, but despite this waywardness the original clearness of its witness shines forth with brightness" (von Haering, 65). "Perhaps worse than sin is the denial of sin" (Faust, "A Crown of Thorns," 68).

17. Jannaris, 240, s.v. "moral."

18. In our modern application, *ethic* is the "philosophy of morals;" while *moral* pertains to "behavior from the point of view of right and wrong, an obligation of duty" (*Webster's Dictionary*, 436, s.v. "ethic"; 826, s.v. "moral").

19. von Haering, 7.

20. Mathews, 294, s.v. "moral obligation."

21. James E. Faust, "A Crown of Thorns," 69.

22. Cowley, *Wilford Woodruff: History of His Life and Labors*, 650.

23. Richard G. Scott, "Peace of Conscience," 16.

24. "The Hebrew language contains no specific terms for 'duty' and 'conscience'" (Cheyne, *Encyclopædia Biblica*, 4:5331.

25. Meyers, *History of Past Ethics*, 162.

26. Cheyne, 4:5331.

27. *Diaspora* means a dispersion of people from their cultural homeland. Emigrant Jews that were scattered across many countries following the Babylonian captivity were termed "Jews of the Diaspora."

28. Psychology is composed of two Greek words, *psyche* (ψῦχή), meaning breath, life, or soul; and *logia* (λογία), meaning study.

29. In the Greek and Roman world, "even the gods had to be improved on, and the old god contended with the new one for the right to exist" (Nash, *Genesis of the Social Conscience*, 77).

30. Sophocles (Σοφοκλῆς 496–406

BC), Greek dramatist.

31. "The Greek city state was the creator of the Greek conscience. . . . Conscience was very little involved in that part of his life, which lay outside of the civic sphere. It was solely as a member of a city community, which was to the Greek what the church was to the man of medieval times, that he could live the truly moral life and attain the highest virtue" (Meyers, *History of Past Ethics*, 169–170). "Socrates' aim was to replace the artificial conventional conscience of his contemporaries by the natural rational conscience; in other words, to replace customary communal morality by reflective individual morality. His fundamental doctrine was that virtue is dependent upon knowledge. He maintained that one can no more see the right without doing it than one can see a proposition to be true without believing it. Therefore without knowledge—insight—there can be no virtue" (Ibid., 198).

32. "The teachings of a philosophy such as Stoicism and the universal idea of Oriental religion tend alike to individualism" (Carter, *The Religious Life of Ancient Rome*, 73).

33. Ibid.

34. Ibid., 72. "The origin of this idea of the personal soul is obscured in great mystery. It was not present at the time of the Punic Wars. We see only scanty traces of it in the literature of the Ciceronian age, and yet in the time of Seneca it was absolutely prevalent" (Ibid).

35. Cheyne, 4:4030.

36. "The Sermon on the Mount announces the awakening of the true prophetic spirit in Israel after a sleep of five hundred years" (Meyers, 163).

37. Ibid. 255.

38. "Alongside the primary Christian virtue, whether this be regarded as correct belief or charity, were grouped a cluster of secondary virtues, such as humility, meekness, gentleness, compassion for weakness, resignation, and renunciation of the world. What is especially noteworthy respecting this body of moral qualities making up the Christian ideal of excellence is that all these were virtues which in general were undervalued or held in positive disesteem by the Greeks and the Romans" (Ibid., 263).

39. Nash, 79–80.

40. "Neither Socrates nor the Greek philosophers in general recognized that this self-knowledge comes through right living rather than through right thinking" (Meyers, 199).

41. Strong, #3820.

42. Bresslau, *A Compendious Hebrew Grammar*, 287, s.v. "leb."

43. Hicks, *Traces of Greek Philosophy*

and Roman Law in the New Testament, 11.

44. "Language is an imperfect vehicle of thought, and that incomplete, or even misleading expression need not be erroneous statement. To study the illogical associations and misleading suggestions embodied in the history of words is to discover that a portion of search for truth consists in disentangling what a speaker means from what he is obliged to say" (Wedgwood, *The Moral Ideal*, 323).

45. "It is difficult to estimate, and perhaps not very easy to overrate, the extent to which Stoic philosophy had leavened the moral vocabulary of the civilized world at the time of the Christian era. . . . To a great extent therefore the general diffusion of Stoic language would lead to its adoption by the first teachers of Christianity" (Hicks, 118).

46. Neal A. Maxwell, "Yet Thou Art There," *Ensign*, November 1987, 30.

BIBLIOGRAPHY

Adam, Robert. *The Religious World Displayed*; or *A View of the Four Grand Systems of Religion*. 3 Vols. Philadelphia: Moses Thomas Publishing, 1818.

Adams, John Quincy. "What is Slavery?" Published in John Greenleaf Whittier's *The Conflict with Slavery, Politics and Reform, the Inner Life and Criticism*. Feb. 9, 1837. Retrieved Oct. 15, 2009, from http://infomotions.com/etexts/gutenberg/dirs/ etext05/wit3610. htm.

Aland, Kurt, Matthew Black, Carlo M. Martini, Bruce M. Metzger, and Allen Wikgren. *The Greek New Testament*. 3rd edition. Münster, Westphalia, Germany: Institute for New Testament Textural Research, 1966, 1975. United Bible Societies, Württembergische Bibelgesellschaft, Stuttgart, Germany.

Anonymous. World English Bible. Based on the 1901 American Standard Version, Greek Majority Text, and Hebrew Biblia Hebraica Stuttgartensia, 1997. Retrieved Oct. 15, 2009, from Project Gutenberg at http://www.gutenberg.org/etext/8294.

"Apostle Titus," *Orthodox Messenger*. Vol. 8. July/August, 1997. Retrieved August 2010 from http://home.iprimus.com.au/xenos/titus.html

Aristotle (Ἀριστοτέλης 384—322 BC). *The Ethics of Aristotle*. Translated by Alexander Grant Bart. 2 Vols. London: Longman's Green & Co., 1885.

Asay, Carlos E. *In the Lord's Service*. Salt Lake City: Deseret Book, 1990.

Authorized King James Version of the Bible. Salt Lake City: The Church of Jesus Christ of Latter-day Saints, 1979.

Bagster, S. *The Apocrypha: Greek and English in Parallel Columns*. London: S. Bagster & Sons, 1857.

Ballard, Russell M. "The Atonement and the Value of One Soul." *Ensign*, May 2004.

Barnes, Albert. *Notes, Explanatory and Practical on the Epistles of Paul to the Thessalonians, to Timothy, to Titus, and to Philemon*. New York: Harper & Brothers, 1849.

Barrs, Jerram. *Apologetics & Understanding—Transcription for Lesson 20*. ¶11. St.Louis: Covenant Theological Seminary, Spring 2006. Retrieved July 11, 2009, from http://www. covenantseminary.edu/worldwide/en/CC310/CC310_T_20.html.

Bartman, Elizabeth. "Hair and the Artifice of Roman Female Adornment." *American Journal of Archaeology*. Boston: Archaeological Institute of America, 2001. Retrieved Dec.

19, 2008, from http://www.ajaonline.org/archive/105.1/pdfs/AJA1051.pdf.

Bassler, Jouette M. *Abingdon New Testament Commentary—1 Timothy, 2 Timothy, Titus*. Nashville: Abingdon Press, 1996.

Behra, W. and B. Księgarni. *Dokładny Słownik Polsko-Angeilski i Angielsko-Polski*. Polish-English Dictionary. London: Barthes & Lowell, 1851.

Benseler, Gustav Eduard. *Griechisch-Deutsches Schul-Wörterbuch*. Leipzig: B. G. Teubner Druck & Verlag, Leipzig, 1891.

Benson, Reed. *So Shall Ye Reap: Selected Addresses of Ezra Taft Benson*. Salt Lake City: Deseret Book, 1960.

Bernard, J. H. *The Pastoral Epistles with Introduction and Notes*. Cambridge: Cambridge University Press, 1899.

Betteridge, Harold T. *Cassell's German–English / English–German Dictionary*. New York: Cassell, 1978.

Brenton, Lancelot C. L. *The Septuagint with Apocrypha: Greek and English*. London: Samuel Bagster & Sons, 1851; Peabody: Hendrickson Publishers, reprinted 2009.

Bresslau, M. H. *A Compendious Hebrew Grammar*. London: John Weale, 1855.

British & Foreign Bible Society. Tiomnadh Nuadh ar Tighearna agus ar Slanuighir Iosa Criosd Eadar-Theangaichte O'n Ghreugais Chum Gaelic Albannaich [Scottish]. London: British & Foreign Bible Society, Richard Watts, 1840.

Brockelmann, Carlo. Lexicon Syriacum. Edinburgh: T. & T. Clark, 1895.

Brockhaus Verlag. Die Eberfelder Bibel [German]. Witten, Germany: Brockhaus Verlag, 1905.

Brown, Ernest Faulkner. *The Pastoral Epistles*. London: Methuen, 1917.

Bunkowske, Eugene W., editor. God's Word Translation. Iowa Falls: World Bible Publishers, 1995.

Bunnin, Nicholas, and Jiyuan Yu. *The Blackwell Dictionary of Western Philosophy*. Oxford: Wiley-Blackwell Publishing, 2004.

Callimachus of Cyrene (300—240 BC). *Callimachus: Hymns and Epigrams, Lycophron and Aratus*. [Translated by A. W. Mair and G. R. Leob. Vol. 129. London: Loeb Classical Library; William Heinemann, 1921. Retrieved May 11, 2009 from http://www.theoi.com/Text/CallimachusHymns1.html#a3.

Calvin, John. *Commentaries on the Epistles to Timothy, Titus, and Philemon*. Translated by William Pringle. Edinburgh: Calvin Translation Society, 1856.

Carcopino, Jérôme. *Daily Life in Ancient Rome—The People and the City at the Height of the Empire*. Translated by E. O. Lorimer. New Haven: Yale University Press, 1940, 2003.

Carry, M., and H. H. Scullard. *A History of Rome*. London: Macmillan Press, 1975, 1984.

Carter, Jesse Benedict. *The Religious Life of Ancient Rome*. Houghton Mifflin Company, Cambridge: Riverside Press, 1911.

Cassell's Latin Dictionary. London: Cassell, 1959, 2007; McMillan, 1982.

Catholic Biblical Association of Great Britain. Revised Standard Version of The Holy Bible—Catholic Edition. London: Catholic Truth Society; Oxford University Press, 1966.

Catholic Encyclopedia, The. Edited by Herberman, Charles G., Edward A. Pace, Conde I. Pallen, Thomas J. Shahan, and John J. Wynne. 15 Vols. New York: Robert Appleton, 1907.

Catholic News Agency. "St Paul Burial Place Confirmed." Dec. 6, 2006. Retrieved Sept. 8, 2009 from http://www.catholicnewsagency.com/new.php?n=8221.

Catholic Online. "St. Titus." Saints & Angels. Retrieved Feb. 2010 from http://www.catholic.org/saints/saint. php?saint_id=2352.

Caton, Richard. *The Temples and Ritual of Asklepios at Epidauros and Athens*. Liverpool: University Press of Liverpool, 1900.

Charles, R. H. *The Book of Enoch*. London: Society for the Preservation of Christian Knowledge (SPCK), 1917, 1987.

Cheetham, S. *The Mysteries Pagan and Christian*. London: MacMillan & Co. Ltd., 1897.

Cheyne, T. K., and J. Sutherland Black. Encyclopædia Biblica. 4 Vols. London: Macmillan, 1903.

Church of Jesus Christ of Latter-day Saints , The Book of Mormon—Another Testament of Jesus Christ; The Doctrine and Covenants of The Church of Jesus Christ of Latter-day Saints; The Pearl of Great Price. Salt Lake City: The Church of Jesus Christ of Latter-day Saints, 1981.

Conybeare, William John, and John Saul Howson. *The Life and Epistles of St. Paul*. Grand Rapids: Eerdmans Publishing, 1984; Hartford: S. S. Scranton, 1897.

Cooper, Maurice Ashley, Edward Spelman, William Smith, and Isaiah Fielding. *The Whole Works of Zenophon* (Xenophon of Athens, Ξενοφῶν circa. 431–355 BC). Philadelphia: Thomas Wardel, 1840.

Cowley, Matthew, and Wilford Woodruff. *History of His Life and Labors*. Salt Lake City: Deseret Book, 1909.

Darby, John Nelson. Darby Bible Translation. Grand Rapids: Christian Classics Ethereal Library, 1890.

Davies, John Llewelyn, and David James Vaughan. *The Republic of Plato*. London: MacMillan, 1921.

de Almeida Atualizada, João Ferreira. A Bíblia Sagrada: Antigo E O Novo Testamento [Portuguese]. Edition 2a. Edicao. São Paulo: Sociedade Biblica do Brasil, 1993.

De ganse Heilige Schrift—het Oude en Nieuwe Testament [Dutch]. The Netherlands: Jongbloed editie, Staten-Generaal der Verenigde Nederlanden, 1637, 1715. Retrieved November 2008 from http://www.statenvertaling.net/

Det Danske Bibelselskab. Den Hellige Skrifts Kanoniske Bøger [Danish language Bible]. Copenhagen: Det Danske Bibelselskab [The Danish Bible Society], 1931.

Die Bibel—Schlachter Übersetzung [German]. Geneva: Genfer Biebelgesellschaft, 1905, 1951.

Dinneen, Patrick S. Foclóir Gaedhilge agus Béarla [Fochlór Gaedhilge agus Béarla]—An Irish-English Dictionary. Dublin: Irish Text Society / Educational Co. of Ireland, 1927, 1975.

Division of Christian Education, National Council of the Churches of Christ in the United States of America. Holy Bible: New Revised Standard Version with Apocrypha. New York: Oxford University Press, 1989.

Dyer, Alvin R. *Who Am I?* Salt Lake City: Deseret Book, 1966.

Ellicott, Charles John. *A Critical and Grammatical Commentary on the Pastoral Epistles, with a Revised Translation.* London: John W. Parker & Son, 1856.

Erdman, Charles R. *The Pastoral Epistles of Paul.* Philadelphia: Westminster Press, 1923.

Etheridge, John Wesley. *The Apostolic Acts and Epistles from the Peschoto, or Ancient Syriac.* London: Longman, Brown, Green, & Longmans, 1849.

Eusebius Pamphylia [Eusebii Pamphili] of Caesarea (circa. AD 260–339). *Historæ Ecclesiastæ—The History of the Church.* Translated by G. A. Williams and Andrew Louth. London: Penguin Books, 1965, 1989.

Eusebius Pamphylia [Eusebii Pamphili] of Caesarea (circa. AD 260–339). *Evangelicæ Præparationis (Preparation for the Gospel).* Translated by Edward Hamilton Gifford. 5 Vols. Oxford: Oxford University Press, 1903. Retrieved Sept. 11, 2009 from @ http://www.tertullian.org/fathers/eusebius_pe_00_intro.htm.

Evangeliska Fosterlands-Stiftelsens. Bibeln eller Den Heliga Skrift—Gamla och Nya Testamentet de Kanoniska Böckerna [Swedish]. Stockholm: Evangeliska Fosterlands-Stiftelsens, 1917. Retrieved July 14, 2009 from http://runeberg.org/bibeln/#1996.

Fairbairn, Patrick. *The Pastoral Epistles.* Edinburgh: T. & T. Clark, 1874.

Falconer, Robert. *The Pastoral Epistles—Introduction, Translation, and Notes.* Oxford: Clarendon Press, 1937.

Faulring, Scott H., Kent Jackson, and Robert J. Matthews. Joseph Smith's New Translation of the Bible—Original Manuscripts. Provo: Religious Studies Center, Brigham Young University, 2004.

Faust, James E. "A Crown of Thorns, a Crown of Glory," *Ensign*, May 1991.

First Presidency of the Church of Jesus Christ of Latter-day Saints. *True to the Faith*. Salt Lake City: The Church of Jesus Christ of Latter-day Saints, 2004.

Folengo, Teofilo. Riveduta Bibba [Italian]. 2nd edition. Bari, Italy: Giuseppe Laterza & figli, 1927.

Fosdick, Harry Emerson. *Twelve Tests of Character*. London: Hodder & Stoughton, 1923, 2003.

Gaebelin, A. C. The Annotates Bible—The Holy Scriptures Analyzed and Annotated. 4 Vols. New York: Our Hope, 1917.

Gibbons, James, and Richard Challoner. Douay-Rheims Version. Baltimore: John Murphy, 1582, 1899.

Golden Jr., Christoffel. "Grace," *Ensign*, Oct. 2003.

Graham, William. *A Practical and Exegetical Commentary on the Epistle to Titus*. London: James Nesbit, 1860.

Grant, Heber J. "Message from the First Presidency." In Conference Report, Oct. 1942.

Suetonius [Gaius Suetonius Tranquillus, circa AD 100] (1957, 1986). *Suetonius: The Life of the Twelve Caesars*. Translated by Robert Graves. Harmondsworth: Penguin Books, 1957, 1986.

Green, Jay Sr. The Interlinear Hebrew—Greek—English Bible. 2nd edition, 4 Vols. Lafayette: Sovereign Grace Publishers, 1975, 2000.

Green, Jay Sr. Green's Literal Translation. Lafayette: Jay Green Sr., 1993.

Groves, John. *A Greek and English Dictionary*. Boston: Hillary, Gray, Little & Wilkins, 1828, 1830.

Hackett, H. B. *Dr. William Smith's Dictionary of the Bible*. 4 Vols. Boston: Houghton, Mifflin, 1892.

Harvey, H. *Commentary on the Pastoral Epistles, First and Second Timothy and Titus; and the Epistle to Philemon*. Philadelphia: American Baptist Publication Society, 1890.

Henne am Rhyn, Otto. *Mysteria—History of the Secret Doctrines and Mystic Rites of Ancient Religions and Medieval and Modern Secret Orders*. Translated by J. Fitzgerald. Chicago: Stockham Publishing, 1895.

Henry, Matthew. *An Exposition of the Old and New Testament*. 9 Vols. London: James Nisbet, 1890.

Hicks, Edward. *Traces of Greek Philosophy and Roman Law in the New Testament*. London: Society for Preservation of Christian Knowledge (SPCK), 1986.

Hillard, A. E. *The Pastoral Epistles of St. Paul*. London: Rivingtons, 1919.

Hinckley, Bryant S. *Sermons and Missionary Services of Melvin Joseph Ballard*. Salt Lake

City: Deseret Book, 1949.

Holland, Jeffrey R., and Patricia T. Holland. *On Earth As It Is In Heaven*. Salt Lake City: Deseret Book, 1989.

Holland, Jeffrey R. *Christ and the New Covenant*. Salt Lake City: Deseret Book, 1997.

Holy Bible, New International Version. New York: International Bible Society, 1978.

Holy See Communiqué, "Conferenza stampa de presentazione dei lavori che hanno riportato all aluce il sarcofago de San Paolo, nella Basilica de San Paolo fuori le Mura," Dec. 11, 2006. Retrieved Sept. 8, 2009, from http://212.77.1.245/news_services/bulletin/news/19405.php?index=19405&po_date=11.12.2006&lang=en.

Holzner, Joseph. *Paul of Tarsus*. Translated by Fredric C. Eckhoff. St. Louis: Herder Book, 1959. Original title *Paulus, Sein Leben und Seine Briefe*, 1944.

Hooke, Samuel Henry. Bible in Basic English. Believers Resource, 1941. Retrieved from http://www.believersresource.com/content/pdf-bible-basic-english.html.

Hopkins, Keith. *Conquerors and Slaves—Sociological Studies in Roman History 1*. Cambridge: Cambridge University Press, 1981.

Horne, Thomas Hartwell. *An Introduction to the Critical Study and Knowledge of the Holy Scriptures*. 4 Vols. London: Longmans-Green, 1877.

Humphreys, A.E. *The Cambridge Bible for Schools and Colleges—the Epistles to Timothy and Titus*. Cambridge: Cambridge University Press, 1895.

Hunter, Milton R. *The Gospel Through the Ages*. Salt Lake City: Deseret Book, 1945.

Huther, John Edward. *Critical and Exegetical Commentary on the New Testament*. Edinburgh: T & T Clark, 1881.

Huther, John Edward (Titus and Timothy epistles) and Göttlieb Lünemann (Hebrews epistle). *Critical and Exegetical Handbook to the Epistles to Timothy and Titus and the Epistle to the Hebrews*. Translated by David Hunter and Maurice J. Evans. New York: Funk & Wagnalls, 1891.

International Standard Version 1.4.8. Paramount: Davidson Press LLC, 1996, 2008. Retrieved Feb. 2009 http://isv.org/downloads/index.htm.

Jannaris, A. N. *A Concise Dictionary of the English and Modern Greek Languages*. New York: Harper & Brothers Publishers, 1895.

Jerome (Eusebius Sophronius Hieronymous, AD 405). Biblia Sacra Versio Vulgata (Latin language Bible) and Biblia Sacra juxta Vulgatam Clementinam (electronic version). Edited by Michaele Tvveedale. London: Council of Bishop's Conference of England & Wales, 2005. Retrieved Sept. 11, 2009 from http://vulsearch.sourceforge.net/vulgate.pdf.

Jerusalem Bible, The. Edited by Alexander Jones. New York: Image Books / Doubleday,

1969. Based upon La Bible de Jérusalem. Paris: Les Editions du Cerf.

Josephus, Flavius. *Complete Works of Flavius Josephus—Antiquities of the Jews; Wars of the Jews; Flavius Josephus against Apion; Dissertations.* Translated by William Whiston. London: Pickering & Inglis, 1867; Grand Rapids: Kregel Publications, 1960.

Juvenal (Decimus Iunius Iuvenalis, 1st-2nd century AD). *A Translation of Juvenal and Persius.* Translated by Edward Owen. London: Rivington & Sons, 1786.

Kelly, William. *The Pastoral Epistles of Paul—An Exposition of the Epistle of Paul to Titus and of that to Philemon.* 3 Vols. London: Thomas Weston, 1901.

Kimball, Spencer W. "Beloved Youth, Study and Learn." Quoted in *Life's Directions.* David O. McKay, Marion G. Romney, J. Reuben Clark Jr., Harold B. Lee, LeGrand Richards, Delbert L. Stapley, Henry D. Moyle, Ezra Taft Benson, Hugh B. Brown, and Joseph Fielding Smith. Salt Lake City: Deseret Book, 1962.

Kimball, Spencer W. *The Teachings of Spencer W. Kimball.* Compiled by Edward Kimball. Salt Lake City: Bookcraft Publishing, 1982.

Kirk, Harris E. *The Religion of Power.* New York: Hodder & Stoughton, George H. Doran, 1916.

KJV-21, 21st Century King James Version. Gary, South Dakota: 21st Century King James Bible Publishers, Deuel Enterprises, 1994.

Koester, Helmut. Einführung in das neue Testament: Im Rahmen d. Religionsgeschichte U. Kulturgeschichte d. Hellenistischen U. Römischen Zeit. Berlin: Gruyter Lehrbuch, Walter de Gruyter GmbH KG, 1980.

Köhler (1795). Quoted in James Strachan's *The Captivity and the Pastoral Epistles.* New York: Fleming H. Revell, 1883.

Kyle, Melvin Grove. *The International Standard Bible Encyclopedia.* 4 Vols. Grand Rapids: William B. Eerdmans Publishing, 1915, 1986.

La Biblia—Versión Reina-Valera [Spanish]. Grand Rapids: Christian Classics Ethereal Library, 1569, 1909. Retrieved May 2009 from http://www.ccel.org/ccel/bible/esrv.html.

Lamsa, Grorge M. *Holy Bible: From the Ancient Eastern Text.* Philadelphia: A. J. Holman, 1933.

Lateran Treaty (Concord) of Feb. 11, 1929, between the Holy See and the Italian Republic. Retrieved Sept. 8, 2009, from http://www.whitehorsemedia.com/docs/THE_LATERAN_TREATY.pdf.

Le Quien, Oriens christ., I, 125 & II, 1061. Paris, 1740. Quoted in *The Catholic Encyclopedia*, v.15, 106. Edited by Charles G. Herberman, Edward A. Pace, Conde I. Pallen, Thomas J. Shahan, and John J. Wynne. New York: Robert Appleton, 1907.

Léon-Dufour, Xavier (1962, 1973). *Dictionary of Biblical Theology.* Translated by J. Cahill and E. M. Stewart. New York: Seabury Press; Desclee; Geoffrey Chapman Publishers; and Crowell Collier Macmillan Publishers, 1973. Original title, *Vocabulaire De Théologie Biblique*. Paris: Les Editions du Cerf, 1962.

Lewis, C. S. *Mere Christianity*. New York: Harper & Collins, 1952, 2001.

Ovid (Publius Ovidus Naso). *De Artis Amatoriae (The Love Books of Ovid)*. Translated by J. Lewis May. New York: Rarity Press, 1930.

La Biblia de las Américas [Portuguese]. Anaheim: Lockman Foundation, 1997.

Liddell, Henry George, and Robert Scott. Greek-English Lexicon. Oxford: Clarendon Press, 1901, 1996.

Lightfoot, Joseph Barber. *St. Paul's Epistles to the Colossians and to Philemon*. London: Macmillan, 1875.

Lipsius, Apokryphe Apostelgeschichte, Brunswick 1883. Quoted in The Catholic Encyclopedia. Edited by Charges G. Herberman, Edward A. Pace, Conde I. Pallen, Thomas J. Shahan, and John J. Wynne. v15. New York: Robert Appleton, 1907.

Livermore, Abiel Abbot. *The Epistles of Paul to the Corinthians, Galatians, Ephesians, Philippians, Colossians, Thessalonians, Timothy, Titus, and Philemon*. Boston: Lockwood, Brooks, 1881.

Livius, Titus. *Livy: the Early History of Ancient Rome*. Translated by Aubrey de Sélincourt. Vols. 1–5. Harmondsworth: Penguin Books, 1960, 1987.

Livius, Titus. *Livy: the War with Hanibal*. Translated by Aubrey de Sélincourt. Vols. 21–30. Harmondsworth: Penguin Books, 1960, 1987.

Livius, Titus. *Livy: Rome and the Mediterranean*. Translated by Henry Bettenson. Vols. 31–45. Harmondsworth: Penguin Books, 1976, 1983.

Lock, Walter. *A Critical and Exegetical Commentary on the Pastoral Epistles—1 & 2 Timothy and Titus*. Edinburgh: T. & T. Clark, 1924.

Ludlow, Daniel. *Encyclopedia of Mormonism*, 5 Vols. New York: Macmillan Publishing Co., 1992. Digitized copy at Harold B. Lee Library, Brigham Young University—Provo, 2006. http://www.lib.byu.edu/Macmillan/

Luther, Martin. Heilige Schrift des Alten und Neuen Testaments—Luther Übersetzung [German]. Stuttgart: Württembergische Bibelandstalt, 1545, 1964.

MacCarthaigh, Maitias. Ⲁⲛ ⲃⳝⲟⲃⳡⲁ Ⲛⲁⲟⲅⲁ (*An Bíobla Naofa*) [Irish]—CD edition. Baile an Mhuilinn: Fios Feasa, 1970, 1998.

MacKnight, James. *Apostolical Epistles—with a Commentary, and Notes, Philological, Critical, Explanatory, and Practical*. 4 Vols. London: Longman, 1809.

MacLaren, Alexander. *The Expositors Bible—Colossians and Philemon*. London: Hodder & Stoughton, 1892.

Madden, John. *Slavery in the Roman Empire—Numbers and Origins.* Vol. 3. Dublin: University College Dublin, 1996. Lecture given at the Annual Summer School of the Classical Association of Ireland in Galway, August 1994. Retrieved 22 September 2008 from Classics Ireland [http://www.ucd.ie/~classics/ClassicsIreland.html], document: ISSN 0791–9417 http://web.archive.org/web/20031211005259/www.ucd.ie/classics/96/Madden96.html.

Magiera, Janet M. *Aramaic Peshitta New Testament.* 3 Vols. Erwin: Light of the World Ministry, 2009.

Marcus Valerius Martialis (AD 38/41–102/104). *Martial: Epigrams.* Translated by Walter C. A. Kerr. 2 Vols. New York: Leob Classical Library, G. Putnam's Sons, 1920.

R.S.V. Interlinear Greek—English New Testament. Also a marginal text of the Revised Standard Version. Basingstoke, UK: Marshall Morgan & Scott, 1958, 1985.

Martin, David. *La Sainte Bible—l'Ancien et le Nouveau Testament* [French]. 1744. Retrieved 28 December 2008 from http://www.biblemartin.com/bible/bible_frm.htm.

Mathews, Shailer and Gerald Birney Smith. *A Dictionary of Religion and Ethics.* New York: Macmillan, 1921.

Maxwell, Neal A. "Care for the Life of the Soul," *Liahona.* May 2003.

Maxwell, Neal A. "Yet Thou Art There," *Ensign.* November 1987.

McConkie, Bruce R. *Mormon Doctrine.* Salt Lake City: Bookcraft, 1958, 1979.

McConkie, Bruce R. *A New Witness for the Articles of Faith.* Salt Lake City: Deseret Book, 1985.

McManus, Barbara, F. "The Flavian Coiffure." Retrieved 21 September 2009 from http://www.vroma.org/~bmcmanus/flavian.html.

Messia, Hada. "Pope: Basilica bones belong to apostle St. Paul," Cable Network News (CNN), 29 June 2009. Retrieved 8 September 2009 from http://www.cnn.com/2009/WORLD/europe/06/29/vatican.st.paul.bones/index.html.

Metzger, Bruce M., Ed. *The Apocrypha of the Old Testament—Revised Standard Version.* New York: Oxford University Press Inc., 1957, 1977.

Meyers, Philip van Ness. *History of Past Ethics—An Introduction to the History of Morals.* Boston: Ginn, 1913.

Mikołajewski, Daniel, *Biblii Gdańskiej* [Danzig Bible]. 1632. [Polish]. Retrieved 21 November 2008 from http://pol.scripturetext.com/.

Murdock, James. *The New Testament*; or, *The Book of the Holy Gospel of Our Lord and Our God, Jesus the Messiah—A Literal Translation from the Syriac Peshito Version.* New York: Stanford & Swords, 1852.

Murphy, Arthur translator [Tacitus, Publius/Caius Cornelius, AD 56–117], Tacitus, 4 Vols.

London: Henry Colburn & Richard Bentley, 1831.

Murphy-O'Connor, Jerome, "Community and Apostolate: Reflections on 1 Timothy 2:1–7." *The Bible Today*. October 1973. Quoted by Ben Witherington. *Letters and Homilies for Hellenized Christians: A Socio-Rhetorical Commentary on Titus, 1–2 Timothy and 1–3 John*. 3 Vols. Dowers Grove: InterVarsity Press, 2006.

Nash, H. S., *Genesis of the Social Conscience*. London: MacMillan, 1897.

New American Standard Bible. La Habra: Lockman Foundation, 1963, 1995.

New Testament in Modern Speech, 3rd edition. Grand Rapids: E. Hampden-Cooke, Kregel Publications, 1912.

Nouvelle Édition de Genève [French]. Geneva: Société Biblique de Genève, 1910, 1979.

Numenius the Pythagorean from *On the Good*—no longer independently extant. Quoted in Eusebius Pamphylia of Caesarea, Evangelicæ Præparationis [Preparation for the Gospel]. Translated by Edwin Hamilton Gifford. 5 Vols. Oxford: Oxford University Press, 1903.

Ostervald, Jean Frédéric, la Bible [French]. 1744. Retrieved 28 December 2008 from http://biblos.com/

Ovid [Publius Ovidus Naso], *De Artis Amatoriae* [The Love Books of Ovid]. Translated by J. Lewis May. New York: Rarity Press, 1930.

Owen, Richard, "Basilica bones are St Paul's, Pope declares after carbon dating tests," *Times-Online*, 29 June 2009. Retrieved 8 September from http://www.timesonline.co.uk/tol/comment/faith/article6601375.ece

Pausanias: Description of Greece [Παυσανίας: Ἑλλάδος περιήγησις]. Translated by W. H. S. Jones and H. A. Ormerod. 6 Vols. New York: G. Putman's Sons Publishing, 1918.

Perry, L. Tom, "The Need to Teach Personal and Family Preparedness," *Conference Report*, April 1981.

Pervanoglu, John. *A Dictionary of the Greek and English Languages* (Λεξικον Ελληνοαγγλικο). Athens: D. Sakellarios, 1894.

Plummer, Alfred. *The Expositor's Bible: The Pastoral Epistles*. London: Hodder & Stoughton, 1891.

Plutarch of Chæronea. *Plutarch's Lives*. Translated by Bernadotte Perrin. 11 Vols. Cambridge: Harvard University Press, 1917, 1955.

Reid, Alexander. *A Dictionary of the English Language*. Philadelphia: D. Appleton, 1845.

Revised Version—Standard American Edition, (ASV). New York: Thomas Nelson & Sons, 1901.

Riddle, John T. *A Latin-English Dictionary*. Boston: Ginn, 1898.

Riddle, Joseph Edmond and Thomas Kerchever Arnold. *A Copious and Critical English-*

Latin Lexicon. New York: Harper, 1864.

Roberts, Alexander and James Donaldson. *The Ante-Nicene Fathers.* 24 Vols. New York: Scribner, 1886, 1913.

Romney, Marion G. "The Basics of Church Welfare," *Priesthood Board,* 6 March 1974, 2. Quoted in Perry, L. Tom, "The Need to Teach Personal and Family Preparedness," *Conference Report.* April 1981.

Roth, Carolus Ludovicus. *C. Suetoni Tranquilli: De Vita Caesarium.* Lipsiae, Leipzig: B. G. Teubneri, 1858.

Sadler, Michael Ferrebee, *The Epistles of St. Paul to the Colossians, Thessalonians, and Timothy—with Notes Critical and Practical.* London: George Bell & Sons, 1896.

Salkinson, Isaac E. and Solomon L. Ginsburg. The New Testament in Hebrew (החדשה הברית). London: Bibles.org.uk, 2001, 2005. Retrieved 20 December 2009 from http://www.bibles.org.uk/HebrewNT-Salkinson-Ginsburg.pdf.

Scheidel, Walter. *The Roman Slave Supply.* Palo Alto: Stanford University, May 2007. Retrieved 12 September 2008 from http://www.princeton.edu/~pswpc/pdfs/scheidel/050704.pdf

Scott, Richard G. "Peace of Conscience and Peace of Mind," *Ensign.* November 2004.

Smith, Joseph Fielding. *Doctrines of Salvation.* 3 Vols. Salt Lake City: Bookcraft, 1954.

Smith, Joseph Fielding. *Teachings of the Prophet Joseph Smith.* Salt Lake City: Deseret Book, 1976.

Smith, William. *Dictionary of Greek and Roman Antiquities,* 2nd edition. Boston: Little, Brown, 1870, 1891.

Smith, William. *A Smaller Dictionary of the Bible.* London: John Murray, 1876.

Smyth, J. Paterson. *The Story of Saint Paul's Life and Letters.* London: Sampson Low, Marston and Co., 1939.

Sophocles [Σοφοκλῆς]. Translated by Thomas Francklin. New York: Harper & Brothers, 1840.

Stelten, Leo F. Dictionary of Ecclesiastical Latin. Peabody: Hendrickson Publishers Inc, 1995, 2003.

Strachan, James. *The Westminster New Testament—The Captivity and the Pastoral Epistles.* London: Fleming H. Revell Co., 1883.

Strong, James. The New Strong's Expanded Dictionary of Bible Words. Nashville: Thomas Nelson, 1890, 2001.

Suetonius. *The Life of the Twelve Caesars.* Translated by Robert Graves. London: Penguin, 1957, 1986.

Tacitus, Publius and Cornelius Caius. *Tacitus.* Translated by Arthur Murphy. 4 Vols.

London: Henry Colburn and Richard Bentley, 1831.

The Book of Jasher. Salt Lake City: J. H. Parry, 1887, 1973.

The Living Bible—Paraphrased. Carol Stream: Tyndale House Publishers, Inc., 1971.

Today's New International Version Bible. Colorado Springs: International Bible Society, 2001.

Webster's Dictionary—2003 Encyclopedia Edition. Köln: Verlag Karl Müller GmbH, 2003.

United Nations High Commission for Human Rights, Supplementary Convention on the Abolition of Slavery, the Slave Trade, and Institutions and Practices Similar to Slavery. 30 April 1956. Adopted by a Conference of Plenipotentiaries convened by Economic and Social Council resolution 608 (XXI) of 30 April 1956 and done at Geneva on 7 September 1956. Retrieved 20 September 2008 from http://www.unhchr.ch/html/menu3/b/30.htm

United States Department of State. "Trafficking in Persons Report." United States Department of State Publication 11407. Washington D.C.: Office of the Under Secretary for Democracy and Global Affairs and Bureau of Public Affairs, June 2008. Retrieved August 2008 from http://www.state.gov/g/tip/rls/ tiprpt/2008/

Vardaman, Jerry. "A New Inscription Which Mentions Pilate as Prefect," *Journal of Biblical Literature.* Vol. 81. Atlanta: Society of Biblical Literature, 1962.

Vaughan, C. J. *The Wholesome Words of Jesus Christ.* London: MacMillan, 1868.

Veláquez de la Cadena, Mariano. A New Pronouncing Dictionary of the Spanish and English Languages [Nuevo Diccionario de Pronunciación de las Lenguas Inglesa y Española], 2 Vols. New York: D. Appleton, 1852, 1900.

von Haering, Theodor. *The Ethics of the Christian Life.* New York: Putmans Sons, 1909.

Wedgwood, Julia. *The Moral Ideal—A Historic Study.* London: Kegan-Paul-Tench-Trübner, 1907.

Wesley, John. *Notes on the Bible.* Grand Rapids: Christian Classics Ethereal Library, 1754, 1765.

White, John T., A Latin-English Dictionary. Boston: Ginn & Co., 1898, 1904.

Winfield, Nicole. "Pope: Scientific analysis done on St. Paul's bones," *The Guardian*, 29 June 2009. Retrieved 8 September 2009 from http://www.guardian.co.uk/world/feed-article/8581822

Wirthlin, Joseph B. "What is the Difference between Immortality and Eternal Life," *New Era.* November 2006.

Witherington, Ben. *Letters and Homilies for Hellenized Christians: A Socio-Rhetorical Commentary on Titus, 1–2 Timothy and 1–3 John.* Dowers Grove: InterVarsity Press, 2006.

Wordsworth, Christopher. *The New Testament of Our Lord and Saviour Jesus Christ in the Original Greek.* 4 Vols. London: Gilbert & Rivington Printers, 1859.

Wuest, Kenneth S. *Word Studies in the Greek New Testament.* 4 Vols. Grand Rapids: William

B. Erdmans Publishing Company, 1980.

Cooper, Maurice Ashley, Edward Spelman, William Smith, and Sara Fielding, eds. *The Whole Works of Zenophon*. Philadelphia: Thomas Wardle, 1840.

Young's Literal Translation. Grand Rapids: Baker Book House, 1862, 1898.

ABOUT THE AUTHOR

William Victor Blacoe comes from Ireland where he became a member of the LDS Church in 1978. His early career was in mechanical engineering design and thereafter as a cartographer with Irish off-shore oil exploration. He obtained a degree in business management from the University of Phoenix. For the past few decades he worked as manager of several Church operations in Europe. Currently he is the manager of LDS Family Services in Europe.

Living in Germany since 1982, William has served in a several capacities in US Military Wards—including twice as bishop and three times as counselor in bishoprics. He is married with three children. William and his wife Reingard live near Frankfurt, Germany.

For over twenty five years, William has had a passionate interest in the New Testament and has conducted extensive research into the life and epistles of the Apostle Paul. This new translation and commentary on the four epistles of 1 & 2 Timothy, Titus, and Philemon is the first in what may become a series on the New Testament.